Páidí

About the author
Seán Potts has worked as a journalist with Independent
Newspapers for the past ten years and is currently deputy
sports editor for the *Evening Herald*. He lives in Dublin.

Páidí

The life of

Gaelic football legend

Páidí Ó Sé

as told to

Seán Potts

TOWN
HOUSE
DUBLIN

First published in 2001 by

TownHouse and CountryHouse Ltd
Trinity House
Charleston Road
Ranelagh
Dublin 6
Ireland

3 5 7 9 10 8 6 4

A CIP catalogue record for this book is available from the
British Library.

ISBN: 1 86059 147 75

Cover design: Terry Foley
Typeset: Claire Rourke
Printed: Omnia Books Ltd, Glasgow

Contents

Acknowledgements

IT ALL started because of music really and a tough
assignment from the Celtic Department of the Queen's
University, *seal sa Ghaeltacht*, back in April 1989. I was
enjoying the immense hospitality of Séamus and Máire
Begley in glorious Baile na bPoc, just over the bridge
from Feothanach, eight miles west of Dingle. The high
point of the week at that time was, unquestionably,
Sunday night at Ard an Bhóthair, in Tigh Pháidí Uí Shé.
The journey from the Begley's is about twelve miles
south, twenty minutes across Ireland's most spectacular
corner in Séamus' old white Escort.

On Sunday nights, Séamus and Steve Cooney would
hold the pub spellbound with their magical music.
Locals swelling with pride with every polka, with every
key change, with every lift of Begley's mischievous brow.
This was their music, the music of Kerry, magnified by
Cooney's pulsating strings. Steps would be battered out
with feverish tempo, in time. It was very passionate
stuff, typical of the locality. At one corner of the counter
the lads would be gathered, Diarmuid, Allisdair, John
Taimí. Páidí would be on patrol behind, pacing up and
down. The Ventry Sentry, surrounded by yesterday's
memories: Egan, Mullins, Hickey, Sheehy, Paddy Bán.
When the dust settled from the night's music, the talk
invariably turned to football when, with ease, Páidí

7

would transport us to Croke Park, into the half-back line and a skirmish with David Hickey, or to Gaelic Park in New York for a rumble with the Dubs. This was Páidí Ó Sé at his most comfortable, in company telling hilarious yarns about football, about life as a footballer. "Will you kick a few balls down on the strand with me?" asked Páidí one evening, intent on making the starting line-up for the Munster final. Scared the shite out of me. Best days . . .

I teamed up with Páidí four years later when he became the Gaelic football analyst for the *Irish Independent*. It wasn't long before I realised the intent in his heart. With each setback Kerry suffered, his quest to land the job of manager became more intense. He promised faithfully and repeatedly that he'd deliver the Sam Maguire back to his native county. At the time, I was far more concerned about seeing it paraded around O'Connell Street but I never doubted him for one second. Páidí wasn't a man for convention though. He was never comfortable in the press box with his opinion being sought at every turn or someone in his ear. No, he was the unconventional type. We often ended up on the sideline in the heat of championship battle rather than in the stand, me with notebook in hand trying to take notes for him while players were landing in on top of us. All gates opened for Páidí. He never hid his affection for Dublin people and Dublin football. When they eventually won the 1995 All-Ireland after a tortuous journey, Páidí put me on his shoulders in the Hogan Stand so I could witness John O'Leary and Paul Curran lift the Sam Maguire. He didn't think twice about it. Páidí, with eight All-Ireland medals in his arse pocket, five of them at Dublin's expense. "Get up on my shoulders, don't mind those fuckers behind. Get up!" That's Páidí: Gaelic football analyst, in the middle of the Hogan Stand, with his ghost writer sitting up on his shoulders.

Páidí didn't forget either. He took me on his journey; he confided in me; shared his triumphs and failures with my family. Páidí offered me an invitation to the edge.

After four years pressing, I gave in. It was time to share some of this incredible trip with GAA folk everywhere. Thanks Páidí. And thanks particularly to Máire for your patience, support and generosity. Thanks to Beatrice and all the Ó Sés for always making me feel welcome at Ard an Bhóthair.

I am deeply grateful to Pat Courtney, group sports editor, Independent News and Media, and his son David, sports editor of the *Evening Herald*. Their backing and encouragement made the whole project possible, made life a lot easier for myself and my family. I am also indebted to Independent News and Media and Gerry O'Regan, editor of the Evening Herald, for facilitating me. Thanks also to Pat Keane for stepping into the breach.

I kicked to touch with this book for years. Scared of it, I suppose. From the outset some people never stopped pressing. The late Mark Lane was one. Some years afterwards Paul Kimmage added his voice. Himself and Tom Humphries cleared away any woolly notions I had in my head; there were many. Don't get me wrong, I'm not saying Humphries did anything. Thanks Paul, in particular, for introducing me, the book and the expletive-charged world of sports to Treasa Coady of TownHouse. Thanks Treasa, for your stoical support. Tactically, you're a match for any manager. Thanks to Claire Rourke and Helen Gleed.

Meeting the extraordinary photographer Colman Doyle was a great privilege. To have him throw himself so whole-heartedly into the book was an honour. Colman has been a talisman for Páidí for twenty years, something to do with a local druid. The rest of the country will have to stop him taking pictures the week before they play Kerry.

My personal editors suffered most. Besides having to read the copy, they had to endure the endless ranting. I am most grateful to Kevin Nolan who kept me and the text honest. Thanks to former Cliftonville striker Aaron Shearer who tried to listen to two voices. To the Warsaw Pact; first thumbs up I got. Kept me going. To Tomás Ó

Flaharta, West Kerry Dub, thanks for your generous assistance.

My gratitude to John Martin, for always being on hand. Also for getting me to work on time and breaking the land speed record between Dunshaughlin and Dublin. Thanks to Paudie Lynch, Frank Keenan for the Kerry video I stole, J J Barrett, the Haughey family for their kind hospitality, Gay O'Driscoll, Frank Roche, Shane Scanlon, Tom Rowley, Karl MacGinty, Eoin O'Sullivan @ the Kerry website, Ray McManus and Sportsfile, John Costelloe in Limerick, Liam Aherne in the Palace Bar, Tom Collins' Bar in Limerick, Tommy Martin, Paul Hyland and Gay McKeon.

Ba mhaith liom mo bhuíochas a chur in iúl do mhuintir Chúil Aodha; Rachel agus Sorcha Ní Riada, Eoghainí Maidhcí Ó Súilleabháin, Hammy Hamilton agus Noirín ach go háirithe. Tá buíochas tuillte chomh maith ag Séamus Ó Beaglaoi, a chur Gaeltacht Chorca Dhuibhne agus, ar ndóigh, Páidí Ó Sé in aithne dom i dtús báire. Buíochas leis do Robbie Hannan i mBéal Feirste. Ba é Pádraig Ó Siocfhradha (An Seabhac) 1883–1964, a bhailigh na seanfhocail atá luaite sa leabhar seo; *cf. Seanfhocail na Mumhan*, eagraithe ag Pádraig Ua Maoileoin, An Gúm (1984).

Finally, to Cora Flynn and Fiachra Potts who endured most. Profuse apologies for banishing you from your own home. Thanks to Kitty and Anthony Flynn and Seán and Bernie Potts for providing refuge.

Go mbuaile Dia seans maith chugaibh go léir.

SEÁN POTTS
SEPTEMBER 2001

1
Where The Heart Lies

Níor chaill fear an mhisnigh riamh é

Foot and mouth disease, spring 2001

SOMETHING'S not right. It's March, I've been off the drink for nearly a month, shed over a stone – should feel great. Don't. Bloody head cold, bloody weird weather. I mean, it has been beautiful in west Kerry, blue skies, sharp crisp days, snow-covered peaks. One wag in the pub suggested that we plant a ski lift on top of Mount Brandon. "Ya, 'tis aall the crayze at the moment," agreed his pal, "t'would be great to see 'em shoot off de cliffs into the sea at Cuas."

Bloody weird. Foot and mouth disease. League in chaos, which is just as well for Kerry who've been away with the fairies since we brought Sam home in October 2000. Plenty of feet in mouths. Sam's not enough, there's no real closure anymore. Not that there ever was. Plough on and try and win it again, fail, go at it again. That's football.

Weird. Grief. Too much grief. Maurice Fitzgerald's not happy. With no matches, every scribe in the country is analysing myself and Fitz. There can be no winner in this situation. Some experts have called on me to resign. Jeezuus. No, Sam's not enough. You have to play it their way. A young reporter in a Sunday paper says that, for Páidí, football is all about "getting fit, giving and taking hits". I can't communicate and, my God, how could

someone who preaches pride and passion in the jersey
understand greatness, understand beauty in a footballer?
Jeezuus! Knows his stuff that boy.

Must 'explain my decisions'. Take a group of twenty-
six lads, amateurs, sacrifice every minute of your free
time, forget your job, your business, work to the bone,
live in a goldfish bowl for four or five months, gamble
with your reputation, gamble with your sanity, gamble
with Maurice. He's as good as it gets – his goal against
Armagh, can't defend against that. Win an All-Ireland
and now explain myself? Fuck off.

Why bother with it all? Well, I know why.

Tuesday evening. An air of normality has returned as a
thick mist blows in off the Atlantic. Rain, drizzle and fog
. . . story of our lives. I turn the cart towards Dingle and
sweep through Ventry. Winding around by the marina, I
shoot through a gang of sodden early-season tourists
with bemused faces marvelling at the narrow streets of
this magical, old market town. Give them a little
reminder on the horn. One of 'em smiles. Delighted with
himself. He'll be red-cheeked by 11 o'clock after he's had
his two glasses of Guinness and bellyful of crab claws.
Foot to the floor now as I sweep out of town. Heading
east. Give the new motor a serious grilling on the horse-
shoe bends after Lispole. On towards Annascaul. Not
much happening on a wet Tuesday evening in March.
Live for summer we do. Veer right for Castlemaine before
the village. Turn on Raidió na Gaeltachta. Tony
McMahon and Noel Hill are belting out a few fiery reels.
Joined by the clatter of hooves on the floor of Dan
Connell's pub in Knocknagree. Lifts me. Zigzag through
the reclamation work at the cliffs outside Inch, zip
through Boolteens and aim her right for Killarney.
Downhill to Fossa, swing left into the town. Impatiently
steer through the evening traffic, by the jaunting cars, up
the hill to Fitzgerald Stadium. Grab the bag, ten balls.
Head down, belt on in, see the pitch. This is why I
bother.

It is why I've always bothered. It's in your soul. It's
spiritual. Passion, courage, skill . . . these are only

manifestations of what is much deeper. If football is in the pit of your belly then it's difficult to live without. Shapes your life, relegates the important, distorts reality and drags you relentlessly in one direction.

It irritates the supporter and the pundit. Even the most astute can't put their finger on what makes a player tick or what makes a team great. Sure it's easy to define great skill, great heart. But winners and greatness? Footballers know and great footballers know better. Can't always articulate it but they know, can't spin it out with flowery language, don't always look for tidy answers, but they see things most people can't see.

Sure, the beauty of the skilful player is, for many, what makes the whole game worthwhile. The moment of skill rises above the contest itself, a Matt Connor shimmy, Mikey Sheehy's audacious chip over Paddy Cullen, Maurice Fitzgerald tormenting Benny Tierney in the Armagh goal by switching feet in a split second. When the moment of genius secures victory, it becomes irresistible. But the sublime moment is only the icing. I have always been driven by winning. Skill, courage, fitness, intelligence and passion are the vital components, but rarely can any one be isolated if the end – victory – is to be achieved. Quite often I have been painted as a blindly passionate footballer – one who got stuck in, didn't like the nice boys, the lads with the tricks. But this is completely misleading. As a player I never stopped working on the basic skills. As a manager I've never stopped looking for them in players. My philosophy on how the game should be played is that a very high level of skill and intelligence are required. But, if it is to be executed, it must be done so at pace and it must be done ruthlessly. Enter the other components.

Naturally, my obsession now is with the team, the panel, the sum of the parts. As a player I was, typically, far more selfish. I never wanted to let my guard down and the irony of bust-ups with some of my charges is not lost on me. The successful footballer's journey is endless, he's never satisfied with the last victory, must go at it again. I think this is why accepting the end of one's career is so damn difficult and why so many former players go back at it, travelling the endless road again, revelling in the highs but, ultimately, remaining unsatisfied. Hungry.

I'm always read wrong. It seems that, if you wear your heart on your sleeve, well . . . you're a thick fucker. Can't understand some folk. You've got to spell it out for them. I mean, I don't break ranks during the summer, don't do much talking. So no one seems to understand what's going on. Can they not see it on the field? Can they not see it in our performances? If we don't bate our opponents out the gate does that mean we're a bad team, that I'm a bad manager? Do they understand the modern game at all? Tell you, it's not easy. Drop your guard at all and you'll lose. Seven or eight teams, every year. Go in against 'em with anything less than ideal preparation and you lose. No matter how many geniuses you have in your squad. Professional game. Professionals . . . dressed as amateurs.

What drives me? Kerry. It's always been Kerry, since I was a kid. The Green and Gold lured me from childhood. Everything else took second place. Still drives me. Confidence drives me. This is what I know best, football. Makes sense to me. Páidí Ó Sé, a manager short of confidence, of belief? Couldn't be further off the mark. I have great confidence in my own ability. As a player, as a manager. Always believed. If my words and body language don't portray it, well, tough. If the discipline I impose on Kerry teams is taken as a sign of uncertainty, of an over-cautious manager, well, tough. Blame me if the team is badly prepared. Blame me if the team loses a game because of a lack of discipline. Blame me if Kerry ignore their traditions. Blame me if Kerry ignore their responsibility to the basic skills. We do our talking on the field. I don't deny any player the chance to develop his profile through football. I will do anything in my power to improve the lot of one of our players. Anything. But, my philosophy is simple. Forego the chance to seize the once-off moment and reap the rewards that collective success will bring in time. Especially in Kerry.

In most counties, in most regions, success is quite often judged by individual brilliance – to have played for your county, to have caught a great ball in Croker, to have rammed home a great goal in a provincial final. In Kerry if you fail to land the ultimate prize, they remember. Individually, collectively, they remember. You'll be at a wedding or a funeral in another parish and, coming down from communion, someone will elbow the person beside him and say, "There's that fucker who lost an All-Ireland for us."

The bar never stops rising in Kerry. Rich tradition. Every part of the county has its own slant, its own characteristics, but we all drink from the same well. Basics. Catching, kicking, taking scores, making scores, tight defending, heart, courage. Stamp of football in the county. Is for me anyway, no matter what happens on the field. Nowadays, of course, 'tisn't enough to rely on tradition, or rely on the basics. In the world of science, of professional training, video analysis, diets, psychologists, a well-drilled team can squeeze the fucking life out of a talented outfit. Last year's winners are fodder this year. Can't stand still. But, never lose sight of the basics. I don't ignore the modern approaches. Far from it, I embrace them. You have to. Can't yield any ground. But I think people are so caught up with analysing the tactics, the fitness levels . . . that they miss the point. Football. Mick O'Dwyer didn't miss it and I was a good listener.

Why do I bother? Something about the journey east. West Kerrymen, Gaeltacht men representing their county. Going east in the west Kerry car. Decades. Batt Garvey, Paddy Bán Brosnan, Jim Brosnan, Tom Long, Mícheál Ó Sé, Tommy Doyle, Dara Ó Cinnéide, Darragh Ó Sé, Tomás Sé, Aodhán Mac Gearailt. The West Kerry car. John Martin at the wheel. Solid. When the Bán & Co. were in their prime, the west Kerry car was legendary. Playing in a match up the country, stopping off in pubs along the way to offload some fresh fish, probably hauled in by the Bán at dawn that morning.

Then, after the game, the favour would be recalled on the return journey, when each pub would be visited after hours. The west Kerry car. *Spriod, croí, caid . . .*

This is why I bother. Football. Tasting the fruits of success. Young lads carrying O'Neill's balls around with them, soloing along the streets in Dingle, catch and kickout on the beach in Ventry, practising frees in Gallarus, in the Sportsfield. My son Pádraig is out the back, trying to kick the ball over his makeshift crossbar. I pick up the phone. "Hello, *Páidí Sé anso. N'fheadar a' bhfuil Dara Cinnéide timpeall?*

Hello, Dara, any chance you can drop back to the house later, young Pádraig's trying to learn how to chip the ball."

"No problem, Páidí."

Later on I glance out the back window. Young Pádraig is lamping the ball up over the hedge. He's seven. Football. Everywhere. This is what Páidí Sé is about. Mightn't have been the greatest clubman ever, always looked at the broader picture, the bigger stage. Has it's own influence though. Kids need heroes. Look to the bigger stage nowadays, look to their heroes, Kerry heroes. Success.

Don't take for granted what we have. Can't. We're blessed with heroes. All over the county. Maurice Fitz down south, Seamus Moynihan in the east, Noel Kennelly up north . . . no shortage of role models. No shortage of heroes.

My job? To keep it that way. Stay faithful to my beliefs, stay faithful to football. Keep the Green and Gold as close to the top as is humanly possible. Keep the edge. Take the stick, fight my corner, forgive, win, lose, don't hold grudges, move on. Never stop searching, never stop looking, listening, never stop learning, never stop enjoying. Gets harder by the year, harder for management, harder for players. Players need a break, inter-county players. Need a break, in every sense, a time out. Amateurism in a professional context is not an easy thing to juggle. We demand an awful lot from players . . . clubs, counties, supporters. I suppose slowly, things are changing for the better. A new season, new techniques, new support structures. But we can't stop giving. Sponsors, in particular, get most from the players. Sure, all levels of the GAA need the support of sponsors, but it's the players that make it worth their while. Successful players, even better. Nothing for granted.

Head is going now. We need a match badly. This fucking foot and mouth. Suppose it's a blessing in disguise. Give us a chance to catch up. Feeling a bit better, an hour out in the air, hot shower, bit of black magic with the lads in the dressing room. Head is going. Quick briefing from the selectors. No matches, hard to gauge what the fuck's going on. Back into the car. Couple of quick calls. Slip away from the stadium, into the night. Head is going . . . if we can get these boys right, we'll carry our legs against Cork. I know it. Cork. Journey starts again. Same as it ever was.

   On the road again.

2
One-Way Ticket

Is buan fear ina dhúiche féin

A GREY afternoon in November, 1966. Raw. Life in Ard an Bhóthair has changed little in decades. The church, crossroads, shop, road down to the beach flanked by steep hedges, down past the *Duí* to Ventry Strand. Opposite, the road to Dún Chaoin rises steeply over the Clasach, past Mount Eagle.

Eleven years old, oblivious to the world. Except, of course, for football. Galway are All-Ireland champions, beat Meath. Ventry man Tom Long's the local hero – carried the Sam Maguire back west in 1959 and 1962. Another Dingle man, Jim Brosnan, is training the Kerry team in 1966. Jim won two All-Irelands with Kerry in the 1950s. Well-respected, Jim, our local doctor.

I arrive home from school in the afternoon. Normally, it's straight over to the churchyard, start kicking against the wall, commentating like Mícheál O'Hehir . . . "what a great bit of fielding by Mick O'Connell . . . Tom Long, heads for goal". Bit of variation today. Practise my tackling in the field behind the house, with the turkeys. Parents keep a scatter of birds, fatten 'em up for Christmas. Start chasing the unfortunate creatures around the place. Half-demented, I take a mad rush into the middle of them, rugby-tackle one bird. Miss him. Can't stop. Don't. Career over a barbed-wire fence, ripping the calf-muscle on my left leg. Mayhem. Turkeys gobbling, running petrified around the field, young Páidí, sitting on the ground, blood streaming from my leg. Bawling. Beatrice hears the commotion. Runs out, sees me. Sees the leg. Ashen-faced.

Beeline for Dingle with Beatrice, in through Milltown. Kerry trainer, Dr Jim's already got the call. "The young footballer . . . young Páidí Sé, Tom's little brother. Beatrice's youngest." I'm impressed with Dr Jim's surgery. Kerry footballer, Kerry trainer. After cleaning the considerable wound, Jim gets to work with the needle. Sews me up – fifty stitches I tell my friends later. Puts my mother's mind at ease, "He'll be fine, Mrs Ó Sé, don't worry about him." Beatrice isn't convinced. Questions Dr Jim once more. "Will he have a scar, doctor?" she enquires.

Dr Jim pauses, "He will, Beatrice, no doubt. But don't worry about that, the green and gold sock will cover it."

In the beginning, there was football

My own journey started on 16 May 1955 in Tralee Hospital and football was to be a fellow-traveller from the outset. I was named Páidí after Paudie Sheehy, the great Kerry wing-forward who won an All-Ireland later that year and indeed two more in 1959 and 1962.

My mother, Beatrice Lavin, and father, Tommy Ó Sé, had recently returned to Ireland after living in London for a number of years, where my two brothers Mícheál (the eldest and father of footballers Fergal, Darragh, Tomás and Marc) and Tom had been born. My mother was originally from Ballymoate, County Sligo and, as was customary for a child in a large family, she emigrated to England. She married Tommy while in her teens and they ran a guesthouse together. Things had been going reasonably well for them but, like most young Irish people abroad at the time, there was a yearning to return home. However, events were to force the issue for Tommy and Beatrice. While cycling his bike one day, my father was struck by a lorry and seriously injured. It was touch-and-go with him for quite a while, but it was out of this almost tragic misfortune that a priceless opportunity arose for the family. When Tommy started to recover from his injuries, he became very anxious that they return to his birthplace of Ventry, in the west Kerry Gaeltacht. The insurance claim that followed was to provide just the ticket. The money gave them the chance to look for a place back home and, when a shop opposite the church in Ard an Bhóthair, five miles west of Dingle, came on the market in 1952, he and Beatrice made a successful pitch and returned to a new life as shopkeepers.

Some move it turned out to be. The shop not only catered for the people of Ventry but the parish of Dún Chaoin and there was a creamery close by that had up to one hundred and forty suppliers. It was a thriving business. They sold everything, not just your basic groceries. If you needed a can of paint, a shovel, a rake, horseshoes, or five or six fathom of rope, they'd have it. They also supplemented their income from the shop by starting a small farm behind the house where they kept pigs and hens. It was as comfortable an existence as myself, Tom and Mícheál could have wished for. Ireland in the 1950s was a difficult place but life was good for us.

It was my mother who drove the business. My father was a quiet man and he was totally dominated by Beatrice. She was also the prime mover behind everything we did and has always been ruthlessly single-minded. I'm told the term for a woman of her standing is 'matriarch' but somehow I don't think it does her justice as she was more than just the head of our family. Beatrice was to have a profound influence on my life. She, more than anyone, recognised where my raw talent lay and was prepared to nurture it to an extent few parents could tolerate. She also turned a blind eye to my many weaknesses, which came to light later in my life, and was a constant, positive force behind my career as a footballer.

As the youngest, I was left to give Beatrice and Tommy (or Tom Power as he was known locally) a dig-out in the shop and on the farm. My brother Mícheál was

20

in boarding school in St Brendan's, Killarney, while Tom attended the Mon' in Dingle. I was sent to the local primary school at Cill Mhic an Dómhnaigh, about a mile back the road from the house.

It was a happy time for me. I had a better share of interaction with people than a lot of others around due to the shop and the proximity of the church and this, of course, led to talk of football and the great exploits of Kerrymen in Croke Park. The summer was particularly good. Tralee people would drive back by Slea Head and stop off for icecream in the shop. When Kerry wouldn't be playing, John Joe Sheehy would often call in and regale me with stories of big games and the stars of the time. They were vivid pictures in my head and it wasn't long before young Páidí Ó Sé, five years old, was picturing himself nailing the winning goal in an All-Ireland final against Down or Galway. We would listen to the big games on the radio with our neighbour Joe O'Shea who would embellish the commentary for us. After a tense afternoon in our kitchen listening to Mícheál O'Hehir, myself and Joe we would tear off down to the *Duí*, a bit of commanage on the way from the cross down to the beach at Ventry. This was Croke Park.

Batt Garvey used also visit. They say he perfected the solo run. Skilful, won an All-Ireland with Kerry in 1946. Batt, originally from Ventry, would return home for the summers. "Páidí," he'd say, "I wish you were around when I was younger. I wanted to kick ball morning, noon and night." Batt lamented the way football was played in his day. He had touch, class, in an era of bite and bollock. Paddy Kennedy was the midfielder back then, used to horse the ball into the forwards. "Fight for your ball, Garvey," he'd blast. Longed for someone like Connell, place a ball onto your chest. Batt never missed a chance to influence young Páidí. Used to put the ball on the high windowsill outside the shop. "Now, Páidí, you have to learn how to jump and tip the ball off the sill. Take a run, Páidí, and get up there." I never stopped practising. Took me years. I remember the evening I first scaled the height. Couldn't wait for Batt to arrive so I could show him. Thrilled.

Although my mother was to play a key part in my development, the football pedigree lay on my father's side. His nephew Tom Long was a star forward on the Kerry team of the 1950s and 1960s and was a god in the eyes of his young cousin. Another former Kerry footballer, Mick Murphy, taught me in Cill Mhic an Dómhnaigh. Mick was full-forward on the All-Ireland winning team of 1955. Maureen Geaney also taught me at primary level and her son Seán, from Dingle, went on to play with Kerry.

It mightn't have been the football heartland of the Kingdom at the time but I was hardly isolated and the various influences were beginning to steer Beatrice and Tommy's youngest on an inexorable course. Two things helped a lot. In my final year in primary, the Bord na nÓg school leagues were started by Pádraig Ó Siochfhradha and the Gaeltacht Under-14 side was initiated by Joe Curran, Pat Kenealy and Fr McCarthy. I actually captained the first Gaeltacht Under-14 side and these two new under-age structures provided a valuable platform for the young talent of the community. According to my mother, I never left the ball out of my hand and, in the absence of constant companions to play with, the church wall was to act as an able substitute. At one stage, myself and my pal Muiris Fenton collected the refunds on a heap of glass bottles and purchased a proper football in Danny Flahive's shop in Dingle. Cost 19s/11d. We went flat out playing for weeks. Of course by 'proper' I mean the old pigskin balls that weighed a ton. Funny, I later became one of the first players along with my schoolmates to use the new O'Neill's leather ball, introduced in 1972. No wonder we could lamp the bloody thing so far in the 1970s. Anyway, back in Cill Mhic an Dómhnaigh we went mad, tearing around with *our* ball. I remember the day it got burst. Inconsolable.

In 1963 my brother Tom won a minor All-Ireland with Kerry and, as an eight-year-old, I was already hell-bent on following in his footsteps. I was probably showing signs already that I would travel that path, but I would eventually pay a price for my youthful obsession with the game.

I progressed to Dingle CBS for my first year of secondary school in 1969. In that same year a local lad, John Long, won a Hogan Cup All-Ireland colleges medal with St Brendan's, Killarney. I wanted a bit of the action. I convinced my parents that Brendan's, or the Sem as we called it, was the school for me. I had to go there. John's All-Ireland medal, my brother's success with the Kerry minors, it all pointed in one obvious direction – the Sem. The motivation for the move to Killarney was obvious to my mother. She was content with that and helped with the transfer.

I didn't manage to pull off the move immediately. I did some kind of exam which, I've no doubt, I failed. I failed every exam I ever sat with the exception of the garda exams. But I had a fledgling reputation from my under-age football with the Gaeltacht club and, following in Tom's path, I snuck into the Sem as a boarder on the third or fourth round of entries.

Once in Killarney I wasn't long making a name for myself on and, subsequently, off the field. In my first year there, I managed to play on every football team in the college with the exception of the senior championship team, and I was even knocking around that. By the second year, I was playing with every team. It was to be hugely productive time for me as a young footballer. While in St Brendan's, I won three senior Kerry colleges titles, an Under-15 title, two Munster colleges and got my first taste of Croke Park in 1972 when we lost the Hogan Cup final to St Pat's, Cavan. Incidentally, while preparing for that final, our trainer Jimmy Hegarty arranged a challenge game with some of the Kerry seniors as he was a close friend of the county boss Johnny Culloty. Kerry were preparing for the league final against Derry. They mixed up the teams. Great experience. See these guys at close quarters, play with 'em. Mick O'Dwyer, Brendan Lynch, Paudie Lynch, Derry Crowley, Eamon O'Donoghue, Mícheál Ó Sé. Great. Used the new ball as well. Felt important.

A year later as Munster champions again, we were beaten by St Jarlath's of Galway in the semi-final. By that stage I was the best player in the college. I wanted to be the best player in the college. After playing in the half-forward line, I had moved to midfield, leaving the forward headlines to be grabbed by Pat Spillane, a year my senior at the Sem.

By 1973 the county had already come calling. Young Páidí Ó Sé was making some reputation for himself. But it wasn't all good.

Three years earlier, an incident occurred which probably signalled the road ahead. In September, Kerry were taking the Sam home after defeating Meath in the final. DJ Crowley had scored a cracking goal at the death and I was beside myself with excitement. Unfortunately I was barracked in the Sem, so I devised a plan to break out and travel to see the homecoming. I arranged to borrow a bike from one of the day students, robbed a brush and dressed it up as a decoy in my bed and set out for Rathmore. On returning, the college dean, Dermot Clifford, now Archbishop of Cashel, was waiting form me at the entrance. "Ó Sé," he bellowed. "There are more brains in that brush above than in your head!"

He wasn't wrong. Unfortunately that breach of discipline was only a forerunner. I failed my Inter Cert, dismally. In fact I struggled to concentrate in class at all and to this day have difficulty with concentration, a trait I think I share with my mother. On the field, no problem, never dropped my guard. Anywhere else I'm liable to drift off to another planet. But a lack of concentration was a venial sin compared to what happened in fifth year. One day it was announced that something had been stolen in one of the dorms and that there was to be a full check of all the personal lockers. A shakedown! Now, I hadn't stolen anything but the inspection uncovered a porno mag stashed in my locker, a souvenir from a Gaeltacht club trip to London, when I had discovered Soho for the first time! Unfortunately this wasn't really an isolated incident. I had started drinking and, though I was never caught red-handed by any of the teachers, they had a fair idea. Despite my prowess on-field, I had become a tearaway and a bad influence off it and I was to pay the ultimate price. Expulsion from the Sem.

It was a bit of a jolt. I had been in line to captain the senior football team at the end of my fourth year, a great honour for any student of the college, and now I was out on my arse.

Regrettably for me, Dermot Clifford had left the Sem the previous summer and with him went my strongest ally. Clifford had good time for me despite my obvious weaknesses and I feel to this day that he may have been able to turn things around had he been there. He has said as much to me since and the Archbishop has remained a good friend through football. Anyway, in his absence I was goosed.

The news was confirmed to my parents that summer, 1973. I remember sitting anxiously waiting for the postman to arrive every morning, wondering had word been sent from Brendan's. When it did arrive my parents were, naturally, upset. But I do recall my mother asking me, "Did you steal anything, Páidí?" When I told her I hadn't, she was content and herself and Tommy headed to Killarney to plead my case with the college officials. But there was no second chance.

I kind of regret that I didn't finish out in the Sem. Not that my grades were likely to improve but I may have won a Hogan Cup medal the following year. I have also certain regrets that I didn't give education a chance at all; there's a price to be paid for turning your back on the books and I suppose I'm still paying it. However, *is treise dúchas ná oiliúint.*

Fortunately a former Irish teacher of mine at the Sem, the late Bishop Diarmuid Ó Súilleabháin from Millstreet, had been recently promoted to president of St Michael's College in Listowel. I had become friends with Ó Súilleabháin's two nephews Derry and Denis O'Hare while at the Sem. I was particularly good pals with Derry who was captain of the senior football team. Tragically, his brother Denis was electrocuted and killed in an accident while helping to move a set of portable goalposts.

Ó Súilleabháin was a big fan of the Irish language and spent a lot of time back in west Kerry. He agreed to accept me at the school and made the transition as easy as possible. I would move to north Kerry and move in with my brother Mike who was already married and living in Listowel.

My first day in the new school was nerve-wracking. There was a long avenue from the gates up to the school buildings and, when I was met by three hundred unfamiliar faces at assembly, I felt like a new prisoner.

Johnny Flaherty was training the team in Michael's and, as luck would have it, became my new Irish teacher, so there was a bond on two fronts. In fact, football aside, Johnny used to get me to give Irish-language grinds to the town pupils before exams. On occasions, he also gave me the responsibility of training the footballers. His guidance proved invaluable to me at that crucial developmental stage of my career.

Possession

At that time, the school participated in the Munster senior 'B' colleges championship, which we won outright as soon as I joined. Following that success, we concentrated on the O'Sullivan Cup, the Kerry inter-schools competition. After a significant victory over Tralee CBS in the semi-final – a team that included Seán Walsh – we reached the decider against my new enemies, the Sem. The Untouchables?

I was possessed.

It was the first time in my life I had become so taken by any match. There comes a point when a young player must learn how to focus on a difficult challenge but my focus was all-encompassing. I couldn't think of anything else. I couldn't countenance losing this game. I think this obsession served me well subsequently, but it was the spring of 1974, my final run into the Leaving Cert and I was hoping to study physical education in college.

Whatever chance I had of scraping by probably evaporated with that fixture. My motivation was simple: fuck the Sem, I'd show them.

Now things were complicated enough with Listowel's run to the final but I had other commitments. After Christmas 1973, I was invited to line out for the Kerry senior team and myself and Spillane started to get the odd run-out in the league. In fact I ended up in the shake-up for the conclusion of the league. I was excited, sure, but this should have been a momentous time in my life; after all I had dreamed of the Green and Gold since I was first lashing the ball off the church wall in Ard an Bhóthair. Should have been. Wasn't. Why?

Well this is part of what makes Páidí Ó Sé tick at least this was the start of it. Vindication, revenge, a platform on which I can prove I'm better than my opponent, especially if he thinks he's better! The league final, and now the league final replay, were all very well, a step-up for a tenacious footballer from the Gaeltacht. But the showdown with the school that had dumped me. Personal. As far as I was concerned, 1974 was the year of the St Brendan's bother. Kerry could wait.

When the big game arrived, myself and the Michael's boys travelled to Austin Stack Park, Tralee. We were pumped. And it stood to us. We battled hard, I slogged it out mostly in midfield but everyone rose to the occasion, so much so that we were two points in front in the closing stages. Then, disaster struck. Brendan's snatched a goal. I recall, vividly, turning to the referee, Timmy Woulfe from Ahtea in Limerick. "Jeezuus, ref, what's left?" I squealed.

"Well . . ." he paused.

"Ah, ref, just give us one last crack, one chance to level her," I pleaded. We got two.

We won the kick-out and moved the ball upfield where it was deflected wide for a '50'. I stepped up. "This must go dead, lad," said Woulfe. Pressure.

Luckily as a player I never found pressure to be suffocating. I know it can be terribly debilitating but it just didn't bother me. My guard stayed up. This was a big test of my bottle. I stepped up and planted the ball into the wind and over the bar. Test passed. Game drawn.

Now if the demons were on my shoulder for the first clash with the Sem, they were singing in my ear for the replay. Possession. The replay was set for the following Thursday. Once again, there were complications. The National League final was set for the Sunday after the colleges final replay, a mere forty-eight hours after! And worse still, Kerry boss Johnny Culloty had selected me to start against Roscommon at wing-back. Here we go again. First full game for my county as a defender. Croke Park, National League final replay, a blooding. Surely now it would take precedence.

It didn't. Destiny? Destiny could wait.

We took the whole of Listowel with us on that journey. Even the north Kerry lads who were stationed in St Brendan's shouted for us in the replay. John B Keane, whose son Billy played alongside me on the Michael's team, was eulogising. There was a great buzz. I was in the middle of it. Now, it was no one-man team. But I was the middle-man. And I loved it.

One of the problems many aspiring Kerry schools faced when playing the Sem was getting a fair deal from the ref. Brendan's had a reputation, a good reputation. A bit like the Kerry team of the 1970s, known as good footballers; honest; no messing. In the replay we were lucky again. Seanie Burrows from Bóthar Buí, who played with Kerry in the 1968 All-Ireland final and who was also an international basketballer, took charge of the game and didn't ref it on reputation. So we had a chance.

The game was back in Austin Stack Park and again it was tight. I got an amount of punishment in midfield and, in the closing stages of the game, shipped a dead-leg for my troubles. But my heart was pumping on my sleeve. Adrenaline, endorphins or whatever keeps you from lying down, I had 'em, I refused to buckle. As we entered the closing stages we trailed by a point again and this time I fisted the equaliser. Extra time.

Anyone who has ever experienced a game like this can understand what the atmosphere was like. It may be a small, insignificant sporting event, but it is the GAA at it's most beautiful. Local, bitter, passionate, courageous. Beautiful. Paddy Kavanagh understood. And most GAA folk understand.

This was one of those occasions.

Extra time. I moved from midfield to centre-forward. 'Twas a good move. I scored 2–2 over the next ten minutes. Game over. The O'Sullivan Cup was heading to Listowel. The Sem were humbled. Boy was I happy.

The bus arrived back to Listowel and the place was hoppin'. Of course drink was banned but the president of the college handed me a £20 note, a serious divvy for 1974. He said nothing and carried out the formalities, filling the O'Sullivan Cup with the strongest soft-drink he could find. Britvic orange!

With the formalities over, myself and the lads disappeared with the £20 and had ourselves a decent drink. Of course with restrictions in place we had to go off the beaten track, but we had a fair sup nonetheless.

By the time I'd sobered up, I was on the pitch again, putting the final preparations together for the league final that Sunday. It was all a little hazy. I wasn't nervous, not after what I'd been through on Thursday. I played reasonably well against Roscommon, although I remember trying to push forward at every opportunity until Ger Power counselled me. "Take it handy, Páidí, mind your patch."

We won. Celebrations. Back to school.

Unfortunately, it was the same old climbdown for me. Take football out of the equation and it didn't add up. Failed the Leaving Cert. Prospects weren't great. Football good, real life bad.

Still there was Kerry. The Munster Championship. The future. Destiny.

Destiny is now.

3
Step-Up

Cé ná bíonn aon chnámh sa teangain is minic a bhris sí ceann duine

Sunday 20 July 1975

MUNSTER FINAL. I devoured my steak about noon,
give her time to sit. Another misty day in Killarney.
Check the cogs, gloves. No beautiful backdrop of the
Reeks for the commentators to talk about if the match is
bad. Can't see further than the terrace. It's back in
Fitzgerald Stadium again as they're finishing off the new
ground in Cork. Páirc Uí Chaoimh they call it, the old
Athletic Grounds. We're lucky, you know. Dwyer has
stuck with the young lads, now ten of last year's Under-
21s on the panel. Big gamble for a new boss, they say.
Playing at home for the second year running, with a
young crew. Lucky. We know otherwise. They've been
gambling with the kids for a couple of years. Now it's
time and, fuck it, we're flyin' – Power, Egan, Spillane,
Mikey – Jeezuus the speed of 'em. Tuned in too.

Nervous? Nah. Sure I'm nearly two years on the Kerry
team, a veteran! National League medal in my arse
pocket. Won't let these bastards beat me again though,
lay down too fucking easy last year. Keep it simple.
Quick ball, quick ball. Keohane said to me last year;
"Patrick," as he called me, "you're a defender and the
bigger the game, the closer you must be to your man.
Patrick, if I ask you, at *any* stage of a game 'Where's your
man?' You tell me 'HERE'," he roared, placing his hand

30

on my shoulder. Makes sense. I'm supposed to be marking Ned Kirby but they've switched Dinny Allen on to me. Do a job on the young lad I suppose? He's a quare hawk, soccer player, good hurler too. I'll be up his arse. Have to win this one. Mickey Ned talks to us before the match. Funny. Captains never addressed a team until this year. Sounds good. Great speech Sullivan!

Usual start to a Munster final, everyone tearin' and slidin' into one another. Crowd's narky, heavy auld day. Brendan Cross will be busy reffin' this today, I'm thinking. Cork'll try and soften the young lads up. Some job. Brendan Lynch stitches over a free from forty-five yards. Experience. Himself and Johnno have All-Ireland medals. Deep breath, hand on the red jersey for the kickout. Next minute, Allen wanders away right into the corner and picks up a loose ball at the corner flag; impossible angle. Can't score. Scores. Stitches it over, lands it on top of the net, brilliant. "WHERE'S YOUR MAN?" I'm thinking. Well I shepherded him into the corner, can't help it if he's a fuckin genius. Then – disaster. Tim Horse Kennelly tries to drop-kick a clearance. Mortal sin, lazy-man's clearance. Nestles on Allen's chest. Bang. Point. Couldn't get a hand on him. FUCK! FUCK YA HORSE! What a start.

I'm thinking; "Páidí Sé, Páidí Sé, who was he again? Oh ya, youngfella from back west, played a bit in the mid-1970s under Dwyer. Got a roastin' from Dinny Allen in the 1975 Munster final, never heard of again. Played a bit with the juniors last year. Thought he'd make it, they did. But too loose. Too loose. Hadn't the head for it."

Thank God for goading. Allen couldn't resist it. Turns to me and leans into my ear, "They'll be takin' you off now, boy."

Switch trips. I reply, "We'll if I'm goin' off, your fucking coming with me."

Hit him. Crowd erupts. He elbows me back, loosens a tooth out. Now I really get stuck in. Plant him. Cross turns and makes his way to the duelling pair, slips on the way. Crowd goes mental. Poor ref, probably got flustered.

Lucky for me. Warns myself and Dinny. Lucky. Not so lucky for Dinny though. Got me going now, fired up. Going to play this cute Nemo hoor off the field. Do. A flukey goal from Spillane settles everything, Cork buckle. Jeezuus it's not even half-time and we have them. Seven points to the good. Don't let up, says Dwyer. Don't let up, says Mickey Ned. Don't. Sullivan, McCarthy, the Lynches, Egan, Sheehy, Spillane. Attack in waves. Me? I'm in control. Dinny's lost it. My guard doesn't drop for the rest of the match.

Rebel hearts broken. New order is born in Munster. Kerry 1–14, Cork 0–7.

Definition

There is a defining moment in every footballer's life, a pivot on which their whole career turns. It may not be the most famous moment, nor, indeed, the best moment, but it is the occasion when their true courage is tested at the top level for the first time, physically and morally. Pass this test and anything is possible, fail it and you'll always be questioned. This was my moment. It was far from spectacular, and it certainly wasn't glorious, but it was a beginning. A heavy auld day in Killarney in 1975, my reputation was born. Dinny Allen, a talented, intelligent and streetwise footballer had asked the questions. I answered them. Sure the experience I had already gained stood to me, the guidance of men like Johnny Flaherty, Batt Garvey, Joe Keohane and now Mick O'Dwyer was invaluable, but this was make or break. Step-up time.

I had, however, to get to that point. It wasn't as straightforward as history suggests. You see, the tale often begins here; Cork overturned; the breakthrough; the fifteen bachelors. The great Kerry journey was underway, a journey never to be repeated. Great college player becomes great inter-county senior . . . It's not the full story. The step-up wasn't automatic. I had my doubts and they were shared by selectors and family. Could have blown it, you know. My parents knew it, my brothers knew it. Could have blown it.

Rewind to July 1973. I lined out for the Kerry minors in midfield against Cork in the Munster final, did okay. We lost 1–16 to 3–5. Seniors were next up. Mick O'Dwyer still playing, Johnny Culloty in charge. Hammered. Jimmy Barry Murphy runs amok for Cork, scores three goals. Cork 5–12, Kerry 1–15. I think it was after this humiliation that the first rehabilitating steps were taken to plant Kerry back in pole position in Munster. The manager and selectors met in the Victoria Hotel, Cork, after the game and made a list of the best Under-21 players in the county. They would spread the net. Kerry football would look to its youth. The future. I was mentioned.

There were already a number of youngsters on the Kerry senior panel in 1973; John Egan, Mickey Ned O'Sullivan, Jimmy Deenihan, Ger O'Keeffe, Ger Power. (Paudie Lynch had graduated the previous year but was injured.) All these guys were minors in 1970, lost to Galway in the All-Ireland final. They'd made the step-up. More kids, including myself, would line out with them in the Munster senior final the following year and lose again. But, crucially, the policy of developing the under-age players on the senior team was in place. It would, of course, eventually pay off handsomely as Dwyer, elevated from selector to manager for the 1975 season, stuck with the plan. Victoria Hotel, Cork, 15 July 1973. Important night for Kerry football. Important night for me.

Following that meeting I received a letter from Johnny Walsh inviting me to join the Kerry Under-21 panel due to face Cork in the Munster final in Skibbereen (I wasn't on the squad for the first round). I was a sub and came on at midfield during the interval. Kerry were getting a grilling, didn't look good for us. Beaten in the minor, beaten in the senior. And now . . . But we turned it around and I helped do it, quietened their star performer, Robert Wilmot, a skilful left-footer. We won by a goal. It was a big lift for Kerry. Lost prestige regained. Páidí makes another good impression. Can't go wrong for me now, or so I thought. Foolish youth. We were drawn against Offaly in the All-Ireland semi-final in Tralee two weeks later and I held my place in the middle of the field. I didn't hold my head though. Went on the piss and had several late nights in the lead-up to the match. Big mistake. I partnered my Hogan Cup hero from Ventry, John Long, in midfield and boy did I struggle. Moved from midfield to wing-forward. Moved from wing-forward to corner-forward. Taken off. Footballers will know those days, know that particular journey. Nothing worse. Funny, Mikey Sheehy followed me off five minutes later! Mikey had an arse on him then. Funny. Facing home wasn't funny. It was one of the worst days of my life. My brothers fucked me out of it. Beatrice agreed with them. They knew I'd been out during the week, knew I wasn't tuned in. Jeezuus I felt bad. Expelled from the Sem, failed at my studies. There was always football, I thought. Now that was even in question. If I couldn't behave myself in the run-up to an All-Ireland Under-21 semi-final, what hope? Luckily for me Kerry beat Offaly well in that game.

Response? Shortly afterwards I was selected to play midfield for Na hÁghasaigh, a west Kerry side comprising An Ghaeltacht, Dingle and Lispole, in the quarter-final of the Kerry senior championship against East Kerry. I scored 2–11. The two goals came from two penalties and who did I kick them past but Kerry senior boss Johnny Culloty. We then defeated Feale Rangers in the semi-final so I'd already addressed some of the damage. I think it's important that a young player, aspiring to become a county senior, should hold down a central position on his club side. It's a point often debated; where should a good county minor or Under-21 player line out with his club? I think good young players learn about responsibility on the field if they are handed a central role with their clubs. Stands to them in the long run. Stood to me. I still look for it. Anyway, I kept my starting place, though this time at wing-forward, on the Under-21 side for the All-Ireland final against Mayo in Ennis. A fine display from John Long in midfield swung the game our way and we took the title. I was marked by Mayo senior Ger Feeney and he kept me quiet. I kicked a point but contributed little. Lucky to stay on. Another bad day for me, didn't really enjoy it. Step-up? Takes a while. Need to learn.

That Under-21 championship was important. It took me down a peg. I'd been blazing a trail. Cocky. Blind. Now I had a much better idea of what was involved. The need to work hard, stay tuned in, keep the head and watch the sauce aren't always obvious to a *garsún*, especially one of my nature. Now I knew a bit more. It stood to the rest of the lads as well. Gave 'em their first taste of inter-county success. O'Mahony, Deenihan, O'Keeffe, Power, O'Sullivan, Egan, Sheehy. Sweet. Liked it. Paudie Lynch also returned from injury to get a slice of the action that day. He was still a bit rusty, replaced in the final by Martin Ferris. But Lynch was back. That was good for Kerry.

So fortune favoured me. A bad semi-final and a non-descript final could have closed the chapter there and then. It didn't. I survived. A good run with Na hÁghasaigh helped and another chance to win over the selectors and my family presented itself when we took on Austin Stacks in Tralee in the county final. Can't say that I really grabbed the chance though. I improved, no doubt about that. I scored 1–2, the goal was decent but it came late in the game. We were well beaten. Stacks were powerful, inspired by Joe Joe Barrett, their player-manager. I got away with it. I didn't even convince myself or my family that day, but my name stayed in the hat and the Kerry seniors invited me for a run-out after Christmas.

The big chance had arrived. A sniff of the Green and Gold. Now, had I learned my lesson? Well, I was learning it but I was to get away with a bit more messing before it finally hit home. "DISCIPLINE YOURSELF, YOU CLOWN." Didn't quite get it yet. Early in January 1974, a young Denis Ogie Moran from Limerick and Ballybunion (a mate of mine from the Kerry minor team of 1972 and 1973) was back in the Gaeltacht learning Irish and the pair of us gave the west a serious lash. In the middle of that *spraoi* I'd been handed a starting role for the Kerry seniors in a challenge game against Clare. As late as the Friday night, myself and Ogie were living it up at a Wren Ball in Ventry. A fucking Wren Ball, and me with a chance to impress the Kerry management two days later. Once again I got away with it. I played well. Got away with it. The following Sunday we played the Dubs in a challenge in Tralee. I kicked five points from right half-forward. More than got away with it. Impressed them. Never really looked back.

Although I was still at school and playing for the Gaeltacht club, the divisional side, Kerry minors, Kerry Under-21s, college team and, now, the Kerry seniors, I was drinking. *Bhí dúil agam 'sna pínt,* I liked the pints, no doubt. Throw in women and my early appetites were complete. Football, drink, women; kind of in that order. How was I going to manage the step-up if I was drinking? Must have worried my mother no end. Football was my one big shot. She knew it, even then. But those difficult days that summer, when I didn't shine so brightly, probably clinched the deal for me. Saved me, if you like. I mightn't have started to act on it yet but it was in the back of my mind already. "DISCIPLINE YOURSELF, YOU CLOWN." There's a time for football and a time for drinking. They'd have to be separated. They were eventually. And still are.

My first big game for the seniors came at the tail-end of the National League when we played Galway in Tralee. Kerry needed to win or draw to qualify for the semi-finals and had a number of injuries. I was selected at wing-forward from the start. Pat Spillane had impressed for Thomand College in the higher education leagues and was given a run as a sub. I got another big break in that game. The late Eamon O'Donoghue, a real player's player, realised my predicament and brought me into the match, set up two scores for me, two easy points. Looked good for young Páidí. Makes a huge difference when an established player gives a rookie a

dig-out, can make or break you. Made me that day. I've a
lot to thank Eamon O'Donoghue for. Only realised it
later in my career just how kind he was. Players can be
very selfish. He wasn't. It may have had something to do
with the fact that I was playing with St Mike's at the
time, that Listowel, north Kerry, had adopted me. He
was from Ballylongford and a lot of my classmates hailed
from the same parish. He'll never know but I'm grateful.

Stepping back

I was relegated to the subs bench for the semi-final of the
league game against Tyrone as the established players
had recovered from injury. I didn't play that day and
Kerry won easily. However, another important thing
happened to me shortly after that was to have a profound
effect on my career. At a challenge game against Cork in
Dunmanway, I was given half-an-hour at centre-back,
marking Declan Barron. Did okay. On the way off the
field Joe Keohane approached me, "How are you enjoying
your football?" he enquired.

"Very much, Mr Keohane," I answered reverentially.
But some impetuous streak in me came to the fore and I
added, "But I'd love to get a crack at wing-back."

Didn't really give it a lot of thought. Anyway the first
league final in which we drew with Roscommon arrived
in April and I was introduced as a sub late in the second
half. I was very excited, playing in Croke Park, although
my focus at that point really lay with St Mike's and the
chance of a crack at the Sem. Spillane started but was
taken off. I was brought on late for our full-forward
Séamus Mac Gearailt, a clubmate of mine from the
Gaeltacht. I didn't fancy it – telling Séamus I was
replacing him – so I went to Jackie Walsh who was on
the '40' and told him to move to full-forward. It was he
who broke the news to my clubmate. I snatched a point
and John Egan grabbed a goal that secured a draw for us.
For the replay I was selected from the start . . . at wing-
back. My new home. We won the replay 0–14 to 0–8.

Páidí Ó Sé, the new right half-back on the Kerry team.
Step-up? Well we'd see. I was in the right parish anyway.

The gloss wasn't long peeling off that jubilant period.
Leaving Cert, June 1974. I resigned myself to the
inevitable, hadn't a hope. I failed miserably. A place in
college studying physical education would be beyond me.
I had no real notion what to do with myself, I wasn't
exactly driven at the time. The garda exam had been
mentioned but I didn't give it a great deal of thought just
yet. Still, my early elevation to the senior ranks of the
Kerry set-up meant I was part of the 1974 championship
campaign. Football was filling the void, to an extent.

If the 1973–1974 season had marked the first notch in
my belt, nothing tangible was added in the championship
summer of 1974. We surrendered our Under-21 crown to
Cork in Caherciveen when I blasted a penalty so wide of
the target that it shot through the window of Batty
Burns' shop behind the ground (they never invited me
that far upfield again). On the senior front we fell, as
expected, to All-Ireland champions Cork on another rain-
soaked afternoon in Killarney. Balance wasn't right.
Myself, the two O'Keeffes, Sheehy, Power, Egan, Lynch,
O'Sullivan, and O'Mahony all lined out that day. I doubt
if any of us really believed that we could beat Cork. I
certainly didn't. In fact, I thought we would serve a long
apprenticeship to our neighbours, such was the power in
their line-up. They had excellent forwards – in particular
Ned Kirby, Declan Barron, Jimmy Barry Murphy, Ray
Cummins and Jimmy Barrett. We managed to stay in
touch with them for a while until I conceded a goal to
Dave McCarthy. Case closed. Cork 1–11, Kerry 0–7.
None of us really raised a gallop. Ogie impressed in the
minor match, kicked a number of long-range frees over
the bar, against the wind. Later on Mikey missed a
number of kickable frees with the wind from closer
range. One of those days.

A bad summer just got worse. What now? The Leaving
Cert results certainly wouldn't cast any light on the
situation. Failure. Beaten in two Munster finals. Failure.
Páidí Ó Sé. Failure? No, wait a minute. Wasn't I now

mixing with legends? Dwyer was my selector, Connell my team-mate?

Johnny Culloty had invited Mick O'Connell back on to the panel for that championship. Our jaws dropped at the sight of him in the dressing room. He may have been past his prime but we revered him. Connell? God. We were togging out alongside God! Then he asked us our names. "What's your name?" Made us feel very uncomfortable. Half a National League campaign . . . that wasn't enough to talk to this man on an equal footing. Nervous. Uncomfortable. We didn't know what to make of him. And, in truth, his inspiration to us was his very presence. Playing with Connell stuck in my mind for a long time after the dust had settled on the 1974 Munster final. It must have been tough for him though. He was in the twilight of his career, had to haul himself from Valentia to Tralee for training. Long journey, bad road. Not easy. And if a session was due to start at 6.30, myself and Mikey were there at 5.45. Young bucks. Professional footballers, without the loot. Full-timers. Football, football, football. Couldn't have been easy for Connell to accept. He knew those days well. But it must have rattled his cage to be thrust in among a gang of young, blindly enthusiastic footballers.

I won nothing that summer, but I was no failure. I had played with Mick O'Connell.

Now, however, there was no more football. I'd no qualifications and no job. I decided to accept an offer to travel to New York with Eddie O'Sullivan and play football for Carlow in the local championship. Might even stay a while. I should have been beside myself with excitement; nineteen-year-old west Kerry tearaway heads for NY. I wasn't. Don't know why. Ever since I have chewed the Big Apple to the core, but on this occasion I was apprehensive. I landed in JFK and, like any young Irishman at the time, was awestruck. This was the early 1970s, transatlantic travel by choice was a luxury few had tasted. I had been well-briefed by several migrating west Kerrymen who regaled the youngsters back home about life in New York; the magnitude of the place, the well-paid work, the women, the craic. We marvelled at their stories. Then why was Páidí Ó Sé – of all youngsters – not happy? Don't know. Maybe I was just too young to enjoy the freedom, the different culture. I felt detached the minute I got there, couldn't wait to get home. Couldn't wait for the National League. Didn't hang around either. I left for Shannon two days later.

Back to Ard an Bhóthair. Back to the shop. No harm either. I was a powerfully fit teenager at the time but I'd probably spent my first extended period slugging porter. I set in place a personal training programme, which I would dip in and out of over the next decade. Fairly primitive stuff mind you. Probably the most unscientific programme that any athlete ever attempted. Worked for me though. The local landscape of Ventry and the peninsula is mountainous and harsh. Beautiful . . . until you run it. Behind our house a steep road called the Clasach rises to a peak on Mount Eagle and then drops down into Dún Chaoin on the far side. Regularly, especially back in the 1970s, I would set off over the Clasach, run down into Dún Chaoin, and around by Slea Head back to Ventry. Fourteen miles of the most scenic countryside in Ireland. Fourteen miles of the hardest, ball-breaking terrain you can run. I often varied it too. Go off the beaten track, up the side of the hill. Like a fucking goat. Stood to me. I'd jog uphill and try and sprint down.

Improved the speed, this did. Came in handy when I was chasing David Hickey around Croke Park. Another technique I tried on my own was a basic form of hurdling – over gates, brush-handles and fences. I tried to modify hurdling later on as a manager, as I believe it's suited to the stop-go nature of football where speed off the mark and power in the air are vital. Anyway, this training kept me in great shape. It was also good for the soul. Ask footballers. Want to prove to themselves they can endure anything. Especially Gaelic footballers. Often get their heads right by putting themselves through the mill. I did anyway. I even pounded the Clasach during the middle of the championship. Makes no sense at all physically. But mentally. Sharpens you, keeps you tuned in. Hard.

When we reconvened in the autumn, we were managerless. Johnny Culloty had resigned in the wake of the Munster final defeat and county chairman Gerald McKenna actually steered the ship for the first few games. We didn't train together but we continued with our league games. Significantly, in our second outing on 10 November, on a pissy wet day in Killarney, we played Dublin, the new All-Ireland champions. We were well up for it. Few had expected the Dubs to beat Cork in the All-Ireland semi-final but the manner of that victory and their subsequent success in the final had resonated in Kerry. I was at corner-back and Ogie had joined the line-up. We played well and only a seven-point tally from Jimmy Keaveney kept Dublin in it. This meant something to me. We drew with the All-Ireland champions, 0–8 each. That was to help.

So was the appointment of the new manager.

The Waterville line man

In January 1975, Mick O'Dwyer was elected to the role of senior boss. It was a surprise. Sure, he'd been a selector for a year and looked after the Under-21s but we still sort of identified him as a player; after all, he'd only retired at the end of 1973 and was a legendary figure in the county. He brought great experience as a player not only because of his success but because he had played all over the field. Great advantage. However, initially, he kept a low profile. I think he was surprised himself at the appointment and, knowing Dwyer, he wanted to get a handle on the situation first.

There was no sledge-hammer approach, no new training methods, at least not immediately. Rather he chose a number of challenge games to get a feel for the line out, the players. We were exceptionally young so general fitness wasn't really a problem with most of us and, despite our age profile, the majority had been through quite a lot. There was plenty of under-age experience and many of us had graduated to the senior panel early in our careers. We had a lot of cop-on individually. Mikey knew that if he was to make the breakthrough he'd have to shed some weight. I knew I'd have to tighten up, learn the defender's code. The jury was, however, still out. The step-up would only be complete when we turned the tables on Cork. Personally, I felt the Dublin game in Killarney was the first turning point. Dwyer was probably the second.

We qualified for the quarter-finals of the league in March 1975 and were drawn against Meath in Croke Park. Strange. Over the years Meath have often provided a yardstick for us. (It was the same in 2000, and, as for 2001, well . . .) On this occasion, though, we hadn't the strongest of teams out. They beat us by five points, very comfortably. I didn't really care. I was happy enough the way things were going and was happy enough with my own game. I moved from wing-back to midfield. On my toes. The Clasach. Full-timer. Fittest man on the team. The defeat didn't really put any pressure on the team either. Kerry had won the previous four National League titles. It was time to set our sights on Cork. Now Dwyer could get down to business.

Things were looking up for me on the employment front. When I returned from my two-day *deoraíocht* in the States the previous summer, I had been eventually persuaded to sit the Guards exam. I passed. Hard to believe. Not the hardest exam in the world but, when it's the first you've ever passed, got to be pleased. I started in the Garda Training College, Templemore at the beginning of May 1975. Páidí Sé, Garda. Two weeks after starting, on 16 May, my birthday, I won my second Munster Under-21 medal after we hammered Waterford. The game was played in Templemore. Felt like it was there on purpose. Seemed to fit in with my preferential treatment. I was well looked after by the garda officials. The Kerry County Board also played its part. Chairman Gerald McKenna was a flamboyant, ambitious character – he had appointed Dwyer – and it was arranged that I would dine separately in the Templemore Arms Hotel to

ensure my diet was healthy. Always ate well. Beatrice
made sure, now the County Board made sure. They say I
was bred for football. *Tógadh le caid mé*. Seemed that
way.

My boss in Templemore was John Mitchell, a big
Wexford man who won an All-Ireland hurling medal
with his county in 1960. Mitchell was an affable
character. He had been stationed in Killgarvan for several
years and I think he had a soft spot for Kerrymen.
Anyhow, he treated me well and I appreciated the
latitude I was given to pursue my football and the blind
eye that he frequently turned to my indiscretions.

Before we got to turn the tables on Cork in the
Munster final that year, we had an interesting outing
against Tipp. Dwyer was preaching caution prior to that
first championship game in Clonmel. The reason?
Michael Babs Keating and a good dose of complacency.
Babs was a big powerful footballer; dangerous. He had
cemented his reputation on the hurling fields in the
1960s but he could cause havoc with the big ball. Did!
John O'Keeffe was ruled out of the game through injury
and Ger deputised at No. 3. I was right corner-back. Babs
ran amok. Fifteen minutes into the second half we were
still behind. Just shows you. History; eight All-Ireland
medals, sporting immortality. What if?

We survived but in the process Babs taught me a
valuable lesson. Ger O'Keeffe played a looping ball
through to me just before the break. Hospital pass; teed
me up for Babs who accepted the invitation. *Bang!* Awful
clatter to the ribs. I couldn't speak properly at half-time,
couldn't speak properly for a week. I was in a heap. But I
couldn't let Dwyer know just how I felt when he rushed
on to see how I was. Like a stubborn boxer I fought on
and it proved worthwhile as I had a hand in a couple of
goals that eventually killed the game off. Egan, as usual,
did the business. Interesting day though. Not glamorous,
important stuff rarely is. Two years training had stood to
me, the Clasach had stood to me but Babs prepared me
for the real rigours ahead. After all, Brian Mullins & Co.
were lurking around the corner, intent in their hearts!

Approaching the Munster final I was flying. Living the life of a professional footballer in Templemore. Early to bed, drill, swimming, physical education, nothing too taxing on the head. Well fed. I regularly carried a couple of footballers in the college back to the Templemore grounds for a kick around. Their repayment would be a steak in the Arms Hotel, courtesy of the Kerry County Board. Professional footballer from the time I failed my Leaving. Professional. Still have 'em now in the GAA. Students.

By this stage Dwyer had upped the ante at training but it was nothing compared to what he'd put us through some years later. Now, I was well able for it. He'd often arrange a full weekend of football and I would be first out of the traps on Friday night having hopped off the train from Templemore. Dwyer was learning his trade. Everybody was treated the same, he didn't like whinging or excuses. Discipline was good but it would be a number of years before he understood the differences and complexities of each individual's physical make-up. He didn't have the scientific methods that are now at every modern manager's disposal. He'd know later how Ger Power's hamstrings would tighten. Quickest man we had, didn't need to run all day. Natural. Didn't need all the donkey work. Donkey work took the edge off someone like Power. Eventually copped it.

Dwyer had seen the turnaround in Dublin. Interpreted it. He'd seen how they'd turned Cork over. The pace, strength, movement. Sure, he was working with incredible raw material. Incredible. The greatest collection of athletes you're likely to see in Gaelic football. He knew the skill was there, knew the talent was there. Saw Mikey's touch; how Egan struck a shot on the run; how young Spillane, nineteen years old, could plant the ball over the bar from anywhere; the hands on Paudie Lynch and Pat McCarthy. But Dwyer wanted everything done at pace. Wanted to instil the killer instinct. Wanted to win.

A few weeks before the Munster final, I travelled to Dingle to line out for West Kerry in a county championship match on Sunday afternoon. Played a blinder, wing-back. That evening on my way back to Templemore I played for Kerry in a challenge game against Galway in Limerick, the Denis Moran Perpetual Cup. Blinder again, wing-back. Still hopping. Selectors had seen enough. I was moved out of the corner to right half-back for the Cork game. The dress rehearsals were over. I was ready. We all were. And what was even better, we weren't expected to win. Cork were on for the three-in-a-row. Pressure? None. My family and friends didn't think we'd win. We didn't even expect it ourselves. Sure I was wound up, but not nervous. Wound up, not nervous. Tuned in.

Before half-time we had the Munster final wrapped up. Hard to believe. Players like Spillane and Ogie, who came on as a sub, were adding a new dimension to the establishment. A forward division of true class was being assembled. Best ever. Craft, accuracy, pace; these would become their hallmarks. In time they'd be unstoppable. Great for us backs. Look up. Always someone showing. Always hungry. Keeps the game simple. Hunger.

After a couple of pints in Killarney, I returned to Templemore that July evening. Got a spin from Michael O'Donoghue and took the scenic route to include a few pit-stops. By the time I got back to Tipp I was a hero. Fêted in the Arms. My joust with Dinny appeared on the box. Cult status secured. Next stop Croke Park.

Before the All-Ireland semi-final against Sligo, it had been agreed that I would be collected in Templemore on the Saturday as the team made their way to Dublin on the train. However, the week of the game I decided I'd shoot home to Ventry on the Friday night. I suppose it made little sense but I wanted to check in at home, get the blessing of the family for my first championship outing to Dublin. There was a bit of craic too given my mother's Sligo roots. In fact I travelled to Croke Park with plenty of respect for the opposition. Micheál Kearins was a very talented player and was known all over from his frequent Railway Cup appearances for Connacht. I remember he was one of the first players I'd ever seen strike a ball with the outside of the boot. He was known later on, of course, as an inter-county referee. Sent Keith Barr off after the incident with my old sparring partner Dinny Allen in the 1989 All-Ireland semi-final between Dublin and Cork.

Sligo were also a hardy bunch. Men like John Brennan, Barnes Murphy. Had a reputation. We knew they'd get stuck in and at the start they did. But the game degenerated into a total mismatch. Having won their first Connacht title in forty-seven years, Sligo had obviously drained every last drop of satisfaction from that success. They were in Croke Park to enjoy themselves. They couldn't even begin to match us for fitness.

It wasn't the best day I ever had, mind you. Gave away an early penalty for a stupid obstruction with the elbow and was generally a little loose. Fortunately, Paudie O'Mahony saved the penalty and Sligo fell apart. The old way was dying. Big strong Sligo men chased shadows around Croke Park that day. Beaten by seventeen points.

Given how the Dublin–Kerry rivalry developed into a national obsession over the following ten years, it's hard to believe just how relaxed we were with the prospect of facing the Dubs in the All-Ireland final. Nothing was really expected of us, especially not in Kerry. Needed to mature, they said. We were only kids, all bachelors, average age just over twenty-two. Munster title was a bonus. That's the way it was. No pressure. We trained frequently for the final and it was brilliant. Flying. Summer evenings, tearing after one another. We developed quickly as a defence. The O'Keeffes, Deenihan, Horse Kennelly, Power; had to cope with the quickest and craftiest forwards the game had ever seen. We mightn't have realised it just yet, but we were feeding off one another. Didn't realise it but we were ready. Dwyer kept everything simple. Preached to us to defend, defend. Don't get sucked up front. Defend. Trust the forwards. We did. We'd seen them at first hand. The only time Dwyer told us to go forward with the ball was during Railway Cup games. This was solely for the benefit of our Cork team-mates.

As we were such a young panel, relationships between players were only really developing. There were, of course, cliques based on locality, personality, interest. But close bonds only grew in time. I knew Ogie, Mikey, Kennelly and, of course, Spillane. I also knew panellist John Long, my neighbour. But I didn't know a lot of the players well, certainly not socially. And I never really got to know most of them, remarkable as that may seem. Only on the pitch did we all gel. On the pitch we were as tight a bunch as you'll ever get.

At that time I didn't know Paudie Lynch well. The All-Ireland final would change that forever.

The talking point the week of the match was Sheehy being switched to full-forward. John Bunyan had lined out against Cork and Sligo, Ger Driscoll was in the shake-up; there were a few players in with a chance. The last man we thought would be on the edge of the square was Mikey. Ogie was also a surprise on the '40' though, Dwyer must have had Dublin's Alan Larkin in mind with this selection. Larkin was a big powerful man but he wasn't the most mobile. Ogie, the youngest player we had, could run all day. We prepared with a series of trial games, backs and forwards, probables versus possibles. We also trained in public and this added to the excitement of the occasion, added a great atmosphere. I lament the passing of open training. Dwyer always welcomed it, built up a great rapport with visitors over the years, especially with visitors from the north.

Unfortunately, times have changed. The demands of the media and public are now so great that managers have had to close shop. There was a beautiful innocence back then. I suppose life was a lot less complicated, seemed that way. I recall before an All-Ireland several years later, Peadar O'Brien of the *Irish Press* and Paddy Downey of *The Irish Times* were delayed travelling to one of our press nights. They were greeted at the dressing room door by the then county chairman Frank King,

"Jeezuus, lads, we thought you were never going to make it." King told us to make sure they were made welcome. Nowadays I'd be only too happy to escape the glare. Different ball game nowadays. Everyone's looking for an angle. Not enough to explain yourself on the pitch or the line, have to give 'em an angle as well. Professional really. Professional demands.

I spent the last week before the final at home. Again I wanted to set off from Ventry, wanted them to be part of it there. In the lead up to the game, one man who helped me greatly was Donie Sullivan, a squad member at the time. Donie didn't really fancy Dwyer's new training regime and didn't make any secret of his dissent. Didn't turn up for several of the sessions. So he never really got a look in, but he encouraged and cajoled me. Helped me to tune in for the day.

The Kerry minors travelled with us on the Saturday, they were playing Tyrone in the final. When we got off the train at Heuston, a photographer approached me and asked me which carriage the senior team would be getting off. No one really knew us. There was a decent crowd of Kerry supporters waiting to welcome us, which got the blood going. Exciting. Grin on my face. The old Dublin–Kerry rivalry was about to be resumed for the first time in twenty years. Kerry people exiled in the capital were keen to make themselves known to their neighbours.

Still, there was no pressure. We had a guard to the knave, an excuse, we were kids. First-timers. We stayed at the Grand Hotel in Malahide, north Dublin, a new venue for Kerry teams. The Grand was off the beaten track and it was chosen as a quiet pre-match venue where Dwyer could apply the final touches in peace. It was the beginning of an annual routine for us. The Grand, a walk on the beach, a chat with Dwyer, a kick around. Naturally, over the years, Kerry folk started to populate the place on the eve of big games. Weddings aside, it wasn't a bad venue, depended really where in the house you were billeted. Overall the build-up routine worked so well that it's hard to distinguish the different years now, it's all a bit of a blur.

The bachelor boys

On the Sunday we'd arranged to meet in the lobby of the Grand at 1 pm for a light snack before heading to Croker. I shot down about 12.45 to where the selectors and county board officials were meeting for a proper four-course lunch. Our midfielder Pat McCarthy also arrived down on his own. Thinking it was lunch for all, Pat tucked into a feed of roast beef and spuds, FUCKING APPLE PIE AND CREAM. The works! Never realised it. Two hours before lining out against Brian Mullins and Bernard Brogan in his first All-Ireland final. Had it eaten before any of us knew. Went on to play a stormer. Just shows you. Science.

The first signs of tension appeared as we filed into the dressing rooms beneath the old Cusack Stand. We had just watched part of the minor game and were getting togged out when Bishop Éamon Casey approached the room to use the toilets and, I suppose, to give us a word of encouragement. There was quite a bit of nervous banter going on at the time and someone shouted, "Sssshh, lads, hold on, lads, easy. The bishop is coming in." But there was a sharp reply from the corner. "Fuck the bishop, let's win the match." Got us going. Disrespectful sure, but it broke the ice. I don't think the person in question meant to be insulting in any way but, in fairness, an All-Ireland dressing room is no place for a bishop! Mickey Ned then got up on the table and made a terrific speech. As it was still new to us, the captain's speech motivated us greatly. Dwyer then put the finishing touches to our preparations by passionately pleading with us to do it for ourselves. Both collectively and individually, Dwyer always told you what you wanted to hear. Always motivated us. We took to the pitch in our new tracksuit tops. I was fairly wired. Not blindly psyched up though. People often read me wrong. I was tuned in. My brother Tom, who'd played with the minors in the 1963 final, had warned me not to be overawed by the occasion, the atmosphere. Nerves got the better of him; struggled to get his second wind. During the warm-up I ran solidly for ten minutes; a seriously good blow-out. Second wind well got.

Prior to the game, my old teacher and trainer in St Mike's, Johnny Flaherty, wrote me a letter in Templemore explaining that my direct opponent that day, David Hickey, often received signals from the Dublin keeper Paddy Cullen before kickouts. If Cullen tugged his togs twice, Flaherty explained, it meant the kick would be directed towards Hickey. Anytime I saw Cullen's hand drop at all that day I was out of the traps like a scalded cat. I didn't win the first two balls that came down our wing but I got a hand on them. Settled. Remember making a kick block on him. Wouldn't be allowed today. After the block, the ball bounced up and I volleyed it down the field. Felt great. Big roar.

Mickey Ned made a blistering start to the game. He was picking up a huge amount of ball and consistently running at the Dublin defence. What happened to him afterwards, when Seán Doherty eventually nailed him, has been well documented. It was a pity for Mickey and for Kerry. He was a very exciting player. Never the same again. Sure, we completely dominated Dublin that day. After Egan slipped the defence for a brilliant goal, they buckled – couldn't live with our movement. Spillane kicked some mighty scores, Sheehy showed his class; the chip-up. Class. It was to spell the end for a number of their players. The old school. Near the close of the game, I grabbed a hold of Mullins' jersey. He swung back at me but missed. Lucky Páidí. The Dubs laid down a few markers in the process. Markers which we failed to heed initially and would haunt us over the next two years until we added the final touches to our make-up as a team.

After the game, Hickey was utterly gracious in defeat. It was a great personal triumph for me as he was a big powerful man. It was thrilling to get the better of him. Of course he turned the tables on me the following year when he won the battle hands down and we went on sparring for several years. He was probably my toughest opponent but I always felt rather fortunate in our duels. Had David Hickey had more confidence in his own shooting he'd have scored a lot more off me. I got away with that. My record in keeping my final opponents in check is misleading as far as I'm concerned. Hickey should have nipped it in the bud. Helped my confidence. Lucky.

Young, fresh, naive. Unfettered. With nothing to lose, we won the lot. All-Ireland champions 1975.

Unlike the 'townies' on the team, I headed straight back to Malahide on the team bus after the game. Shared a good skip of porter with my brother Tom. Hadn't touched a drop in months. Jeezuus I enjoyed them. My uncle Joe, over from England, also met me that evening. "Well done, Páidí," he bellowed as he hugged me. "This is a great day for the Ó Sés. We're too long in the shadow of the Longs. Great to get a medal from the other side of the family!" Tom gets a great kickout of that. I changed into my three-piece beige suit that Beatrice had bought for me. I looked like a newsreader. Decked out. Stuck into the pints. Remember little else.

Monday morning, twenty years of age, All-Ireland champion. Newspapers belting it out: "Kingdom's Fusillade KOs Heffo's Army." Still not sure what a fusillade is, certainly didn't know that morning with the head lifting off me. After a reception in the garda club in Harrington Street that afternoon, we headed south on the train. Strange; over the years one of the few places the whole panel gathered socially was on that carriage. Even on tours, which were supposed to help us bond, we never all really got together. Now we did. There was fierce ball-hopping. Slagging. Fierce. Boys' stuff. Black magic, as we called it.

There was great fanfare on our arrival home. The minors had won as well so there was double delight. Killarney was buzzing. A parade was planned around the

town on the back of a lorry. I was looking forward to it –
well I thought I was. I'd spent the previous six hours
with Paudie Lynch on the train journey home so just
before we hit town, he said: "Come on, Páidí, we'll give
the parade a miss." We jumped off the train and crossed
the tracks behind. Lynch knew Killarney like the back of
his hand. He carried me off to some quiet pub.

My mother had travelled to see me in the parade and
was well shocked when she couldn't spot me on the
lorry. A search party was dispatched. I was eventually
tracked down. Tom Long was put marking me for the
rest of the night. Our next stop was Tattler Jack's, a pub
owned by Eddie O'Sullivan, currently a selector with me
on the Kerry team and the man who'd carried me to New
York in 1974. After giving it a lash and off-loading some
of the drink, we progressed to Teddy Connor's where four
or five of us re-enacted the final along with John Cronin,
Kery centre-back from the 1953 and 1955 winning teams.
We marched around the pub behind a box player before
eventually standing for the national anthem. "Face the
Tricolour," roared one of the boys. The flag in question
was an old paper hat in the Kerry colours. Tom Long
eventually carried me home to his house in Fossa.

The following morning, in a shockingly delicate state,
I made my way into Killarney. Decided to walk. Needed
to. Still in my new beige suit. Tie was lost. Along the
way, a large black Mercedes pulled up. Bishop Éamon
Casey. "Hop in, Páidí." He took me to the Palace for
breakfast before dropping me off at Scott's Hotel where I
was due to meet a few friends. He double-parked and
stepped out of the car and approached me. Handed me
£50. "You deserve that. Buy a drink for your class back in
Templemore," he said, "and well done again." I returned
to Tattler's and Eddie drove me back west to Dingle
where I had a drink in Paddy Bán Brosnan's pub,
although the Bán was still in Dublin. We returned to
Tattler's where I met up with Dan Kavanagh, a powerful
forward from the 1972 team. He was in the running for
the full-forward berth in 1975 too; great hands, fearless.

Dwyer didn't fancy him though. Not disciplin
for Dwyer. Must have been tough on him.

Eventually shot off on the train for Temp
Changed at Mallow where I squeezed in a
Arrived back at the Garda College expecting
for being late. Didn't. Got a terrific welcome. Three
later Ogie and Dwyer arrived up to the college with the
cup. Nice touch, but I knew what Micko was at. After
getting concessions all year, there was yet one more
request to ask of the authorities. The Under-21 final
against Dublin was to take place the following week in
Tipperary town. Dwyer was in charge of that team as
well. My immediate boss in Templemore, Donal
O'Sullivan, wasn't amused but thankfully, and not for
the first time, he was overruled by his superior John
Mitchell. We beat the Dubs by six points to complete an
incredible minor/Under-21/senior treble for Kerry.

The only sour note at that time was struck on the
Sunday between the two finals when a piss-take article
appeared in the Micheline McCormack Diary in the
Sunday World. In a shit-stirring piece entitled "A
Terrible Shower", McCormack described how the Kerry
players didn't wash after games. Ha Ha. Unfortunately
the article was accompanied by a picture of my bare arse
that had been taken, unbeknownst to me, on the press
night before the senior final. I got some stick in Dingle
that weekend and for weeks afterwards. The family were
none too impressed either. I remember getting a letter
afterwards from the late Brendán Ó hEithir, a
tremendous character. "Let it off, Páidí, don't let them
get to you," he wrote. Thankfully this kind of rubbish
didn't really catch on in Irish journalism, but it is
unfortunate to see elements of it resurface again in
recent years.

I was coming to an end of my twenty-two-week stint
in Templemore. Very enjoyable time. Productive. As well
as living like a professional footballer, I managed to
repeat and pass two subjects in my Leaving. Also enjoyed
the company of my room-mates, two unrelated

onnollys, Tom and Stephen. Good guys. Saved a bit of cash in a Post Office book too. Settled a bit. Sure there was still the odd blow-out on the porter, but life was good. Parents were impressed as well. Couldn't believe I'd saved so much, eight or nine hundred pounds. Passed out then as a garda. Proud day for Beatrice. She travelled up with my two brothers and my nephew Fergal.

It was both a beginning and an end. Success in Croke Park, job as a garda – high hopes marked the start of a new era in my life. But the schooling was over, the first leg of the journey complete. We'd buried the old ball and along with it the old ways. Four county colleges medals, two Munster colleges medal, a National League medal, two All-Ireland Under-21 medals, a Munster championship medal, an All-Ireland senior medal.

Step-up complete.

4
Thin Blue Line

An té nár ól riamh cárt ná cnagaire bíonn ainnise lá a bháis air

March 1979

"You'd better head, Páidí, aren't you on duty in the morning?"

"The morning," I reply, "you mean in a couple of hours." Left Lynch and the boys behind me in Cork, shot back to Limerick. Had a good sup after today's National League game. Fierce craic back there. Slugging all evening. Hit the sack. Alarm sounds almost immediately. "Oh, Jeeezus, I'm dying." Crawl into the station grab the keys and head out to the squad car. I know what I'll do know, I'm thinking. Point her west and head out the Dock Road. See a gate to a field. Pull in, open the gate, throw the car into the field. Out of sight. Roll the seat down and throw the head back. Out like a light. Crafty one, me. Two hours later as the spring dawn slowly brightens the gloomy morning, I turn my thumping head to one side. Hear the noise of a car pulling up outside. And another . . . and another. Raise the head to look out. Squad cars. Fucking everywhere. "JEEEZUUS CHRUUYSSHT. WHAT THE . . . ?" A garda squelches over the mud and raps the window of my car. I leap out of the seat and stagger into the stark, damp morning. Assistant Commissioner is standing in front of me with a posse of gardaí and officials. Assistant

Commissioner. "Howarya, Páid, did ya nod off there?" asks one of 'em.

"Ya," I mumble. "I had an auld match yesterday, I'm a bit wrecked," I add, attempting to explain my presence. "Tell me, lads, what are ye doin' out here?" I ask; bewildered, desperate.

"Well, Páid, we're checking out the venue for the Pope's visit to Limerick next September. The Holy Father'll be sayin' a mass out here, we're sussin' out the place for the security plan." I slip sheepishly back into my squad car and head back to town.

The Ventry sentry

After passing out in October 1975, Garda Páidí Ó Sé was dispatched to William Street station in Limerick. Unit C. Jimmy Deenihan, who was a student in Limerick at the time, brought me around to show me the barracks and later that evening I kicked off in the force on a week of nights. I enjoyed it, at least at first. It wasn't long before I settled into garda ways. On my very first night on duty, a colleague suggested we slip in for a pint at break time. I refused, felt it would be wise to keep my bib clean – at least for a while. I lasted until night two when I had my first taste of Limerick's late night hospitality. Drink while you work, some craic.

At the beginning of my stint in the city, I was housed in the Railway Hotel. My mother was keen that I wouldn't end up in a flat with a gang of students, wouldn't be good for the discipline, she thought. She was right too. Fortunately, on my second night at work, I was approached by a Kerryman named John Costelloe who was stationed with me in William Street. John, from Lixnaw, knew I was looking for digs and was prepared to offer me a bed at his home in Corbally for a couple of weeks until I found a place of my own. He didn't know what to make of me before that. He thought I was a very serious individual, had seen me ignore a few autograph hunters after the Under-21 All-Ireland. However, that night when he stuck his head in the car to introduce himself, he smelled the porter off my breath and thought, "Well at least that's one thing we have in common." I moved in with John, Anne and their family, intending to stay a couple of weeks. I stayed for four years. It became my home. I couldn't have been happier. John and his wife Anne provided me with far more than hospitality, they became good friends. The best. It also provided a stable environment for me, which helped. It was a wild enough couple of years in Limerick and without the luxury of my family residence with the Costelloes, who knows?

If this arrangement sounded a bit cosy for comfort, well it wasn't. John and Anne were remarkably easygoing people and I was away quite a lot with the Kerry team, so we all had enough space. To this day John remains the 'official' Kerryman in Limerick and has taken a host of players under his wing over the years. Of course my mother was delighted with the arrangement. She hardly knew that myself and John would often go on some serious tears around the town. Maybe she did. But she definitely knew there would be a cut-off point, that the routine of life in Corbally would keep me straight and ensure my football didn't suffer. No doubt, meeting the Costelloes was the best thing that could have happened to me. As part of their family, I shared my friends and team-mates with them and John became great pals with Paudie Lynch & Co. and would often be in the thick of the post-match action. Costelloes. Kept me inside the line . . . just about.

Work on the force as a young garda, as a young Kerry footballer, was fine. I was well looked after and, as championship time appeared on the horizon, my days on the beat would be curtailed. As the years progressed, however, I got fed up with night duty, with shift work, in fact I got fed up with work. It was getting in the way of football. It would eventually force me to hang up my tunic. Football and work aside though, the craic was unreal. There were plenty of footballers based in the town at the time . . . Mullins, Ryder, Deenihan, Spillane,

Talty. Thomand College lads. Often met some of the boys at the wrong end of the shift. One night the station received some complaints of a disturbance; reports of a barrel of beer being rolled down Henry Street and up the Dublin Road (later the contents would be emptied into a bath). I was dispatched with a colleague to check out the *rírá*. When I discovered it was a student flat and who was inside, I made a quick detour back to base. Could you imagine it? Young Páidí walking in on top of a gang of footless footballers. In uniform!

Break time or the close of a shift often meant porter, particularly during nights. However, one had to learn the nocturnal habits of the force. I was dispatched one night to inspect a pub that was reportedly selling after hours. I was very raw, and when I arrived at the premises I was told to check it out before entering. "I'm here now, over," I radioed back to the station.

"Is there any activity there?" questioned the officer.

"Yes," I replied. "I can hear people shouting, I can hear laughter and I can hear glasses clinking."

"And can you hear a cash register going?" asked the officer.

"No," I replied.

"Ah you better leave it off, Garda Ó Sé, it could be our own crowd!"

The early days in the job were lucrative for anybody prepared to put in the hours. The Dutch industrialist Dr Tiede Herrema had been kidnapped and guards were being deployed all over the place. I was shy enough though. Couldn't really be bothered. My philosophy hadn't changed from my time in St Brendan's. I really only wanted enough money to get by, play fooball, win medals and buy porter. I wouldn't have been the keenest garda ever to walk the streets of Limerick. In fact the handy life in Templemore had set the scene for me. Work hard on the pitch and nowhere else. I still believe it's almost impossible to play football to a very high standard and work in a demanding job. Especially a job that included shift-work, irregular hours and nights. I mean, you didn't have to do anything, just driving around all night was enough to piss me off. It gnawed away at me over those four years. Football was good, real work was bad.

I have certain regrets about my attitude to life in the guards, just as I regret my attitude to education. Policing, after all, was in my blood, on both sides of my family; I'm related to two assistant commissioners – Joe Long, a first cousin of mine on my father's side and Kevin Carthy on my mother's. I even married a guard's daughter. But despite being steeped in this tradition, I didn't embrace it. Football really saw to that.

My eventual aversion to life as a policeman had nothing really to do with the gardaí. I was exceptionally well-treated. The Kerry network always ensured that Garda Ó Sé was detailed according to the season. Pat Spillane's first cousin, the late Paddy Spillane, was a chief super' in Edward Street and big Ger O'Sullivan was a detective inspector. They helped influence my superiors and, come 1 April, Páidí was given a handy number in the super's office. Nine-to-five. Pulled off the unit. And, in fairness, my colleagues were all understanding. Initially, no one seemed to begrudge the flexibility afforded me. It probably wasn't the most lucrative arrangement – I did precious little overtime – but I didn't care. And with the Costelloes looking after me, I wasn't strapped. In fact if I were to pay John Costelloe back for all he did for me I'd still be doing it today. And there are plenty of Kerry footballers past and present who are in the same boat.

We went through the motions in the 1975–1976 league and Cork eventually put an end to our involvement. No one cared. We were on our way to the States in May for our first transatlantic trip to face the All Stars.

We travelled to San Francisco, LA and New York and, while it wasn't as wild as some subsequent trips, it was still some craic. We stayed mostly with families along the way, which tempered things a little. I teamed up with John Long and Paudie Lynch, but we also fell in with John O'Gara and Martin Carney who travelled out

with the All Stars. We did Tiawana, San Diego, drank
tequila by the tumbler and harassed a few poor Mexican
singers.

We wouldn't have been the most worldly-wise bunch
around. Naturally like any group of young men away on
holidays, especially footballers, women were high on the
agenda. But the perspective of the young Kerryman was
unlike any other. While in New York, one of my team-
mates managed to woo an admirer in a Manhattan bar
and disappeared without trace for the night. We waited
with baited breath the next morning at breakfast to see if
he'd arrive back and, when he did, we pounced on him
demanding he reveal everything. Now, quite often,
everything we spoke about at the time was measured in
Gaelic football terms and a woman's underwear would
be no different. You see, the GAA is not the most radical
body around and one of the landmark changes of our
childhood in the 1960s was the great Down team's
decision to wear black shorts instead of the traditional
white. So in this context our team-mate finally showed
up in the hotel whereupon he was hauled in front of our
specially convened tribunal. "Well, tell us . . . what was
she like?" I demanded.

"Well, Páidí, you wouldn't believe it boy, you
wouldn't believe it. SHE HAD BLACK TOGS ON HER
LIKE DAN McCARTAN!"

The Dubs, of course, had also broken ranks with the
white-short rule and it wasn't long before the Blue and
Navy appeared on the horizon again.

The underlying problems we faced going into the
championship weren't obvious to most. The manner of
our All-Ireland victory over Dublin the previous year
suggested a sustained period at the top but the warning
signs were there. As champions, we'd been fêted
everywhere all winter but during the summer of 1976 we
were guests of honour at the Tralee Races. Shouldn't
have been there. We asked Mickey Ned to get on to
Dwyer to cancel training so we could attend. Discipline
was dropping. From my own experience as a manager
you can't afford any slips in this department. Everyone

must be tuned in and the sacrifices have to be made. Nowadays, most young players are far more aware of the physical and psychological requirements for championship football. Twenty-five years ago we weren't. We thought we were and we would eventually learn the difference between thinking you're right and actually being tuned in. In 1976 the guard dropped, collectively. Sure we went through the motions, said the right things but standards had fallen.

Another tell-tale sign as to where we were heading that summer was our relationship with the media. Dwyer was brilliant at handling the press but a lot of the players weren't. Stories about injuries, often contradictory, were emerging. It was sloppy stuff. I have always had something of an ambiguous relationship with the media. I know its importance and I have enjoyed the company of several journalists. But I also learned about the dangers lurking in an open relationship. Sure, some young fellas treat criticism and praise the same way, but not many. As a manager you can use criticism to motivate, even if the criticism is accurate and well founded. But, quite often, it is the praise which is more difficult to deal with. In 1976 we had our share of praise, we were young and we were teeing ourselves up perfectly for the fall.

We retained our All-Ireland Under-21 crown early that season when we defeated Kildare. I lined out at full-back again. Augured well for more senior success.

After hammering Waterford in the Munster semi-final, we faced Cork in the new Páirc Uí Chaoimh in July. The disastrous overcrowding that occurred that tense Munster final day is well recorded and it got to a lot of our players. There were a couple of thousand people, primarily Cork fans, camped on the perimeter of the pitch and many of our boys felt intimidated. I didn't, in fact I was glad I was on the field when I saw just how packed the terraces were. But I was lucky to stay on the pitch as I capsized Dave McCarthy with an awful high tackle that took him out of the game. I should have got the line. Didn't help relations between the Kerry players and the Cork fans in close company. Ridiculous when you think about it. We were blessed to survive and we told ourselves that when we escaped back to the matchbox dressing rooms.

If that drawn Munster final is remembered for all the wrong reasons, the replay is fondly recalled. It was back in Páirc Uí Chaoimh, as we had enjoyed home advantage two years on the trot. It was a great game, a rollercoaster. With the crowd safely back behind the wire, the players really got stuck into it; great pace, great goals, drama, faulty scoreboard, denied victory in normal time as the ball sailed over the bar, disallowed goals, dodgy goals. Young Seán Walsh from Tralee came on and scored 1–3, Pat McCarthy horsed into it – made the difference those boys. 3–20 to 2–19 after extra time. Brilliant. Ranks with the best that Munster final replay. It was a good Cork team, one that probably could have gone the distance. Killed 'em that day.

One of the reasons for our longevity as a team was the structure and nature of the championship in the 1970s and 1980s – we only had to peak twice a season. However, it was also our downfall on a number of occasions, and 1976 was one of them. After surviving our two visits to Cork, we travelled to Dublin to play Derry in the All-Ireland semi-final and annihilated them. Told us nothing, looked like we were well on our way again. Dublin were unsettled, they'd changed their half-back line and we'd show them last year was no fluke.

Didn't work out that way. Jimmy Deenihan and Ger O'Keeffe were both doubtful starters for the final and news of their ailments was all over the papers before the game. Everyone was talking freely and everything felt loose. Even our haven in Malahide wasn't as peaceful on the eve of the final, word had got out and a scatter of fans had showed up. I wouldn't take an ounce of Dublin's success away from them in 1976, they thoroughly deserved to win but we could have put up a better show. If our raw talent and enthusiasm had surprised Dublin the year before, our immaturity and complacency would play into their hands this time around. I mean we still had the fucking Sam Maguire with us on the bus to Croker on All-Ireland final day. I have a picture of little Leo Griffin carrying the cup over to the Hogan Stand as the teams headed for the dressing rooms!

Sloppy. Dwyer was still learning too, didn't cop it early enough. We took to the field, bandages, heads away with the fairies. Bang!

City limits

The new half-back line of Tommy Drumm, Kevin Moran and Pat O'Neill made a huge difference to the Dubs. Never let us settle, kept us on the back foot. Powerful. Hanahoe did a lot of off-the-ball work and they seemed to have loads of space. Hickey had the better of me that day. No doubts. Kicked a good point and got out in front every time. He was up for it. Well-tuned in. And Mullins? Mullins was outstanding, destroyed our midfield. Pat McCarthy had recently returned from a holiday and had shed an amount of weight in an attempt to be right. He was well off the pace while Paudie Lynch more or less ended his days in the middle of the field. Dublin 3–8, Kerry 0–10. Well beaten. Spillane and Egan were the only two to do the business that day.

Dublin horsed us out of it. They were prepared for us, they were stronger than us, stopped us moving the ball, stopped our short-passing, killed us in midfield.

Kerry prodigies got a serious foot in the arse.

The fallout? Well Dwyer saw the guard had dropped, told us so. But he was still learning and, while he knew that we needed to re-examine our approach and line-up, it would be sometime yet before everything would fit into place. Seeing the Dubs parade the Sam at the Listowel Races helped put defeat into context.

By this stage football had become a two-horse race. Ourselves and the Dubs were streets ahead of the rest in fitness terms, and this carried us through matches and hid the positional weaknesses. We sailed through the National League, learning little along the way. However, when we beat Dublin in the 1977 National League final by two points, we thought we'd rectified some of the problems. The reality was Mullins didn't play that day and Dublin without Mullins were not the same team. Never were and, to this day, never have been. It was another false signal. We experimented with John O'Keeffe in midfield, with Paudie Lynch at full-back. In truth Dublin had chances to win that game. It was nothing more than a pre-season joust, the highlight of which saw myself and fellow Garda, John McCarthy, put our crowd control expertise to good use after a couple of republican protesters landed on the pitch. It's widely remembered that incident, probably because the GAA have had few pitch invasions in their day. Went down well in Unit C. Starksy and Hutch!

I'm still haunted by the post-match interview that has been preserved on *Kerry's Golden Years* when a freckled-faced Páidí Sé, with a tie as wide as a gate, tells the world that "we needed to show Dublin that we were as good, if not a little bit better, than them". I smile as I'm delivering my line, just to show what a cute hoor I am. Unfortunately a suave Tony Hanahoe replies prophetically that, "Well . . . later in the year, if we can get a good run in the championship, we'll see what happens. We may be able to reverse that decision." Thanks be to God that we eventually turned the tables back on them.

Heading into the championship of 1977 there was a big rethink about our midfield pairing. Mullins was now the yardstick and we had to match him. Paudie Lynch had been moved successfully to the '40'. Pat McCarthy was struggling to regain his form and paying the price for his slip-up a year previously. We were a versatile bunch – myself, Ogie and Lynch had already played in several positions – but we had to find a settled line-up. At the time I was doing a lot of auld talk about giving the middle of the field a rattle and I was tried out there with new recruit Jack O'Shea, a full-forward on the successful minor team of 1975. The thinking behind the move probably stemmed from the successful 1959 season when the late Seamus Murphy had complemented Mick O'Connell successfully in the middle. Murphy was good at winning breaks and delivering quick, telling passes. Dwyer was wing-back on that team and decided to give it a shot. I was extremely fit and, although I lacked height, the selectors felt my strength and tenacity might yield a lot of possession for us while young Jacko would do the high fielding. Against Tipp in the Munster semi-final, I ran amok and even kicked three points. In the Munster final I had the better of Dinny Long as we destroyed Cork. It looked promising. After all we had, more or less, killed off the Cork team of the 1970s and wouldn't really be tested by our provincial neighbours again for another five years. Now we had to cross the Blue Line again. The All-Ireland semi-final of 1977.

The spotlight that day was on myself and Jacko in the middle of the field. It was a dull, humid day, there wasn't a breath of wind in Croke Park. Suffocating. Uneasy feeling. Couldn't forget the trial game. The fucking trial game. And who was that overweight beardy boy Dwyer called up as an unofficial substitute? Liston, from Beale, a junior club in north Kerry? Final piece of the jigsaw actually, Páidí. God, a year is a long time in football.

The trial game took place the week before we travelled to Dublin. Jacko and Páidí against Pat McCarthy and John Long in midfield. We came out second best. Despite our Munster championship success, action should have been taken there and then. We failed against Dublin. Had the selectors started Pat or even given Long, a strong fielder, a run, we may not have lost that famous game. I wasn't a bad fielder and, in time, would come to fear no one in an aerial duel but that day Mullins and Brogan won out. Fran Ryder had started in the middle for Dublin and I probably held the upper hand against him but when the game opened up in the second half Bernard Brogan's pace came into its own. Jacko was too raw for Mullins, I wasn't good enough and Pat McCarthy came on too late. Dublin, to their credit, played their aces ruthlessly. Tony Hanahoe had masterminded their tactics in Heffo's absence. Their forward plan and substitutions won the match for them. Anton O'Toole had a dream day. Again they exploited the central channel by pulling their men wide.

Was this the best game of all time? I'm probably the worst person to judge the merits of this game historically. I mean, when you play in a match it's very difficult to view the game objectively – even a quarter of a century later! When I watch the 1977 semi-final, "The Greatest Game Ever Played", I cringe, I see the mistakes I made – when I was caught out of position, when Brogan left me for dead as he 'drilled for oil'. When I try to put my objective cap on I see a first half that was only a pale shadow of the second. Sure the intensity of the second thirty-five minutes was breathtaking but this is where it all goes wrong for me and Kerry. This isn't sour grapes. I don't subscribe to the theory that the game is ranked so highly because Dublin prevailed in such dramatic fashion.

It *was* dramatic, full stop. We had the edge on them and they landed two cracking late goals. What rankles with me is not the fact that Dublin won *the* greatest game ever played but that we didn't win *that* game. We could have and midfield was the most critical sector. After creating the space up front, Dublin launched most of their offensives from the middle. However, over seventy minutes, I think the game has probably been surpassed since. Dublin–Meath in 1991, Down–Derry in 1994 and even Kerry–Armagh in 2000 are games that spring to mind almost instantly. Anyway, the final word on any such debate will always be delivered in the small hours of the morning after a gallon of porter.

Regardless of how good and how close the game was, the fallout from the 1977 defeat was severe and it was very fortunate that Dwyer survived the heave at the county convention. As usual our arch critics were Kerrymen themselves, experts to a man after a century of success. Those who had suggested we'd caught the Dubs on the hop in 1975 seemed to have called it right. Dwyer's opponents included a lot of his former team-mates who didn't like the style of the Kerry team and didn't like

Dwyer's leadership. The knives were out. A senior All-Ireland title, three Munster titles, a National League title, a couple of Under-21 crowns, beaten finalists and beaten in the *greatest game ever played* and the knives were out. I know now how Dwyer must have felt. Only in Kerry.

There was also a concerted effort to oust the chairman Gerald McKenna. He had appointed Dwyer and the pair were seen as an item. Ditch McKenna and Dwyer will go. A lot of eminent Kerry football men were behind the move. They knew best. The great Jack Mahon of Galway had slated Kerry's style of play. Oh, they knew best. But McKenna actually knew best. A shrewd, eloquent man, his opponents underestimated his political clout, ignored his strong base in north Kerry, ignored the 'hurling' vote. McKenna romped home. The hurling vote. Future of the greatest Kerry football team of all time saved by the hurling vote in north Kerry!

The formula

With McKenna secure Dwyer was re-elected as manager. Along with Pat O'Shea three new selectors arrived in the dressing room – Liam Higgins, Bernie O'Callaghan and Joe Keohane. This trio added a serious spine to the decision-making process. Dwyer needed strong, insightful allies and out of the adversity of defeat he got them. Individually, each would impact on me at some stage of my career.

The late Bernie O'Callaghan, who played on the Kerry team defeated by Galway in 1965 was an astute judge of a footballer. He was also the prime mover behind my elevation to senior manager in 1995. He was thick-skinned like myself and, despite the repeated opposition he faced proposing me for the job, he stuck at it. He was to become a close personal friend and one whose loss I feel deeply to this day. Back then, however, I never really knew where I stood with Bernie. I know Dwyer and himself didn't always see eye to eye but Bernie's opinion was respected.

Higgins was a good friend, had taught me briefly in Dingle and was the closest to the players. Still, I never crossed the line with him, never discussed team selections. Keohane had been around the scene when I was making the step-up in 1973 and 1974. A solid full-back who anchored the county in the 1940s, he was uncompromising in his belief in the Green and Gold and in his republican politics. As an army man, his beliefs meant a seriously choppy ride in the early 1970s and only for football, his reputation may not have survived that turbulent period.

Keohane was to play a huge part in turning the Kerry team around. He was staunchly opposed to a slavish hand-passing game and taught us to go toe-to-toe with the Dubs both officially and unofficially – something that Dwyer wouldn't have dreamed of. Keohane helped instil some steel into the Kerry team and preached the simple values of a defender. Like most managers or selectors, Keohane was your friend when you were playing well and I suppose my good relationship with him stemmed from my consistency. I often echoed his sentiments when I gave the team my tuppenceworth.

No disrespect to the previous selectors but we had a stronger outfit on the line for 1978. Dwyer was also a lot wiser after his three years at the helm and he was ready to steer a much more direct course to success. The positional switches he would make this time around stuck and he found his trump card Eoin Liston – The Bomber. Ger Power moved to wing-forward, Paudie Lynch moved back into defence and was comfortable in the corner or on the wing, Seán Walsh moved to midfield to partner a much-improved Jack O'Shea, Egan and Sheehy would man the corner-forward berths, playing off the irrepressible Bomber.

In Gaelic football a lot of truck is placed on laying down markers. In fact I'd venture as far as to say that it's what the National League is all about. Better sometimes to lay down a few markers than to win the bloody thing. Now laying down markers at this stage meant playing Dublin and, to a lesser extent, Cork. Many people

who've charted the history of Kerry football refer to a
heated battle out in New York in 1978 when we played
Dublin in a charity game as being highly significant.
However, there was a significant clash when we met in
the league at Croke Park in the autumn of 1977. We gave
the champions a good rattle in a lively meeting and,
more importantly, they got their first taste of the Bomber
who bagged a brace of goals. Marker laid.

Having been knocked out at the semi-final stage of the
championship it had been a slow run-up to the league
and, to keep my hand in and my fitness up, I decided to
give rugby a go. My colleagues in the unit in Limerick
were at me to travel up to Garryowen; said the social life
was great. When I was stuck in the city, I often trained
with the Limerick hurlers and even went through my
paces with the Limerick soccer team; terrorised their
goalie with some ferocious penalty kicks. Anyway,
showing a rare ecumenical streak, I went up to
Garryowen and joined the panel for training one night.
Didn't like it, wasn't really noticed so I turned to
Limerick's other team, Young Munster. When I landed at
Highfield (or the killing fields as they fondly refer to the
grounds) I was given a warm welcome. I really enjoyed
the craic there. Sure the 'social scene' was slightly
different to their lofty neighbours (I recall denying that I
recognised one of my team-mates in the district court)
but I liked these people. They threw me in full-back and
it wasn't long before I togged out for my first 'real' match
against Skerries in Dublin. I could lamp the ball a fierce
distance, so I was able to hold my own but I remember
well the first and only occasion when I decided to run it.
I dodged a couple of tackles before being hand-tripped. I
landed at the bottom of my first proper ruck and like an
eejit, held onto the ball. Jeeezuus. Thought I'd suffocate.
I swore to myself, "If I get out of this fucking ruck alive
I'm never running with the ball again."

Immediately after that first match against Skerries, we
sat down to dinner with our opponents where the referee
and the club presidents spoke. I couldn't get over this. I
thought initially that it was the greatest heap of shit I'd

ever seen. But in hindsight it was anything but. I mean the GAA could do worse than encourage something similar. I didn't speak a civilised word to Dinny Allen until I was three years retired and here I was slurping soup with my direct opponent a half-an-hour after the game. Naturally my rugby career was a short one, but I still have a soft spot for Limerick rugby and the game in general. I have often tapped into rugby's training techniques and even used a video of Mike Gibson as part of my preparation for the All-Ireland final of 2000 (I was explaining unselfishness and the work ethic to one of our forwards).

Away from the killing fields, I lurched through the National League with Kerry. We narrowly avoided relegation and had to listen to endless rubbish from our critics. Dwyer took it all in, wouldn't forget it in a hurry.

Just before the championship of 1978 we flew out to New York to play Dublin in a charity game. The match took place during a monsoon at Gaelic Park and should never have been played. Keohane had been preaching a new creed to us leading up to this game and had publicly scolded Kennelly for 'lying down' after Keaveney hit him in the 1977 semi-final. We were fired up and got stuck into the Dubs, who were probably well hungover by this stage. It turned into an absolute brawl and myself, Bomber and Pat O'Neill were sent off by Seamus Aldridge. I threw a clip at David Hickey, but there were skirmishes all over the place as everyone slid into crashing tackles on a tiny pitch that was bad at the best of times. We hammered them in the end, Keohane was beside himself; this was a serious marker laid down and the Dubs got a taste of their own medicine, he felt.

Well, not quite, as it was mostly our lads who carried the injuries out of Gaelic Park that day. I don't really go along with all the rubbish that this match was a turning point. It meant little to me except a trip to New York and a run-out for a decent cause. Sure I went through the motions but, looking back, the only noticeable achievement that day was Bomber showing Dublin once again that he wouldn't be pushed around. The 'bitterness' which lingered after Dublin had apparently denied our walking wounded first-hand medical treatment has become the stuff of legend but it was blown out of all proportion. We needed a moral victory and this became one. Managers, selectors, players . . . you do anything to sharpen the mind, whet the appetite. So a narky challenge game in the pissing rain became the Battle of the Bronx.

As the summer arrived, the omens were good. We started winning every challenge game and had a tidy victory over Cork in a friendly in Bishopstown. The movement up front was unbelievable. I can rarely remember, from this stage on, ever coming out of defence and not seeing one of our men showing for the ball. Spillane, Egan and now Bomber. You could throw any type of ball into Bomber. On the far side Power now had the freedom to run all he liked. We destroyed Waterford and were in great nick for our annual clash with Cork in the Munster final at Páirc Uí Chaoimh.

There was a serious niggle to the 1978 game and while it wasn't the most glamorous I think it was one of our best performances. Jacko and Walsh started to gel in the middle and I'll never forget the speed of Power. Unreal. In the last couple of years watching Galway's Michael Donnellan tearing at defenders reminded me of Ger. Fearless. Great pace. Cork were already a broken team but they put up stubborn resistance that day and I felt the brunt of it when one of their subs walloped me in the face as I was coming out of the square. Actually broke my jaw though I kept it quiet. Had to. When I put my hand up to my face to complain, Horse Kennelly grabbed me and threw me back into position. Get on with it. The new Kerry.

We faced Roscommon in the semi-final and it marked one of the lower points of my career. I was generally winning the battle to keep my guard up, stay focused, stay fit and stay off the drink in the lead up to important games. The league was a different matter, I was living on my wits during the league. But the championship? We arrived in Dublin early on the Saturday before the All-

Ireland semi-final and booked into the Grand Hotel that afternoon. Dwyer arranged a team meeting for 11 pm that night. Seemed an eternity away. Anyway, not wanting to stray, myself and Paudie Lynch headed into town to watch the film of the moment – *Saturday Night Fever.* We had to kill the time somehow. We joined a massive queue for the Savoy cinema but by the time we got near the top they closed the doors. What now?

Well we were starting to get recognised by the odd Dub so we decided we'd better head towards the hotel. However, en route, we stopped off in Campion's Pub in Kinsealy and decided to have a pint. I overdid it. The night before an All-Ireland semi-final and I had a fucking feed of pints. Jeezzus! It's more than embarrassing now when I think of it, it's downright scary. We arrived back at the meeting and I was snared straight away. Dwyer was furious. I was going to be dropped. Disciplined. Was I mad? Yes.

The following morning I felt really bad. I decided I'd better try and show some remorse. Up until 1978 there used to be a mass said in the hotel on the Sunday morning, specially for the team. Kerry jerseys and footballs at the offertory, things like that. But having lost to Dublin two years in a row, Dwyer knocked it on the head. Full of *piseoga* Dwyer, like myself. So I decide I'd better show my face at the local mass in Malahide along with the rest of 'em. I wouldn't be the most religious man in the world but, this morning, I was playing it straight. It was in the balance whether I'd be starting, I needed every credit I could get so I went up and received communion. While I was returning to my seat, Dwyer gazed at me from the back of the church and murmured, "Loook at himmm . . . LOOOK AT HIMMM . . . JOHN TRAVOOOLTA!"

Fortunately we got the benefit of the doubt from the selectors and myself and Lynch lined out and played well. We got away with it. Lucky . . . again. It was 1978, the championship was still a two-horse race and we were super-fit. We beat Roscommon by twelve points. In time standards would level out and lapses in discipline would be punished. But we lived on our wits then. Scary. Players nowadays wouldn't dream of it. Don't need to see 'em at mass.

The blitz

The build up to the final against Dublin was much tighter this time. Dwyer had kept a lid on things and the relationship with the media was much more disciplined. So you can imagine the look on Micko's face when, after arriving at Heuston Station, he saw on the back of a Dublin evening paper "WE'LL EAT THE DUBS – JACK O'SHEA". Jeezuus, he was furious. It didn't matter by that stage. The team had found its groove and was moving like no other. There was, however, one last wobble before we cleared the hurdle. We started badly against Dublin in the rain the next day. They pushed up something shocking and we were trying to hold our shape. Nervous. Keaveney was stroking them over. Fortunately they lost the plot. With their defence well out of position, Spillane set up Egan who stung 'em with a goal before the half hour. Probably the most important in our history. Dublin may not have been good enough to go the distance that day but Egan ensured that the serious questions weren't asked. You know the rest. Paddy Cullen clashed with Powery before the break, Mikey chips him – the most famous goal in the history of the game. Stage was then set for Bomber's blitz. We had crossed the Blue Line once and for all. 5–11 to 0–9. It was the end of the road for the Dubs of the 1970s. Sure they bravely returned the following year but, without the suspended Jimmy Keaveney and with several new faces, they were a spent force.

Vindication. Dwyer lapped it up. At Mallow train station on the way back to Killarney with the cup he gave forth. His critics, officials who'd connived to have him removed, his enemies. Gave forth. He would do so for each of the next six All-Ireland successes. "Didn't waaant meee, THEYYY didn't and here weeee are with the Sam, didn't waaant meee. And I think weee'll bee baaaack agaaainn!!" Vindication. We all wallowed in it. A lot of the players had been under the cosh at home after 1976 and 1977. Being in Limerick took the heat off me a bit but the rest gave it a serious lash. The snipers ran for cover.

Before the year was out we played Dublin again in a league match in Croke Park. By this stage the story about myself and Paudie Lynch's escapade the night before the Roscommon game had been blown out of all proportion. Legendary. So the night before the league game, the pair of us decided we'd give the fuckers something to talk about. We visited every regular Kerry haunt in town and put on a display for the chattering fans. The night culminated in the early hours with myself and Lynch lifting former athlete and *Irish Independent* journalist Tom O'Riordan up on our shoulders to tap on the window of the Palace Bar and let our good friend Liam Aherne know who was looking for the late one. Crazy.

Played okay the next day too.

5
Dropping The Guard

Ní mar síltear a bítear

I KNOW now what Dwyer was going through. It may be a two-horse race in Munster most years but the manager's biggest fear is drowning in the shallow pool. Mickey Ned knows it, beaten by Clare in 1992. Revenge for 1979? Well 1979 was their own fault. Clare played a big part in that game or at least that's what Dwyer had us believe. Every year Micko would present thirty reasons why Clare, Tipp, Limerick and Waterford would beat you – how they'd show no respect, make life hellish for you. Moving the first round of the Munster championship in 1979 from Cusack Park in Ennis to the football heartland of Milltown Malbay in west Clare was to screw us up. Dwyer told us. Coach had to snake its way through the windy roads from Ennis over the hills into Milltown. "Injustice – make 'em pay," he told us. "They've dragged us out here to level it." Poor Clare. With Dwyer's fire in our bellies and stiff competition for starting places, the Banner felt the brunt of a merciless hammering. 9–21 to 1–9. Jeezuus.

1979. Probably the easiest championship Kerry ever won. Knocked out of the league by Roscommon in the semi-final, our preparations were perfect. Carrying a ridiculous 36-point victory to the Munster final probably spooked an already weakened Cork. They buckled. Ger Power ran amok. 1979. Easiest championship? Well one thing didn't fit. Páidí Ó Sé wasn't playing well. You see life was coming to a head for carefree Páidí. The relationship between work and football had started to collapse over the preceding year. As Kerry grew in stature that summer, I was shrinking. 1979. Most difficult championship Páidí ever won.

Four years of favours in Limerick, four years of cover, four years of the sergeant writing Garda Páidí Ó Sé out of the equation, four years of football, of training, of switches, championships, leagues, of no overtime and skites to the States. Four years of not giving a fiddler's fuck where my money was going to come from. No more! I was refused permission to attend a training session. Garda or footballer? Which was it to be?

It's easy enough to see it from their perspective now. The gardaí in Limerick, particularly in Unit C, had been very good to me. Accommodated me for years. But there's a limit to everyone's generosity and they had to keep all the troops happy. By the summer of 1979 I had stretched them to breaking point; they were getting nothing in return and were fed up with it. My intentions weren't bad as such but I wasn't delivering and had exhausted every last favour. The pressure was on, my football started to suffer. It was decision time. The night I was refused permission to travel to Killarney for training, I rang John Costelloe immediately. "You have to go to training, Páidí, go on," he said. John knew. My mother knew as well. This was no bolt from the blue. There was no bust-up, no major confrontation with any of my superiors. I hadn't stepped out of line. As far as I was concerned playing football was something I had to do. They didn't see it that way and wanted a change of direction. I went training.

In truth it had been a long time coming. Football being compromised was the last straw but as far back as 1977 I had started to look to a different future, a future back west. Using the contacts I had made on the rugby fields I convinced a bank manager to lend me a share of money and the day after Dublin defeated Armagh in the All-Ireland final, and with the help of my family, I purchased a small site of land opposite our home in Ventry. The field had belonged to a local character, Peaitín Caoimheán, who had recently died. My brother Mike bid at the public auction and secured the plot for £6,500. This was now my future. My family provided the platform. Beatrice, Tommy, Mike and Tom all played a significant part in shaping my life from now on. Beatrice saw the writing on the wall, Tommy and Mike did the business and Tom arranged the opt-out clause. Now it was up to me to face the ball.

Having thought about the alternatives I decided to apply for a licence to build a pub on the site. It was a prime location. Ard an Bhóthair is situated on the spectacular Slea Head drive. Now, I thought, why not make it impossible for tourists to pass the crossroads without stopping at Páidí Ó Sé's? The application was rejected. 1 November 1978 – the day the Munster rugby team scored their famous victory over the mighty All Blacks, the day Dick Spring excused himself from the District Court to attend the match, my first bid to become a publican, to hang up the tunic, was halted. A local publican objected which, in retrospect, was totally understandable. Didn't really see it that way at the time. It was a huge disappointment. Highlighted in the papers too. Made it worse. "Páidí Ó Sé Applies, Refused Pub Licence". I was still a garda in Limerick. My intentions were no longer a secret.

Luckily for me my brother Tom, an inspector with the Department of Agriculture, had also returned home from his travels. He was a regular visitor to Kruger Kavanagh's, a famous pub in Dún Chaoin over the mountain from Ventry. The proprietor at the time, Páidí Ó Néill, had been finding the business a little wearying and asked Tom would I be interested in leasing the premises. The seed was sown. While I couldn't move on the site in Ventry there was now a short-term plan.

Fast forward to the summer of 1979. Now the championship was different. Now there was the site, now there was the hassle in Limerick, now there was Kruger's, now there were choices. What do I do? On the fourth Sunday in July, we defeated Cork comfortably in the Munster final in Killarney. At best I was 'okay'. But things got worse. Three week's later we destroyed Monaghan in the All-Ireland semi-final. I was taken off. Ogie Moran was on the bench, breathing down the necks of half-a-dozen players. I was one of them and paid the price. Ogie replaced me and the first thing he did was move up the field and kick the ball over the bar. My edge was gone. I was going through the motions, about as bad as it gets for a footballer. Now I was staring at an All-Ireland final against Dublin on the bench. Easiest championship my arse! Carefree my arse! I've been critical of the use of psychologists in football over the years but, had one been around at the time, he would have seen one stressed-out young lad. There was only one thing for it. Go west.

The engine room

As before, I touched base with parents and brothers. Into the engine room at Ard an Bhóthair. I'd been refused a pub licence, I was about to jack in the guards, should I take the lease, what about a small hotel? People thought I was mad. Give up the guards? Give up a permanent, pensionable job? Mad. My head was all over the place. I'd lost form, big time. Solution? Well, I thought, I'd have to carry my legs out of this situation as best I could and winning an All-Ireland would be a damn good start. Being taken off in the semi-final was like putting a gun to my head. Now I had a month. I would train twice a day. Squeeze in work in Limerick and get home as often as I could. Hit the Clasach, hit the hurdles. Focus. My mother all but supervised my rehabilitation. Settled my mind. "Páidí, you must forget about your pub, forget about your job. Football, Páidí."

When I'd return from training, a vinegar bath would be prepared and a glass of sherry would be sitting waiting for me. Sounds a bit quaint. Well it worked. I got my head right. Two weeks before the All-Ireland everything fell into place. I started playing. In the final trial game in Killarney a week later with my No. 5 shirt up for grabs, I won the first seven balls that arrived my way. Cleanly. I was taken off after thirty minutes, they'd seen enough. Ogie got his place all right, deservedly so, but at centre-forward and at the expense of Vincent O'Connor.

Back in Limerick things were tense at the station. Earl Mountbatten had been killed by an IRA bomb in Sligo on 27 August and checkpoints were set up all over the place. I was instructed to conduct one such checkpoint on the Ennis Road. It was to be my last serious duty call in the Gardaí. It was a scary procedure really. I mean an unarmed Garda conducting a checkpoint during the Troubles was crazy in my view. Anyway, I had my ways and there were always the 'friendly' registration plates. During my search, however, I inadvertently made my last cop. I stopped one particular car and instructed the driver to open the boot. He did so and to my astonishment I found about sixty pigeons shot that evening out in Cracklow and bound for a restaurant in Limerick! Knew the place well too!

Having spared some unsuspecting punters a few portions of gamey chicken I turned my back on the force. For eight months now, practically everyone I knew tried to tell me otherwise. But I stood firm. My future was in Ceann Trá. Tom negotiated the terms of the lease for me at Kruger's.

First, of course, there was the small matter of 16 September. I don't know if it's medically possible, but I think I had too much energy going into that game. I was pumped which was hardly necessary. Kerry were peaking and, without a suspended Jimmy Keaveney, Dublin were a pale shadow of the previous years. They were also a team in transition, no match for us really. Still, as each layer of frustration peeled off me during that game I went at it harder. Marking David Hickey again I won this bout hands down. I owned the ball. David's brother Mick had the unenviable task of filling in for Keaveney. Before the break, our full-back John O'Keeffe was concussed in a tackle. When play resumed, Tommy Drumm went on the overlap and, knowing full well that Johnno was out of it inside in the square, I clattered into him with a late shoulder and picked up a booking from Armagh referee Hugh Duggan. I didn't take any notice and, despite reports that Croker was clamping down on rough play that year, nothing was said to me at the interval. As normal Murt Galvin towelled me down. Nothing said. We emerged for the second half defending a big lead which inevitably led to a loss in concentration. About ten minutes later, Johnno was gone and Dublin had pulled a goal back when Bobby Doyle set up sub Jim Ronayne.

It wasn't the prettiest score ever taken but it lifted Dublin. Hints of a comeback. Shortly afterwards Anton O'Toole picked up a ball on the turn and was about to set up Dublin's second, or that's what went through my mind. I went for broke and grabbed Tooler around the neck and pulled him down. Duggan rushed over. *Sent off.* So I'd made the bench after all. As I arrived at the dugout, the chairman Gerald McKenna put his arms around me. Well it had to be done didn't it? I wasn't really bothered one way or the other, we remained in control. I sat there for the remaining twenty minutes as the boys completed an 11-point victory over Dublin.

Afterwards I went to the Cat and Cage pub in Drumcondra with Paudie Lynch. It was bedlam so we adjourned to the Skylon Hotel across the road for a couple of pints before heading back to Malahide for the dinner. Then it hit. My guard dropped. *Fuck it. Sent off.* I got very down. I looked for a room in the Skylon to go and steady myself. I was ready to head off home, back to Kerry. The emotional turmoil of the preceding weeks had reached a crescendo. I felt I had let myself down. I'd just won my third All-Ireland medal and I was pissed off. However, I wasn't gone fifteen minutes when Lynch arrived up to the room. "Pa Joe, cop on, boy." I did. Lynch could be persuasive. Crisis over.

A week later I resigned from An Garda Síochána.

6
Into The West

Ní raibh cuibheasach ina thaoiseach maith riamh

Easter Bank Holiday Monday, 1980

SUN BEATING down on Dún Chaoin. Doesn't come much nicer. Shadow of the Blaskets cast across the sea, Ceann Sléibhe rising majestically to the right, Three Sisters jutting up to the left, Smerwick Harbour sweeping up to mighty Brandon. Kruger's is hopping. Warm spring breeze swirling around the car park, short-sleeved punters having the craic outdoors, mostly locals though the first of the season's visitors are starting to arrive, enquiring about grub and glasses of Guinness. "Do you do food?" Pub grub's in its infancy. The ready-made burger with the sauce already applied, bunged into one of these fancy new ovens. Not quite yet a microwave. No fresh seafood platter, no chowder. The local fishermen are still throwing monkfish back into the sea. "Ugly bastards." Open the front door, open the back. Four or five youngsters horsing it out behind the bar. The chat is interrupted as the chopper arrives overhead and swings towards Barra na hAille at the top of the pier. Ten minutes later, An Taoiseach arrives with his family and friends. Into Kruger's. "Howarya, Charlie?" It's a comfortable entrance, smiles all round. I edge the young lads aside and take charge of proceedings. Twenty-five-year-old footballer and rookie publican welcomes An Taoiseach. "Well, Charlie, *conas 'tán sibh? Thá fáilte róimh go Dún Chaoin.*"

"How are things here, Páidí? How is business?"

"Very good," I reply. "Sure Kruger's is flying, Páidí Sé or no Páidí Sé. I'm happy, couldn't be better." The conversation continues, polite, football talk but Charlie enquires more of my lease, of my situation in general. "Well . . . to be honest, 'tis a pity this place is not my own. You may know, Charlie, I applied for a pub licence back home, for Ard an Bhóthair, but 'twas rejected. I'm actually now thinking of building a small hotel on the site. Fourteen or fifteen rooms."

"That's great, Páidí, I know someone who could give you some advice on that matter. Vincent Doyle. I'll arrange for you to meet him, leave it with me." Twenty-five-year-old footballer and rookie publican gets a dig-out from the country's premier.

Who wouldn't be impressed? Charlie never hid his fondness for west Kerry and its inhabitants. Now I could see it first hand. I was his neighbour, so to speak, the first port of call from the island. And he offered me his time. Nothing juicy, nothing underhand. He arranged a meeting for me in Dublin with leading hotelier, the late PV Doyle, who would advise me on how to organise my business. Naturally I took up the offer and travelled to Dublin where I met with PV in the Skylon Hotel in Drumcondra. He told me he'd been contacted by Charlie and proceeded to spell out for me how I should apply for my Bord Fáilte grant, a kind of list of dos and don'ts. Made sure the application was solid. He also explained how Roinn na Gaeltachta would match the Bord's grant pound for pound. Following that meeting, I had a chat with my brother Tom and then arranged to meet with Bord Fáilte. Fully armed with my facts and figures and with solicitor and Dublin rival Tony Hanahoe on toe, I met with Bord Fáilte. No one present knew I had been well briefed in advance so they were suitably impressed. I left the meeting with two thirds of the funding for my Ventry hotel more or less in place; I would borrow the remainder. An architect in Tralee had already drawn up initial plans for the building to Bord standards so it was all systems go.

On my way home from Dublin, I decided to play a courtesy call on John Costelloe in Limerick. I explained my plans in detail and told him that I'd made up my mind. John digested what I had to say and replied. "Well, Páidí, is football second now?" My heart sunk. Wallop! "Are you like the rest, leave the guards and throw yourself full-time into making money?" Wallop! My drive from Limerick to Ventry that night was cruel. My head was spinning. Everything had been hurtling along. An Taoiseach, P V Doyle, Bord Fáilte. Surely I was only being responsible, ambitious? But John spoke the truth. Once again I took his advice to heart. It was the middle of summer and there was another All-Ireland to be won. The planning rumbled on for a couple of weeks. Half-hearted stuff. But, before a sod was turned, the hotel idea had been levelled. Football won again.

Life was good. Make no mistake. Since leaving the guards and taking out the lease on Kruger's, business was thriving. With Tom's help and with a lot of goodwill from the locals in Dún Chaoin, I settled in quickly. The goodwill seemed to stem from the older residents who had built up a relationship with my parents from years of travelling over the Clasach to visit the creamery and stop by the shop. It was also in stark contrast to many of my closer neighbours who seemed to think I had gotten too big for my boots. My job in Kruger's was also made a lot easier by the tenants, who demanded a fairly strict regime. I was single and in charge of the key to a pub, so strictness and discipline were handy bedfellows at the time.

The turnover in Kruger's was unreal. Already an established tourist mecca the pub also had a great reputation among the influential visitors to the west, in no small way due to Haughey's frequent calls. The late Kruger Kavanagh, a bit of a cad in his time, had come back from the States to his house in Dún Chaoin after making his wedge. Kruger was full of it. On returning from his honeymoon he was asked did he enjoy himself;

he infamously replied: "For Cáit, a big surprise but nothing new to Kruger!" He was ahead of his time. He had a grasp of tourism long before anyone else, knew how valuable a liquor licence would be in such a scenic location. He had to battle it out with the local clergy before he eventually got the licence and a young Charlie Haughey advised him as he went before Judge Barra Ó Briain. After Kruger's death, his nephew Páidí Néill took charge of the pub. By the time I leased it from him, his mother Peig and Kruger's wife Cáit had become part of the furniture and remained on for a couple of years after I took charge. And, you know, the two elderly women were a great asset to have around. I mean, no one was going to argue with an 80-year-old woman when it came to closing time. I'd disappear into the kitchen at 11.40 and Peig would go at the place. "Time now, gentlemen," as she poked them with a brush. Cáit also taught me a lot about running a pub. "Did you meet any new friends tonight, Páidí?" she'd ask as we cleaned up. "New customers, Páidí, you must encourage new customers and influential ones. But you must not offend the locals while you're doing that. Never turn your back on a loyal customer while wooing another. Take your time, work your way over."

For the first time in my life I was into some serious money. Bought a couple of derelict houses opposite the shop in Ventry for £20,000, had them restored; crashed a couple of cars, replaced them with better models. Hardly playboy stuff. I mean, that's about as far as it went. Could have gone on decent holidays, chased some bigger money, driven the business. Kruger's . . . unreal. Had I gone the extra step and driven it . . . who knows? Same old obstacle though. Football, football, football.

The benchmark

I toyed with the idea of shifting the emphasis. Tom was kind of behind my attempts. He'd ensured I applied myself to the job behind the counter, so much so he actually convinced me to opt out of the league semi-final that year. Can you imagine? The day before my discussions with Charlie, Kerry played Tyrone in the National League semi-final. Easter Sunday. Tom had stressed the need to give the pub a good shot and he wasn't as lenient as the guards. He explained how important Bank Holiday weekends were to the pub trade in west Kerry. I had to be in the pub that Sunday. I made myself unavailable for the semi. I had ditched the guards on account of football but, according to Tom, I needed to stand up and be counted in my new business venture. I stayed west as Kerry overcame Tyrone.

The upshot? It gave Dwyer the opportunity to give me a rap on the knuckles; a chance to play games with me for the National League final against Cork. He dropped me. A young Ger Lynch from Valentia was thrown the No. 5 jersey. Poor Tom. He had to face the wrath of Beatrice following his earnest advice. However, I had gone with the decision. The word about me around the place was that I couldn't study, I'd left the guards, wanted nothing but football. I'd show them. My decision would turn a few heads, I thought. Tom was only doing what he thought was right but, of course, I should have played in the semi-final. No doubts. What made it worse was the fact I hadn't consulted with Beatrice before taking the decision. Ouch!

The league final was played in front of a large crowd in Killarney and I approached the bench along with Paudie Lynch who was also a sub that day. Now here was a change of tack. There was no Páidí slowly revving himself up for the fray, no dry gawks, no visits to the toilet, no psyching up. As the pair of us were about to sit down in our tracksuits, Lynch turned to me, "Pa Joe . . . there's an awful lot to be said for walking on to the field in this frame of mind." We laughed. With Dinny Allen running riot, I was eventually brought on and the game finished in a draw. I was reinstated for the replay, which we lost by a point in Páirc Uí Chaoimh. I didn't cover myself in glory. Financial success would only come at a cost, one I wasn't prepared to pay.

Going into the championship later that summer, the defeat in Páirc Uí Chaoimh was all we had to sustain us as we were given a bye into the final. Without an outing prior to facing Cork on 6 July, Dwyer had us well wired. He was constantly preaching the injustice of the decision to give us a bye and the fact that Cork had turned us over in the league final. Cork obviously fancied their chances but, after a lively opening, a goal before half-time by Bomber gave us our platform. We ran away with it in the second half. Following that game and subsequent championship outings, a share of the north and west Kerry lads would often travel back home with me – Bomber, Ogie and his cousin Mick Moran along with Paudie Lynch and Seán Walsh. Some craic, back in Johnny Frank's pub on the pier in Baile Dáibhéid. I recall the fun the boys knocked out of a story that a good friend of mine, Toos Mac Gearailt, tells about my existence in Ard an Bhóthair. In those days, my mother kept students in the house during the Coláiste Samhraidh so I was evicted to a caravan behind to make room. Suited me really as it became my pad; planted my three-in-one stereo in the corner. One day a vet arrived to inspect some cattle in the field behind the caravan. It was 12 noon. Going about his work in the normal fashion he was accosted by Beatrice who insisted he stop immediately. "Ssshh," she said, "you might wake Páidí."

Recalling victories over Cork has a poignant resonance for me. From the time I took over Kruger's I had got to know a man from west Cork, a character who was to become a true friend and whose tragic death subsequently, was to leave a deep void for me. Diarmuid Maidhcí Ó Súilleabháin was a traditional singer of note from Cúil Aodha, a member of the famous family whose music profoundly influenced the late Seán Ó Riada. He had moved to Dún Chaoin to work as a broadcaster for Raidió na Gaeltachta and it wasn't long before I realised the common ground I shared with Diarmuidín. He was a fiercely passionate man about life – football, language, music. Sharp and intelligent, he stood loyally by me over the years and was always on hand to advise, cajole or argue the toss. Thankfully, it's a vivid memory . . . Diarmuidín stubbornly arriving back into Kruger's having had to stomach another collapse in Killarney or Páirc Uí Chaoimh. He'd eyeball me with his piercing glance, gulp a healthy slug of his pint, skilfully wipe the froth off his ample beard and protest, "*D'anam ón diabhal, bhfuil deireadh leis an gcrá so in aon chor?*" Is there no end to this torment?

Given our bye into the Munster final and a fairly emphatic win over Cork, 1980 was shaping up to be a handy All-Ireland. Three matches. However, it didn't work out that way. Offaly had ended Dublin's six-year reign in Leinster and we didn't really know what to expect. It turned out to be a rollercoaster of an All-Ireland semi-final. While we always held the upper hand, Offaly exploded on to the Croke Park stage and signalled that they had serious firepower up front and a resilience to hang on. How those traits would come back to haunt us. The general public were treated to the delights of Matt Connor's skills for the first time. He scored an incredible 2–9 that day and caused consternation for Mick Spillane and Ger O'Keeffe. We had our own gems though. Egan and Sheehy were top class and Pat Spillane led the way, kick-started our performance with a really brave first-half goal. Myself, Horse and Ogie did okay, kept the half-forwards busy enough. We dropped our guard a little towards the end and Offaly made up some serious ground. Few of us heeded the warning. Sights turned quickly to Roscommon and three-in-a-row.

Conceding a huge score to Offaly had its plus side for me. Paudie Lynch hadn't kicked a ball in our short championship run. He had his own troubles in college and, no more than the rest of us, his personal difficulties followed him on to the training ground. I felt edgy with Lynch on the bench. He was my soulmate and touchstone. I wanted to march behind Lynch in the parade, get psyched up with him before the final, hear him roaring on the pitch, skull porter with him afterwards. Footballers will know what its like when their mate is dropped. Fucking awkward. A week before the game, he was heading to his local for a quiet pint when Pat O'Shea stopped him. The team to face Roscommon in the All-Ireland final had been named. Lynch was in, right corner-back. He turned on his heels and went home. Matt Connor had opened the door for himself and Jimmy Deenihan.

Two days later, however, we were struck by a hammer blow. Bomber was admitted to hospital in Tralee after training with an acute pain in his side. Turned out to be appendicitis. He'd have to go under the knife. Dwyer was inconsolable. The three-in-a-row was on, Bomber was flying and we needed a big target man against a physical Roscommon team. Micko arrived at training on the Thursday night before the final like an antichrist. In hindsight, it was hilarious. He'd been talking to some GP in Waterford who suggested that the operation could be suspended. His head was wrecked. "JEEZUUS . . . YOUU KNOOW, THEEY COULD PUUT THAAT OPERAAYTION OFFF 'TIL MONDAAYY."

We knocked a great bit of craic out of poor Bomber's misfortune that night. We were already connected with the adidas label in some shape or form and most of us wore adidas boots. To this day I'm not sure what the nature of the tie-up between the brand and Kerry was at the time. Like where the money was going, if any? Despite our adidas affiliation Mikey used wear Puma boots and actually had to cover 'em with polish to disguise the brand name. So when Bomber was laid up in the Bons' somebody piped up at training: "Lads, the photographers'll be rushing to the hospital to see which pyjamas the Bomber's wearing . . . Puma or adidas!" The three-stripe controversy!

The day before the final we followed what was now our routine. Myself, Paudie and a scatter of the North Kerry lads went for a kick around in the park in Killarney, ate a light snack and shot up to Jimmy O'Brien's to collect our gloves. Jimmy was a great fan, owned a pub and a sports shop in Killarney, great spot for traditional music and a favourite haunt of the west Cork crew from Cúil Aodha and Baile Bhúirne. He'd rarely miss a training session in Killarney and would always like to be kept up to date with tactics and such. So when we landed in the shop he enquired, "Well, boys, have ye made your switches for tomorrow?" In Bomber's absence I think Dwyer wanted to muddy the waters a bit for Roscommon and so named Ogie at full-forward, although the plan was to switch to the '40' almost immediately and throw Tommy Doyle into the square.

"Who's full-forward?" asked Jimmy.

"I'm going in full-forward," responded Ogie.

"Oh, Jeezuus," cried Jimmy, "won't Pat Lindsay be kept on his toes!"

We fell around the place laughing. O'Brien couldn't wait to get rid of us so he could go down to the bar and pontificate to the assembled about our crazy plan.

The Roscommon bother

Final day was horrible and blustery. There was a bit of baggage carried into the game, stemming from the 1978 Under-21 final when Roscommon got stuck into Kerry to prevent a fourth title on the trot. In truth I remember little of that occasion. It was a week after the All-Ireland. I hadn't seen a bed the night before and had to line out in a Ceann Áras final before the Under-21 game. I know that the red mist descended on Keohane and there was a bit of scelping. I, on the other hand, was away with the fairies and was withdrawn in the second half. Bernie O'Callaghan remarked: "Does Páidí realise there's a ball involved in this game at all?"

According to the legend, 1980 was a continuation of that bother. However, I don't really subscribe to the rubbish about bad blood between the counties. Personally I never had a problem with Roscommon, having struck up a friendship with John O'Gara out in the States in the mid-1970s. I didn't have a problem with the 1980 final either. It was a lousy day, there was a strong wind swirling around Croker and Roscommon decided they were going to get stuck into us. Can you really blame them? I mean we were tearing at teams, humiliating them with the pace and ruthlessness of our attack. Roscommon were wired and tried to put a halt to our gallop. I harbour no resentment for that. And, you know, they were unlucky not to win that All-Ireland.

They started like an express train, they were extremely fit. Dermot Earley was dominating midfield, they scored 1–2 without reply, unfortunate not to have more scores on the board. The story goes that, as soon as we hauled them in, they became obsessed with hammering into us. Went all negative. But in truth they missed vital scoring chances, from play and placed balls. We didn't. Mikey kicked some great frees in difficult conditions and bagged an important goal before half-time having linked up with Spillane. Charlie Nelligan, crucially, had one of those days between the sticks, pulled off two unreal saves after the break. I kept wing-forward Aidan Dooley scoreless, even managed a last-gasp block on him to avert a goal. I have one big regret though. In the first half I tore up the wing and kicked the best point I ever scored in Croke Park against a strong wind into Hill Sixteen. I must have been forty yards out. Unfortunately the ref disallowed it, said I was barging. I was furious. I mean, a number of players came at me and I gave as good as I got, kept the ball and kept momentum. There were a lot of sore bodies in our dressing room at half-time but there I was, whinging about my disallowed point! Later in the game Roscommon became desperate. They missed a sequence of frees and we edged ahead. Our strong players came into their own; Jacko, Seánie Walsh, Kennelly. God, the Horse came out of defence near the death with two or three men hanging out of him; ball under his oxter. Powerful. Paudie Lynch was also magnificent. Having been out in the cold he delivered in spades. When the going gets tough . . .

No doubts though, Roscommon kicked it away. They were powerfully fit and had plenty of talent. They missed their chances. We only scored 1–9, our lowest winning tally of any of the eight All-Ireland victories. In

fact in ten finals, only against Dublin in the 1976 final
did we score less. But a three-point victory in a tight,
free-ridden game told its own story. Three-in-a-row
secured.

The celebrations were familiarly wild and we gave all
the usual haunts in Dublin a good rattle before
retreating. A couple of weeks after that victory we
embarked on our now annual pilgrimage to the States for
the All Stars trip. For one reason or the other, I still
hadn't made the breakthrough on the All Stars front. I
suppose there were a couple of disciplinary incidents
which hadn't gone down too well with the journalists, so
I remained very much a Kerryman in New York. We
travelled out with the victorious Galway hurlers and
shared some great times with them en route. We had a
lot in common, west of Ireland stuff. Mighty craic. It was
around this time that I first became acquainted with Páid
Donohue and John Riney, who have escorted me around
the Big Apple ever since.

With the celebrations out of the way there was a
welcome return to normality back in Ventry and Dún
Chaoin. However, the winter of 1980 was to mark a
serious turning point in my life. After playing Cork in a
National League match in Páirc Uí Chaoimh I met up
with an old childhood pal, Máire Fahy. Máire was from
over the mountain, from Baile 'n Fheirtéaraigh, daughter
of local guard Steve Fahy and his wife Siobhán. I was
struck by this handsome young schoolteacher and asked
her out immediately. We started meeting up regularly
and it wasn't long before I realised that 'this was the
one', as they say. Dating or sharing a relationship with a
footballer can be difficult at the best of times. Most
football wives will tell you that the patience of a saint is
required just to make a relationship work. Now with
Páidí Sé, not the most orthodox of footballers, this
situation was probably magnified significantly so you
can imagine how impressed I was with Máire's
enthusiasm and understanding from the outset. Also,
given the extraordinary influence my mother had over
me, it was a lot to ask Máire to move in on a situation

like that. She did so with ease. I went on to marry Máire Fahy three years later and have never looked back. She has always filled the gaps left by football's hold over me and this has been especially so since the birth of our three children – Neasa, Siún and Pádraig. When the young players mention the difficulties of holding down a relationship and playing football I often brag about my own situation, "Lads, I'd like to think that I'm not a bad manager but, I'll tell ye, I wasn't a bad selector either."

With Kruger's ticking along nicely, with my aspirations to do 'something' back in Ventry and with my new girlfriend in tow, I faced 1981 with a lot of optimism. I was now in my mid-twenties, that bit more mature. With a chance of a four-in-a-row on the horizon, myself and several of the players were determined to make 1981 a special year. We demanded more. While out in the US on the All Stars trip, a number of us had started to talk about a 'world tour'. After all, the Kerry team of the 1970s had travelled to Australia and we felt we were due something out of the ordinary to mark our achievements. The States had become routine for most of us between flying visits for championship matches in New York, Boston, Chicago and All Stars trips; it was like a second home. So we put it to Dwyer who'd travelled on the previous Kerry world tour in 1970. Dwyer gave the idea his imprimatur.

As soon as the seed was sown, myself and Liam Higgins mentioned it to Tommy McCarthy, a hotelier and shrewd businessman from Annascaul. Tommy, a good friend of West Kerry, and Kerry football in general, was very positive about the trip and agreed to co-ordinate the fund-raising if it could be organised with all concerned – the players, management, county board and supporters. Word quickly filtered around the camp and a meeting was arranged for early in the New Year.

We played Clare in a friendly in Ballybunion and a meeting took place later that night with the county board, then chaired by Frank King, Tommy McCarthy, Dwyer, Higgins, Bernie O'Callaghan and a scatter of players – myself, Bomber, Ogie, Paudie Lynch and Tim

Kennelly. Frank had done a rough estimate on the cost of taking the entourage to America, Hawaii and on to Australia. It was somewhere in the region of £80,000 to £90,000. A lot of jaws dropped. However, Tommy lifted his head and comfortably explained to the assembled, "This is Kerry we're talking about. That's easy money." Some present started to laugh. We didn't. McCarthy's reputation was solid in west Kerry. Coincidentally, New York GAA chief and guru John Kerry O'Donnell happened to be home for the holidays and was invited to attend the meeting. After it was decided that we would go for it John Kerry spoke, "You've decided you're going now so there's no opt out, no choice. We have to make it happen." It added serious weight to our plans and the campaign was launched.

A proper fund-raising committee was formed and Tommy set about promoting the Kerry team. An artist's impression of the three-in-a-row team was painted and sold at £100 a shot. We also toured several counties in Ulster for a series of exhibition matches from which we bagged a share of the gates. There was great respect for the Kerry team up north and thousands turned out for those games. Tyrone, Fermanagh, Donegal, Derry, Monaghan all supported us. Meant a lot.

In Tommy's safe hands the fund-raising was motoring along nicely. It seemed more important to us than that season's National League, which we bowed out of to the eventual winners, Galway, at the semi-final stage. It was drilled home to us, however, that this should not interfere with our football. And, in truth, it didn't. Our championship preparations were meticulous and our focus wasn't blurred at any stage. This is something that I'm working on with the current Kerry players under my charge. I'm often accused of over-protecting them, of stifling their natural profile. This isn't true. As soon as players start to mature I encourage them to avail of everything they can. But maturity is vital. I will always put it to them that they can do anything they want as long as it doesn't affect their game. As mature adults they understand the choice and will only move on something if they can keep their eye on the ball. If there's a few bob to be earned for promotional work, I'm all for it. But nothing can be done at the expense of a player's performance level.

Putting the boot in

When the championship arrived in 1981, the machine just clicked into place once more. In fact it rarely functioned as smoothly. And this was against the backdrop of a change in rules which had seen a redefinition of the hand-pass and the hand-passed goal outlawed, something at which we were particularly good. It is said that the rule changes were to curtail Kerry, open the competition up. It mattered little. This was the year the Kerry team reached its peak. If anything the changes spurred us on. Anyway Dwyer had it well sussed, bringing referee Paddy Collins down to Killarney to explain the changes. Common practice now.

Handy All-Ireland? Well it's only when I take a step back that I slam any notion of the handy All-Ireland. The idea is often mentioned by pundits and spectators, even players. But there's no such thing. Just because the opposition doesn't get it right on the day does not make the process of winning a title easy. The endless preparation, sacrifice and psychological battle is *never* easy. We marched through 1981 because a fucking incredible team was reaching the pinnacle of its potential – mentally and physically. Maturity and experience had given us an even keener edge. I played the best football of my life that year and I wasn't alone.

After the annual destruction of Clare, this time in Listowel, we hammered Cork out the gate in Killarney. They only managed a single point from play and only kicked three in total: 1–11 to 0–3. It was a dreadful game played on a blustery day but we tore them apart after the break. Mayo fared little better in the All-Ireland semi-final. We defeated them 2–19 to 1–6 and they failed to score in the second half. I was absolutely flying. I was so

confident that I don't think I dropped my head once.
Always looking up, always looking for Spillane. If not
Pat, then Powery, Ogie and there was always Bomber.
Spillane was first choice though. And that was largely
due to him, not me. He always showed and a lot of
markers and spectators alike underestimated just how
powerful a man he was. Unreal. I have listened to some
bullshit over the years about how he wasn't the complete
player because he wasn't naturally 'two-footed'. The fact
was he compensated so well that it didn't matter. His
finishing was exemplary and he possessed extraordinary
hunger. As a wing-back there's nothing better, after
riding the first tackle, than to see a player breaking
diagonally for the ball. Consistently. When it was
Spillane you knew he'd win it. Unfortunately for Pat he
damaged his knee badly shortly after the semi-final, an
injury that would hamper him for nearly two years. It
would prove very costly for Kerry as well.

I had an interesting prelude to the All-Ireland final
against Offaly. Earlier in the year we played the Leinster
champions in a friendly in Edenderry one Sunday
evening where I marked wing-forward Aidan O'Halloran.
During that challenge game he won a fierce share of ball
and gave me something of a run around. Going into the
final my head was going overtime. "Jeezuus, if a fellow
beats you once . . ." O'Halloran's display that day wasn't
lost on Offaly manager Eugene McGee who obviously
issued definite instructions to him for the All-Ireland
final. We entered that game with an injured Pat Spillane
on the bench and decked out in our new fancy jersey and
green togs. From the outset O'Halloran went really deep
into his own half. There was pressure on me to stay put,
to remain on hand as a stopper but I ignored it and stuck
limpet-like to O'Halloran. Followed him everywhere. I'd
have gone out on to Jones's Road after him. The old
Keohane dictum was ringing in my head. "Where's your
man?" – "Here!" It wasn't long before I began to wear
him down. Started to beat him to every ball, won the
breaks, even kicked a point. What was more frustrating
for Offaly was that I was beating O'Halloran to

possession while already in an advanced position. However, we had other problems. McGee had detailed one of their midfielders to drop back in front of Bomber every time a free-kick was being delivered into the square. I was taking a lot of the frees from midfield so I had to change tack. In fairness with Spillane sidelined and Bomber under wraps, the rest of the forwards picked up the baton. That was Kerry. Every one of them chipped in with scores. When Jack O'Shea cracked home the crucial goal in the second half he turned to me with his fist clenched, "We're on our way to Australia!" 1–12 to 0–8. Four-in-á-row secured.

Couldn't get any better. Could it? Well there's always immortality. The September shadow hadn't fully crossed the pitch in Croke Park when the talk had already started.

Five-in-a-row!

BROTHERS IN ARMS: My brother Mike with me in his
rms outside the church at Ard an Bhóthair in the summer of
955. Tom is to the left and my mother Beatrice is far right.

CÚRAM OIBRE UÍ SHÉ: The shop run by my parents,
at Beatrice and Tommy, Ard an Bhóthair.

UP KERRY!: Five years old, sporting the Green and Gold.

STUDY TIME: Favourite part of the school day, on the
training ground in St Brendan's College, Killarney in 1972.
Team-mate Pat Spillane is in the background.

HALLOWED TURF: The St Brendan's College (Killarney) panel beaten by St Pat's (Cavan) in the 1972 Hogan Cup final at Croke Park. Pat Spillane is front row, second from left. I'm seated on the far right of the front row.

BOYS IN BLUE: Back in the Garda Training College, Templemore in 1975 with the Sam Maguire and the All-Ireland Under 21 cups on toe. I'm in the centre with the Sam.

THE YARDSTICK: Trying to get around Dublin's Brian Mullins in the 1978 All-Ireland final. Never an easy task.

COUNTER FLOW: Out of the guards and into Kruger's. After taking the lease out on the pub in Dún Chaoin in 1979. My brother Tom was a key player in my career change, here with his wife Roseanna.

HELPING HAND: An Taoiseach Charles Haughey on one of his frequent visits to Kruger's in 1979. *Picture: Colman Doyle*

THE FOUR OF US: (l-r) Jack O'Shea, Anton O'Toole, myself and Paudie Lynch in the 1979 All-Ireland final.

YOU DON'T BELIEVE ME?: Running over Mount Eagle, over the Clasach in 1981.
If the body was right, the head wouldn't be far off.

MO CHLEAMHNAS DÉANTA: With Máire after the announcement of our engagement in 1982.   *Picutre: Jerry Kennelly*

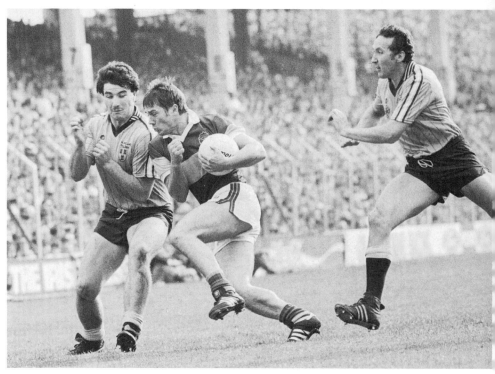

SHOULDER TO THE TASK: Getting to know Big Joe McNally with the Blue Panther, Anton O'Toole, closing in. All-Ireland final 1984. *Picture: Colman Doyle*

RIAN NA gCOS: In the footsteps of a giant. Dingle legend Paddy Bán Brosnan, who captained Kerry in 1944, give's the Ventry captain of 1985 some priceless advice on the beach in Dún Chaoin. *Picture: Colman Doyle*

LEADING ROLE: Captain, 1985.
Picture: Sportsfile

SAM I gCORCA DHUIBHNE: On top of Mount Eagle...on top of the world.
Sam goes over the Clasach after the 1985 victory.   *Picture: Colman Doyle*

GRAND OPENING: At the opening of Tigh Pháidí Uí Shé at Ard an Bhóthair in July 1985. (l-r) Charlie, my mother Beatrice, my wife Máire and the new owner.

WALKING THE LINE: Making the step up to senior inter-county management in 1996.   *Picture: Colman Doyle*

BACKROOM TEAM: (l-r) Our three children, Neasa, Pádraig and Siún, a few years ago.

FAMILY VALUES: Celebrating with my nephew Darragh after our 1997 All-Ireland victory.
Picture: Sportsfile

IN LOCUS PARENTI: Young Pádraig takes the place of his father for the Irish Nationwide 25 year jubilee presentation before the 2000 All-Ireland final. Máire was worried about allowing our six-year-old son on to the pitch until I explained who'd be flanking him for the event – Jimmy Deenihan and Tim Kennelly. Enough said.   *Picture: Sportsfile*

ACE IN THE PACK: About to up the stakes. Maurice Fitzgerald enters the fray in the 2000 final against Galway. Holding Maurice in reserve was a risk few were prepared to take. We felt it was a killer move.   *Picture: Sportsfile*

PHOTOGRAPHER ON BOARD: Full of *piseoga*...after inviting photographer Colman Doyle for a spot of fishing out of Dingle before the 2000 All-Ireland final. Colman is something of a lucky charm for me. Always a welcome sight, particularly so before a big match. The two local fisherman are (left) Paddy Manning and (right) Bobby Kearney.   *Picture: Colman Doyle*

ISLAND DAYS: On Inis Mhicileán with Charlie in July 2001.   *Picture: Colman Doyle*

STANDING THE TEST OF TIME:
The gang of five's 40 All Ireland medals (l-r) Pat Spillane, me, Ogie Moran, Ger Power and Mikey Sheehy.
Eight titles each, a feat unlikley to be matched again.

7
Failure and Greatness

Buann an t-imníomh ar an gcinniúint

NO TIME to pull in the reins. Great fortnight toasting our four-in-a-row back west with Diarmuidín and the boys. No pressure, Kruger's ticking over and most of the tourists out of the way. Now I'm about to head half way around the globe with over £3,000 in my arse pocket. In fairness to the board, they've thrown in £1,800 each spending money for the players. With the pub going well I've been able to match that. Comfortable. So this is payback time. I've watched myself all season; stayed in great shape, best ever; in charge; Kruger's, girlfriend, training; head up when playing, confident; knew when to go, when to stay . . . now it's payback. Craic is mighty in the bar in Shannon Airport when an announcement is made: New York flight delayed . . . for twenty-four hours. Doesn't bother us. Next thing we know we're all shooting down to Durty Nellies pub beside Bunratty Castle. Craic is even better there. Don't let up.

By the time the nose of the jumbo rises off the tarmac the following day, it's goodnight Vienna! Lights out. Touchdown in the Big Apple and I'm like a bear with a sore arse. "Enough. *Lig liom, thá mo dhóthain 'gam.*" Struggle on for a couple of hours before making for the cot. Lights out again. Doesn't go too well. Three hours later I jump out of the sack. "JEEZUUS. THE FUCKING ROOM'S FILLING WITH WAATER . . ." The horrors.

97

There I am, a broken man, standing on the bed in the Statler Hilton, opposite Madison Square Gardens! Got a lot of sympathy, as you can imagine. Uproarious laughter. "Hah! Lads, did ye hear? P Sé's in the jigs." Have to disappear for a while. Get myself sorted. Next day we play Galway in a friendly in Gaelic Park. Give us an awful hiding but at least the game opens the pores, kick-starts us. Get Shannon out of the system. Head off to San Fran' for a bit of R and R before we head down under.

What a trip. This was the real thing. No flying visit. We were away for over a month. Unbelievable freedom. All the hard work fund-raising, all the hard work breaking our arses training. Worth it. We hit Melbourne first and were treated to our first real dose of 'high society' partying. Stationed in the classy Old Melbourne Hotel, we were taken racing to the Melbourne Cup where we supped champagne and grazed on smoked salmon. However, myself and Paudie Lynch decided to ease our way into life down under with a bit of sightseeing. We weren't up to much more after New York, San Fran' and the jetlag to boot. Also we could get our 'cultural' activity out of the way in one fell swoop. After Ned Kelly's jail and Captain Cooke's cottage, myself, Lynch, Tommy McCarthy and his wife Kate rented a car and shot on ahead of the entourage. We drove out into the sticks to explore Victoria, encountering a share of kangaroos along the way. Thought I was back in the horrors! We arrived in Geelong, home of the Aussie Rules team, the Cats, ready to wind things up again, hit the town. With the batteries recharged I was raring to go. Jeezuus, what a come down. Dead. Nothing stirring, not even a bar in the place open. Four of us wandered around, bemused . . . had to make do with a carry-out and a bite to eat. Now, I thought, I know how to knock a bit of craic out of our misadventure. I phoned the hotel back in Melbourne. "Lads, ye'll have to come here to Geelong. There's a six-day festival going on at the moment. It's mighty, barbecues, drink, craic. Get on out here." They fell for it. Three or four cars of the North Kerry brigade landed in the ghost town in time to watch the lights go out. I got some bollocking.

Adelaide was next stop where we played an exhibition game against the local Aussie Rules boys – first half, round ball; second half, oval. I remember going up the wing after the break with a grin on my face, soloing the oval ball. Dwyer roars from the sideline. "Will yoouu looook at himm, he caan't even sooloo the round one!"

Perth . . . on to Sydney in the baking heat. One long sun-drenched party. We played another game in Sydney. I was cute enough not to get too involved in these exhibition matches, happy to trot around the field, pretend. Playing football in the jigs against the Aussies could be a hazardous business. I think poor Pat Sheahan ended up in hospital overnight in Sydney. Could do without that.

Australia, fond memories.

You'd think 'twas time to go home. Not a chance. After Oz we hit Hawaii for a week and that's where the real heavy-metal craic went on. Wikiki Beach, parties, booze cruises. Finally we landed back in San Francisco to try and come down before returning to Ireland. I was gone mad at this stage. Lynch went shopping one afternoon before we left, to buy some presents for the folks back home. His gifts included some women's clothing. When he arrived in the foyer in the hotel, he asked could he leave the purchases in the hotel safe. The receptionist asked him were there valuables in the bags, jewellery and the likes. "No," says Lynch. "But if I leave the clothes in the room, the lunatic I'm sharing with is likely to start wearing them!" Time to go home.

There was little let-up until Christmas but at least the resumption of the National League leant an air of normality to life – just about. We played Dublin in our first league game. As if we hadn't enough craic, Patsy Galvin had arranged that we were guests of the affable Seán Kinsella, a great friend of Dublin football, in his famous Mirabeau Restaurant the night before the match. Perfect preparation. Still, we ticked along nicely despite our indulgences.

Before Christmas I picked up my first All Stars award which capped off a damn fine year for me. I was reaching my peak as a footballer and had marched stridently through the championship. The confidence I now felt on the pitch was reflected, I felt, in the award. In a Kerry context, it had been a fair while coming, though rushes of blood in the past had done me no favours. It was a proud moment being honoured by the game's commentators and observers, though I have to admit that now, as a manager, I hold somewhat mixed views about the All Stars. Sure, it's a super honour for a player to receive. It may not rank with an All-Ireland medal but it goes a long way to justifying the sacrifices and highlighting the individual effort and achievement. However, like most award schemes the selection process is far from perfect and is quite often bound by a sort of political and geographical correctness. I suppose it's hard enough to pick a team with two or three selectors; it must be a nightmare when there's a committee! Still, managers are entitled to gripe about selections. Often, the journalists take this as an affront to their integrity. One reporter on the selection committee took me to task at an All Stars ceremony when I had the audacity to query the choice of players. "Jesus, Páidí, you try and do any better." I had just won my first senior All-Ireland as a manager.

The worst aspect about the annual All Stars debate is that it gives certain observers the chance to indulge themselves, with breathtaking arrogance, in a public selection process that does nothing to honour the achievements of players and managers alike. I find this annual judgement at odds with the spirit of the scheme. That aside, it has proved an enduring and worthwhile event and one which any inter-county player, in form during the championship, will be keeping half an eye on.

Approaching the All Stars ceremony I, of course, turned to my mentor Paudie Lynch – picking up his third award – for advice on protocol. I togged out in a tux for the first time and with my dickie bow secured I set out for the Burlington Hotel with Lynch's instructions ringing in my ears. Needless to say I made a pit-stop along the way, at O'Brien's pub and ended up sprinting to the Burlo, sparing myself some major embarrassment by a couple of minutes. So much for protocol. Turned out to be a super night, a chance to socialise with players from other counties. Brought the curtain down on 1981. Best year yet.

For three months the party had rolled on. Few people will ever get a chance in their lives to experience the fun we had that autumn and winter. The beauty of it for me was that my own situation left me free to roll along and enjoy every minute of it. Now, with Christmas out of the way, it was time to hurt. Party over.

I hadn't held back during that period, I never really did. Still don't. But neither did I shirk when the time came to work. Conscious of our excesses and with the five-in-a-row now looming large, Dwyer reassembled the troops shortly after Christmas and turned the screw. Big time. With my youthful exuberance on the wane I was now detailed as a member of Dwyer's 'heavy gang' – a specially convened group of those players who'd displayed an insatiable thirst, *tart ar bruach leanna*, over the preceding months. He ran us harder than ever. Throw in a few trips over the Clasach with a sharp northwesterly howling in off the Atlantic and it wasn't long before Wikiki Beach became a distant memory. But it was great to tighten the gut again, to feel the power in the limbs, get on the toes. As the body sharpened so did the appetite.

Every silver lining has a cloud

Remarkably we had managed to tick along in the league until the holiday break and kept the momentum going into the spring. Dwyer had us tuned in earlier than normal that year, trying to lay a good disciplined foundation for the distractions that he knew lay ahead. It sounds absurd but we had no business contesting the league final given how well our annual championship preparations had worked up until now. We reached the final in Killarney which was drawn when substitute Tadhg Murphy kicked a point at the death. We won the replay comfortably enough in Páirc Uí Chaoimh. It didn't really augur well. The last time we'd taken the league title was 1977, after which we crashed out of the championship to Dublin. It was already approaching the end of May as the final had been delayed due to the annual All Stars trip to the States. Personally, I was going well. I was back in good shape and even kicked a couple of points in the replay. But involvement in the shake-up for the league can be a double-edged sword. Poor Dwyer was trying to keep the lid on the five-in-a-row hype so the last thing we really needed was a couple of high profile games against Cork so soon before the championship. If ever we needed a low-key build-up, this was the year. We didn't get it. Instead there was talk of the 'double', of a fitting precursor to the five-in-a-row. Perversely, winning the league was the first thing to go wrong in 1982.

Charlie dropped into the pub shortly after our league success. "*Comhgairdeachas a Pháidí*, well done on your success in the league final. You played well." Haughey was in the midst of a political crisis. Having survived a heave, the Fianna Fáil party was on the verge of splitting down the middle. He continued, "What do you think your chances are of being on the steps of the Hogan Stand in September, Páidí?" I couldn't resist. "I think they're a lot better than yours, Charlie!"

The unwanted attention of the league victory seemed trivial a week later when disaster struck. Jimmy Deenihan broke his leg in a freak training accident, he stumbled when we were doing some reverse sprints. This robbed us of a cornerstone, upset the foundation of the team; how we'd miss him in the closing stages of the All-Ireland final. Ger O'Keeffe deputised for the first round of the Munster championship when we shunted Clare out of the way.

Reeling from the loss of Deenihan, Dwyer's hand was dealt an even worse blow after the Clare game when Pat Spillane's knee injury flared up again. Pat wouldn't appear again until the start of the second half of the All-Ireland final and he was, by then, only a shadow of himself. In many ways Spillane was Kerry's lynchpin. His unbelievable hunger, his will to win possession, to kick crucial scores, constantly ignited the Kerry team. His play could be a pain in the arse at times for the corner-forward sitting in behind him but for us in defence and for the team in general there was no substitute for Spillane's qualities. He was also a brilliant Croke Park player. Had he been fully fit that summer we would not have failed. I have no doubt. Offaly's half-back line would not have been so adventurous in the first half had Pat been lurking in behind.

A couple of other niggling injuries further complicated the task. John O'Keeffe was struggling with hamstring and back problems while Tim Kennelly was also injured. This fuelled speculation and the chattering classes had a field day about who should and shouldn't be playing as we aimed to achieve our status as football's immortals.

Poor Dwyer. I can sympathise with him for 1982. All the while the five-in-a-row excitement was building. Many hoped we'd pull it off, genuinely. Others wished we'd fall short including a sizeable section in our own county who disliked our style of play and Dwyer's style of management. "Too much hand-passing, bloody basketball," they complained, five years after we'd started mixing our game.

After struggling to scrape a draw against Cork in the Munster final in Páirc Uí Chaoimh, we knuckled down for yet another replay against the old enemy in Killarney. Being July and the height of the tourist season at home, I decided to get out of west Kerry and spend the night in the Hotel Europe in Killarney. Bomber also wanted out of Ballybunion so he joined me. I remember chatting about the game in the hotel room that night and giving Bomber my tuppenceworth. "Bomber, if you can grab a handy point early in the game, 'tis nearly as good as a goal against Cork. Don't go for the kill and give the keeper a chance to get his hands on it, settle. Then afterwards try and hold it up, draw them to you and see what happens." Jeezuus Bomber was superb next day. Popped over an early score and, before half-time, held it up long enough to feed Mikey who planted it in the net. Sickener. We pulled away after the break to win 2–18 to 0–12.

Armagh were next up and although they honestly tried to stay with us we had too much in the tank for them. Cue five-in-a-row mayhem. Offaly stood in our way, resilient but beatable, I thought. But poor Dwyer. Five-in-a-row songs, five-in-a-row T-shirts, five-in-a-row first-time travellers to Croke Park. Everyone wanted in on the act. It was a little like the Munster rugby European Cup odyssey of 2000 where all the hype of the build-up suffocated the players on final day. You see you've nowhere left to go, no higher gear to click into. It gets to players no matter what guards you put in place. What was worse was, back in 1982, teams weren't naturally as cautious as they are nowadays. I'd hate to have to deal with hype like that but, if we were faced with it, the current Kerry set-up would be much better equipped to deflect the glare. August and September back then were crazy in Kerry and beyond. No team had taken five on the trot, in football or hurling. And there were the doubters. The Kingdom's finest. Experts. Any chink in the armour was getting full exposure. Was Johnno up to it with his back? Was Tim Kennelly still niggled? Was Ogie really a wing-forward? Would young Tom Spillane be up to the '40' on final day? Personally, I think some of this bullshit got through to the management because, in the lead up to the game, Jack O'Shea was detailed to withdraw from the middle somewhat and play a defensive role. There was no need, I thought. We can do the job.

No disrespect to Offaly but you could see where we were heading. The preparation had not gone well. The

slightest margin would decide one of the most famous
football games ever played and it was a margin we
yielded. All the tight games we'd shaded in the past were
due to our superior approach, to our confidence. Missing
Deenihan, missing Spillane, players out of position,
players carrying injuries, inexperience and the all-
embracing hype of 'history'. It was a countdown to
disaster.

Friday 17 September

The night before travelling to Dublin. Started thinking
abou the hotel and Saturday night. Funny, after all the
years staying in the Grand Hotel in Malahide, I realised
that it wasn't the most ideal venue for the Kerry team.
Sure, it was off the beaten track beside the sea, but there
were, quite often, functions taking place while we were
billeted on the eve of the All-Ireland final. The cuter
players ensured they were stationed well away from the
wedding din but I never had the gall to insist to Dwyer
that I was moved. And I was a light sleeper. On the
Friday night before the Offaly game, I went for a light jog
on Ventry strand. I often followed this routine. It had
two benefits.

Firstly I would use it to imagine three or four really
difficult situations that I might find myself in on Sunday
– a squirting ball under my feet; a high greasy ball
coming into the square; a breaking diagonal ball with
two forwards coming at me from different directions.
Imagined . . . imagined myself winning that break, taking
two hard knocks and laying it off. You know, it's
remarkable how often the imagined situations would
arise. I always believed I was one step ahead on the pitch
due to my Friday night jogs.

Secondly, the jog would help tire me out for Saturday
night so I get some kind of a sleep while listening to the
distant strains of *"congratulations . . . and jubilations . . ."*

Saturday 18 September

The day before our brush with immortality and more bloody problems. We went for our annual kick around in Fitzgerald Stadium early that morning and decided to kick some penalties against Charlie Nelligan. I was always hanging around penalty situations, though I never got a look in, not since my Under-21 fiasco in Caherciveen all those years back when I ballooned the ball over the wall and through the window of a shop. Still, I took my share that morning and lamped the lot of 'em to the back of the net. Jacko, the same. Struck a scatter of kicks and beat Charlie nearly every time. The one man who struggled that morning was Mikey – our penalty taker. He had been complaining that he didn't feel quite right, that a cold was bothering him. He didn't look at all comfortable. I was thinking "nothing surer than we'll be awarded a penalty the next day". I wasn't alone.

Then there was the jersey problem. There was a branding row over which gear we would line out in, which jersey we would wear. Can you imagine it? With all our years of experience. *The night before we were supposed to rewrite the fucking history books we didn't know what jerseys we were wearing.* Bad!

Then there was a row between some officials about which town the cup would go to first. *The fucking cup?* Jeezuus. Bad! Bad! Bad!

Sunday 19 September

Well it was a lousy day for starters, so a couple of the difficult scenarios I'd painted on the Friday night were bound to materialise. We started reasonably well. Young Tom Spillane kicked two fine points, might settle the rejigged half-forward line, I thought. Yet it didn't really. Ogie wasn't functioning at wing-forward and the whole Offaly half-back line advanced to kick points keeping the pressure on us. Still, there was no panic, it was an open

game. Egan, the captain, was leading by example. I got in
on the act when I broke down the right wing and cut
inside to kick a point into the Hill.

Pat Spillane joined the fray at half-time. Should have
been brought on shortly afterwards, got the crowd going
though, after kicking an early point, I thought he might
just prove the medics wrong. 'Twas a false dawn. It was
really a day for Vincent O'Connor. Then Saturday
morning's practice proved an accurate barometer after
all. We were awarded a penalty when Egan was bundled
to the ground and Mikey stepped up. He was as hesitant
as I'd ever seen him. Martin Furlong dug deep, used his
experience, kept the pressure on Mikey. Missed it. The
Canal End exploded to life as the Offaly tricolours rose in
response to Furlong's celebration. Truth was Mikey
didn't strike it with enough conviction. A marvellous
placer of the ball normally, this was probably a time for
the plant. He hit it at a good height for the keeper. Game
on again.

Still no need to panic. We kept at it and, when Jacko
threw off the shackles, we began to penetrate again. Egan
was flying and we kept our noses in front. But it was one
of those games and Offaly were one of those teams. We
just couldn't put them away. I was marking Gerry
Carroll this time around and, like the year before, I
owned the ball. The teams swapped scores until Seán
Walsh put us four up entering the closing stages. They
pegged it back again. Then, one more time, I broke up
the right wing, played a one-two with Bomber, thought
about a goal for a split second before tapping over my
second point, a replica of the first. Four points up again,
six minutes left.

Then everything went pear-shaped. Referee P J
McGrath brought Offaly within kicking distance with a
couple of handy frees. Panic set in. For the first time in
five years we panicked. Jacko retreated again, allowing
Offaly to pin us in our own half. Even the forwards
dropped deep. "Get out of it, lads!" It was very
frustrating for the defence as it became very congested
and nervy. Matt Connor's 21-yard place kick left them

two behind with two minutes to play. Enter Seamus Darby. With our entire team seemingly filing back, heedlessly, Offaly full-back Liam Connor was allowed the freedom to push forward unchecked. He should never have been even close to that position. It was nightmare stuff from us. I was tracking my man back from the 50-yard line on the opposite side when Connor picked up a pass on the run and floated his famous lob into the square. The rest is history. Darby, Tommy Doyle, the 'push in the back', goal. We had too many men back, all looking to the other to make the decisive tackle. Although McGrath blew up promptly, we had one more chance to square it but it fell on the inexperienced shoulders of Tom Spillane who snatched at his shot and put it harmlessly across the goalmouth.

Mere mortals after all.

The funny thing was the controversy over Seamus Darby's goal didn't register with the Kerry players at all and still doesn't. We blew our chance that day and have no one to blame but ourselves. Sure, there were a number of incidents that went against us, you live with that. But we could and should have beaten Offaly. To this day I maintain that in 1978 Dublin had the armoury to beat us. They lost the plot that day and we punished them. But they had the material. Likewise Roscommon in 1980. Missed their frees and adopted the wrong strategy. Should have beaten us. We should *not* have lost to Offaly in 1982. I know they'd been on the go for three years at that stage but it would be another seventeen before the county emerged from Leinster again. That left me cold. No, we shot ourselves in the foot. I mean no disrespect; they persevered and deserved their reward. But we shot ourselves in the foot. I have absolutely no doubts. The build-up, the bullshit hype, the jerseys, the cup, the songs, the injuries, feeding the opposition, feeding Eugene McGee, the negative tactics. Dwyer was powerless.

Had more care been taken, the accident of history would not have occurred. *Buann and t-imníomh ar an gcinniúint.*

Many were shocked by our failure. Others rejoiced, relieved by our fallibility. Our arch critics back home, some former players, officials, were resplendent in their justification; self-assured that their reservations about our style and the approach of the manager were correct. "Didn't I tell ye?" I felt for Dwyer. I suppose it's the legacy of a successful county, that ultimate victory is expected, anticipated. At least we were anaesthetised to much of the initial criticism. It was, after all, five days before I made it back to Ventry.

In time I would make great capital out of our Offaly setback, especially as a manager. It rammed home to me, one more time, the philosophy of the defender. I owned the ball, I marched up the field, I kicked two points, we *lost* the game. When Seamus Moynihan pleaded for a more advanced role in the 2000 All-Ireland final replay against Galway I didn't hesitate to refer him to my display the day we had our brush with immortality. "The bigger the prize, the closer your man."

It would be a long time before the aftershocks of 1982 subsided but what the speculators and critics didn't legislate for was the sting in the tail. Dwyer would see to that. There was fallout, sure, but the obituaries were premature. Had we achieved the five-in-a-row it would certainly have been the curtain call. As it was, there was unfinished business.

In failure we would achieve greatness.

8
Weathering the Storm

Deacracht gach deacrachta an ní a cleachtar a chur i ndearmad

IT'S HARD to believe . . . there was a sort of modesty about the Kerry team in the 1970s and 1980s. Well it was a peculiar brand of modesty. Our motivation was compact, we kind of played for ourselves. Sure, we were inspired by the jersey, the county, the wonderful tradition, the supporters. But we never once thought about standing back and admiring our achievements. We didn't dwell on records and this stood to us in the aftermath of 1982. An All-Ireland lost, plough on. When Dwyer addressed a sympathetic crowd in Killarney after our five-in-a-row failure, his passionate sincerity about "giving it another shot" was directed at us, his players. This is partly why Dwyer was so successful. His homespun philosophy which was – and still is – enthusiastically dished out to the media and the public belied a ruthless quest to squeeze every last drop of credibility out of his detractors, his critics. Dwyer understood the channels to the players, this enabled him to breathe life back into the squad. The next twelve months would test his resolve like no other year. Of all his remarkable achievements, steering us through 1983 stands out. We didn't win anything but, to coin a phrase, we hadn't gone away. Dwyer, more than anyone, ensured that we didn't.

What Micko couldn't do was turn back the clock. The base rock of the team was starting to crack. It would

110

need rebuilding. A nondescript league campaign and our annual facile passage to the Munster final in 1983 didn't necessarily highlight these cracks in our defence. However, the curtain was drawing. Deenihan never fully recovered from his unfortunate setback a year previously. Now, Johnno, Ger O'Keeffe, Horse Kennelly and Lynch were staring at the final shot. It had been a long and fruitful road for the finest bunch of defenders the game had ever seen but without victory there would be no survival.

We were attempting to win our ninth Munster title on the trot as we marched around a strangely lifeless Páirc Uí Chaoimh. Poor crowd. The skies had emptied earlier in the day. Though the sun broke through, it was awful muggy, heavy. Our team had a familiar look save for Vincent 'Shin' O'Connor who replaced Seán Walsh in midfield. Now for all our problems shaking off the hangover of losing to Offaly, our creaking defence, our dodgy appetite, we had victory in our grasp again. Once more we were to suffer a lethal killer punch at the end of the game. There was a frightening similarity to the Offaly experience. We couldn't shake off Cork. Our forward unit never functioned at full pelt. Jacko's two goals, one from Walsh, who'd replaced Powery, and Mikey's frees gave us our platform. Still, we were two points up in injury time. Looked like we'd be giving Croke Park yet another rattle. Then I played a cameo role in our downfall. I'd had a good afternoon, maintained the form of the previous year and kept the elusive Dave Barry reasonably tame. Enter Tadhg Murphy in the dying seconds. The ball broke just inside our half and I crudely wrestled Dinny Allen to the ground. Seemed the sensible thing to do; give 'em nothing handy. Game's over, I thought. However, a quick ball over the top caught our boys in the square off guard and Murphy stole in behind to fire it to the net.

Jeezuus. Not again.

It was the end of the road for the Kerry defence as we knew it. John and Ger O'Keeffe, Tim Kennelly, Paudie Lynch. It was a poignant moment. I kind of knew the time had come for some of the players. At that stage though, I wasn't sure whether there was any future for the rest of us either. Head down I ambled towards the tunnel when Lynch took a razor to the situation. He put his hand on my shoulder: "Pa Joe, the next time we'll line out on the same team . . . it'll be for the Jimmy Magee All Stars!" End of an era.

It was a blessing in disguise, that defeat to Cork. We were flat. Our hunger would not have been sufficient to match Dublin and we needed a period to recharge, take stock of our situation, ask ourselves a few hard questions.

Rights of passage

For the first time in a decade the best part of the summer opened up before me. It was attractive enough. Think about it. Freedom was a heady prospect. Club commitments aside, I could relax, take it easy. August was a smashing month back west and now I wouldn't be scurrying around Killarney and Tralee every other night. Funny though, no matter how much football is in the blood, life doesn't wait for it. A few weeks after the Munster final, my father Tommy died of a massive heart attack. It was a Sunday morning during ten o'clock mass when he complained of a severe shortness of breath. Dr Séamus Ó Dónaill was summoned from the church to his aid. But Tommy had weathered a fair few knocks in his day and the system finally gave in.

Strange. It wasn't until we'd buried Tommy that I realised just how influential he'd been in his own quiet way. I saw how hard Beatrice took his death, I was deeply concerned for her. We all were. Sure, she'd been the playmaker for us but she would always bounce things off Tom Power. His advice was solid. He was a great foil to her spiky Sligo personality.

I travelled on a bit of an emotional roller coaster in the wake of my father's death. It wasn't a complete shock, his health had been failing for quite some time. But it took its toll. I also wondered if Beatrice would now remain a central figure in my life without my father's quiet counsel. By this time I had grown very close to my long-standing girlfriend Máire. She'd offered great support around that time. Anyway, near the end of August I was drinking a pint in the Dingle Pub with the late Mícheál Ó Riain, a brother of former Cork manager and current selector Eamon and a close friend of Máire's parents, Siobhán and Steve. Mícheál was a lovely character, positive and full of encouragement. He knew the score with myself and young Máire Fahy. "You can't go wrong there, Páid. Put your recent troubles behind ya now and ask for that girl's hand." I shot back to Kruger's fired up with Mícheál's advice and that evening I proposed to Máire. We didn't hang around either. We married on 10 March 1984.

I still think it's strange how life sort of caught up on me so quickly with football out of the way. It was fortunate in one sense; gave me a chance to take a step back, keep an eye on Beatrice, arrange the wedding.

As the trauma and turbulence of August subsided a little, I travelled to Dublin to watch the All-Ireland with a lot of the Kerry team. Saw the twelve Blue Apostles battle it out with Galway in the bruising 1983 decider. After that game Dwyer convened a meeting to decide on our future. It was perhaps his greatest moment. Having sussed out the mood of the players, he delivered a massive speech about giving it one last shot. We all knew the score, he explained. If we were going to go at it again we'd have to push the bar up another notch. Amazing really. He got the response. Everyone decided to give it one last rattle to see if a reshuffled deck and a few new cards could trump the doubters one last time. We started training immediately.

Kerry hit the ground running in the league that winter. We reshaped the defence and, after some soul-searching with Dwyer, it was agreed that I move to corner-back to help shore up the last line of defence. Having started out in that position, it didn't put me out too much and, at the time, actually suited because my residual fitness wasn't carrying me as far as in earlier days. For me, the move was as much a mental one as a physical shift on the field. It marked a change in my overall attitude. I adopted a pretty cold view that I would sacrifice most of my football for the greater cause of stingy defensive play. Negative stuff. Watch the man full-time.

Johnno hadn't retired from the squad but the writing was on the wall. Consistent injuries dogged him at the end of his career and the management decided that his stature would have to be matched in the square. Seánie Walsh was thrown in to replace O'Keeffe. Seemed logical enough. Big strong man, good in the air, good central player. West Kerryman Shin Connor took Walsh's place partnering Jacko in the middle, though they reversed roles on a number of occasions. Another player in the shake-up was Ambrose O'Donovan who'd made quite a name for himself in the county championship that year. Tommy Doyle took charge of my old number, Tom Spillane settled into the Horse's spot while Ger Lynch nailed down the left half-back berth. Ger Power revisited that line during the league until his natural predatory instincts saw him return, inevitably, to the forward division. Up front there was an injection of new talent with John Kennedy, Timmy Dowd and Willie Maher keeping the old guys honest.

The heartening thing for all of us was that our forwards remained as hungry as ever. Pat Spillane's extraordinary determination paid off and he rejoined the squad. Gave us that invaluable edge again. Mikey, Ogie and Bomber played with renewed vigour. In Jacko we also had the premier midfielder in the land. Why not another rattle?

Nineteen eighty-four, centenary year of the GAA. With a self-effacing, workmanlike approach, optimism filtered through the squad once again. There was one snag though. I wasn't in great nick, the body was groaning a bit. Experience rather than fitness was carrying me through a lot of situations. My heart wasn't exactly in it. Tommy's death had knocked me off stride and I married Máire in March. We honeymooned in New York over St Patrick's weekend and when I returned I was playing catch-up. I also missed the old guard, especially Lynch and Horse. The changes were working – we qualified for the National League final against Galway – but I didn't feel right. There was another big distraction.

The West's awake

Before Christmas a Dingle man named Paul Scanlon, a decent footballer and a former Kerry minor, sounded me out about the possibility of me taking charge of the West Kerry divisional side for the 1984 county championship. Scanlon was a knowledgeable man. He knew there was a nucleus of a decent side. "Come on, Páidí, what about it? Centenary year. 'Twould be great." West Kerry boardmen Derry Murphy and John L O'Sullivan threw serious weight in behind the request. "Anything you need, Páidí," was the line. In fairness to Derry in particular, he sensed that I might have something to offer off the field as well, long before anyone else did.

I was seriously tempted. Traditionally, West Kerry teams contained several of the county's finest players. But they could never put it together when it mattered. "I'd like to put that to bed," I pondered. There was another added incentive. A big one. One I tried not to let become an overriding emotion. In Kerry, the senior captain is appointed by the county champions. Their choice. As player-manager of West Kerry, a county championship success would have the added bonus of securing the captaincy of the county team for me. I didn't want to be selfish, but *that* was attractive. I accepted.

At first I was wary of letting Dwyer know what I was at. He'd have grilled me about my allegiances, about my concentration. Dwyer was damn serious that season. He knew he still had the best panel in the country. If the tribulations of the previous two years hadn't fucked up our heads then he knew – oh he knew – that, one more time, he could prove the critics wrong. One more time he could ride the open-top bus into Killarney sneering at our obituarists. Motivated the same way to this day, Dwyer. Best say nothing about my new managerial appointment.

I took charge and represented the Gaeltacht club along with four other selectors: Eugene Devane from Lispole, Paul Scanlon from Dingle, the late Páidí Sé from Annascaul and Paddy Healy from Castlegregory. The first thing I did in the position was organise a new set of gear for the panel. If we were going to go for it then we would do things right. We lined out in our new white jerseys and red togs. Now wearing red togs was brazen enough in the world of Kerry football but we went an audacious step further – we slapped the position numbers on the togs as well. Soccer style! Jeezuus, the lads started playing better immediately! Just shows you.

It was a decent side, strong spine, good scatter of heavyweights. Kerry panellist Bernard O'Sullivan was our full-back, I manned the centre-back spot, Shin Connor was in midfield, Tommy Doyle on the '40' and John Healy full-forward. Crucially, we also had a good place-kicker up front in Kevin Maunsell, or 'Platini' as he was fondly known at the time.

Of course, before we could get down to the real business there was the small matter of another National League final. The decider, against a Galway side still smarting from their setback against the Dubs the previous September, was played in Limerick's Gaelic Grounds. Winning the league was never our greatest yardstick but the manner of our victory that day was very satisfying. A brilliant goal before half-time, a wonderful concoction by Bomber, Ogie and Mikey kept us in the game. After the break Jack O'Shea led the way as we wore them down, dampened their tenacity. Solid stuff. Signs were right, forget the *piseoga*. Centenary league champions. Kerry were back in business.

Things were looking up for West Kerry too. We enjoyed a few notable victories in the early rounds of the championship, including the scalp of the champions – Rosie's Gneeveguilla. Shannon Rangers were next up in the quarter-final on a Saturday evening in Dingle. It's one of the fondest memories of my career that summer evening. Shannon were a decent team, trained by Jackie Walsh. We were a point down entering the closing stages of the game when Tommy Doyle, the 'Private', threw a long ball into John Healy at the Railway end goal in Páirc an Ághasaigh. Healy rode the tackle and flung it out to me thirty yards out where I met it at full throttle, horsed a few bodies out of my road and lamped it to the net. Fuck it, I enjoyed that. We were due to play Feale Rangers in the semi-final but they objected to the date of the fixture and lost their appeal. So we found ourselves in the Kerry championship final against South Kerry.

I was starting to make my presence felt on the line. There were selection problems prior to the county final and one of them prompted my first big move off the field. Midfield candidate, the late Denisín Higgins, a brother of county selector Liam, had been eclipsed. You see, Denis was one of the best players in his club Lispole and was bidding to nail down the midfield slot he generally held there. However, he lost out when we decided to go with Shin Connor and Gabriel Casey, a first cousin of Brian Mullins. So there was a big move by the selectors to throw him in at left corner-forward, a common tactic on divisional, or even county, sides. I was being out-voted. I hit the table. "Let's put a natural forward in there, why put someone in there that doesn't play there?" I bellowed. "Let's go back out to midfield and look at No. 8 and No. 9 and start again." I got my way. My philosophy? Get the key areas right; play men in their proper positions.

Our progress on the local scene overlapped with a steady onslaught on the county front. John O'Keeffe lined out in his last championship game with Kerry in our destruction of Tipp and was replaced by Walsh for the Cork game. Our own Shin Connor had also lost out to Ambrose in the middle. Dwyer had been sceptical about Shin for some time. It was unfortunate for him, he was a very talented player. However, I would later make capital from that very misfortune.

Going into the Cork match on the first Sunday in July I felt burdened. It was my first really big game back in the corner and the jury was still out. I sensed the Killarney crowd was sceptical. Decided to adopt a sort of 'wait and see' approach, stood off a bit, didn't dive in to the 50/50 situations. Then two good clean catches over my head seemed to settle me. The more confident I became, the more negative my influence, that is from a Cork point of view. I focused increasingly on the man; wouldn't let him breathe. I marked Tadhg Murphy our injury-time executioner in 1983. There was no repeat. Entering the final stages of the 1984 final, I took a hold of his jersey and broke one of my cardinal rules of never speaking to my man. "Tadhg," I said, "you're not going out of my sight this time around." We laughed about it afterwards. With seven points to spare we grabbed back our Munster crown. In the process, I became a corner-back.

Galway retained the Connacht championship and provided the opposition again in the All-Ireland semi-final. By that stage, however, the Kerry machine was whirring once more. We may not have been as ruthlessly efficient as the 1978–1981 compliment, but we still had a savage forward division and the collective determination to put the record straight. Galway were missing some of their top players and were no match. Bomber, Egan, Sheehy were flying. I was settling into my new role getting meaner by the week. Seánie Walsh had made the transition to full-back while Rosie settled into midfield.

It was hardly a classic but I'll never forget that semi-final day because myself and Máire met up with *Irish Press* legend Con Houlihan in Mulligan's Pub afterwards and, along with the assembled, roared on John Treacy to his silver medal success in LA.

Fittingly, we would mark the centenary of the Association in an All-Ireland joust with our old rivals Dublin. Kevin Heffernan had instilled life into the capital again with the heroic victory of 1983. Brian

Mullins had also been a massive inspiration. He suffered disgracefully in the aftermath of the Galway final. His courage in hauling himself back from the brink after a near-fatal car accident was a lesson to us all. It was obviously one that went unheeded by a lot of commentators and reporters. I was always a huge admirer of the big man from my earliest playing days – he was a measure of your worth as a footballer. But I had even more time for him now. In the wake of Tommy's death, Brian rang my mother at Christmas just to give his regards and ask after her. She didn't forget that in a hurry. Nor did I.

In some corner of a Dublin field

Heading into the Dublin game we'd a fair idea that we had enough in the tank to take them. I was well psyched up though. Dublin games always meant more to me than any other. Heffernan received a lot of credit for relaunching the side. We knew they'd be fit, strong, organised and suitably aggressive. What I wasn't prepared for was some pre-match shenanigans.

I lined out to mark big Joe McNally, one of the young stars of the campaign a year previously. There was no doubting Joe's natural talent. He was a super footballer; struck a fine ball, had great hands. However, I strongly suspect someone had a word with Joe before the game. After the usual blow-out, I headed over to the patch between the Canal End and the Cusack Stand for my first All-Ireland final as right corner-back. Joe walked over and I extended the hand. To my amazement he leaned in with the shoulder and put me on my arse. "What the fuck's going on here?" I thought. Big mistake. I was furious. I may have been quare enough on a few occasions myself, but I never got involved in this kind of nonsense. Joe was a kid. I was ten years a senior with a new mission to blot out corner-forwards. Anyway, I thought about this for a minute; waited until the national anthem started. Then, while most of the 68,000 punters in the ground were gazing proudly at the Tricolour flying above the Nally, I gave Joe a fierce root up into the hole. He left the field in the second half, scoreless.

Naturally my tiff with McNally has entered GAA folklore in the two counties and there are some amusing versions of events. In truth, there was little to it. He came back and proved himself the following year when he very nearly pulled it out of the fire for the Dubs. No animosity lingered and Joe, a personable lad, laughs about it whenever we cross paths. Perversely, it was the best thing that could have happened that day. It provoked me into playing like a fucking demon for the rest of the afternoon. If he was carrying out orders then the commander adopted the wrong strategy. You see people often made that mistake about Páidí Ó Sé. I know it. "Go on, get Páidí Ó Sé going, he'll come out swinging and get the line." I know people thought like that. They were wrong. I'd get very wired before a game, sure. I'd sit in the corner of the dressing room after emptying my bowels with a serious scowl on my face. I'd let out the odd manic roar. But this was only my method of tuning in. My head was always crystal clear once that ball was thrown in. I knew my job. Passionate? Yes. Blindly so? No. *Never.* Another aspect I think the Dublin line underestimated that day was my strength. Joe was bigger than me, he wasn't stronger. I got well stuck in. Mentally and physically . . . I felt unbeatable.

That was, of course, until Barney Rock – their only real scoring threat – ghosted in behind Mick Spillane for a second-half goal. I started to worry. You see, there'd been talk. After the last-minute collapses of 1982 and 1983, people had been saying that Kerry's will had weakened, that our hunger to make the line had evaporated. "Not again," I thought. Worse still, shortly after the goal, I drilled a ball straight to Rock who stroked it over the bar. Fortunately, we didn't surrender the initiative for too long. Without the injured Mikey, John Kennedy proved a capable deputy with five points. Ogie prompted the forwards while Bomber was on fire.

Yet again our key man was Pat Spillane. Back from serious injury he seemed even keener than ever; kicked some outrageous scores. No late calamity this time, 0–14 to 1–6.

It was sweet. The pain of the two previous years disappeared in an instant. The future was now. All-Ireland champions again.

There was a sour note, though. John Egan was called ashore after the break to make way for Timmy O'Dowd. It was the last time he wore a Kerry jersey. For all of us, especially the veterans, it was tough to see the back of the Sneem player. Dwyer knew he'd made a mistake. Egan was a quiet man, one I never knew that well. What I do know is that, at his peak, there wasn't a forward to touch him. He was always easy-going, softly-spoken. But behind the exterior he was driven – pushed himself to the limit and did the hardest things well. Powerful. History will look most favourably on Egan's contribution to Gaelic football. So too, will Kerry. In the 1975 final he started the whole magic journey with his wonderful goal. Three years later he stopped us from disappearing into oblivion with an equally quality score to halt the Dubs in their tracks. I cherish one fond memory of Egan: psyched up to the hilt before an All-Ireland final, I had just indulged myself in a bit of hand-to-hand combat with a table, I made my way down the tunnel and was just about to burst on to the turf in Croker when I felt this tug on my togs, "Where are ye going after the game, Páid?" . . . Egan!

Being a newly married man, and player-manager of the county finalists, I was back at training in Dingle on Tuesday night. We faced South Kerry a fortnight after the All-Ireland. They were a powerful side anchored by Jack O'Shea. Without putting the shackles on Jacko it would be almost impossible for us to prosper. However, I'd hatched a plan. On the train to Dublin the day before the All-Ireland there'd been some hullabaloo about tickets. Vincent O'Connor had been cut tickets after being dropped from the starting line-up. He was fairly upset so he had a word with Joe Keohane who eventually sorted

121

something out for him. On hearing about this
arrangement Dwyer approached Shin in the train
carriage. Relations between the two had been somewhat
strained in the wake of Shin's demotion. Dwyer
questioned Shin about his attendance at training. Wasn't
happy. Said some of the senior members of the squad had
complained about his commitment. O'Connor was
furious. Later that evening as we strolled on the strand in
Malahide I got chatting to Shin. He was furious, raring
up with Dwyer. "Páidí, who's saying I don't give a fuck?
Which senior members are complaining about me?"
Without hesitation I replied. "Jacko. 'Twas Jacko!" "I'll
clip that fucker's wings," fumed Shin.

Two weeks later Vincent O'Connor beat Jacko off the
park as West Kerry won their first ever county
championship: West Kerry 1–7, South Kerry 1–6.

Of course it wasn't Jacko. Páidí Machiavelli Ó Sé.
New captain of the Kerry team.

9
The Port Is Near

Fiche bliain ag fás,
Fiche bliain faoi bhláth,
Fiche bliain ag trá

Croke Park, 22 September 1985, 5.20 pm

*"A Mhuintir Chiarraí agus a chairde go léir. Tá
áthas ó chroí orm gur ormsa athá an phribhléid i
mbliana Sam a thabhairt thar n-ais go dtí an
Ríocht agus thar n-ais go dtí'n Ghaeltacht. Tá
áthas faoi leith gur ormsa a thit sé i mbliana,
mar táim ana shásta an corn a thabhairt thar n-
ais go dtí an Ghaeltacht, go Corca Dhuibhne. Tá
fear speisialta inniu agus táim ana bhuíoch
dhó, ní gá dom a ainm a luath; Mick Dwyer. Ní
dóigh liom go bhfuil duine 'n aon áit i mbun
bainistíochta athá chomh maith le Mick Dwyer.
Mar fhocal scoir, ba mhaith liom chomh maith,
mo bhuíochas a ghabháil le Tommy Doyle a bhí
ag imirt lena Ciarraí Thiar agus tá súil agam gur
ag an áit so . . . an bhliain seo chugainn a
bheidh Tommy Doyle. Go raibh míle maith
agaibh go léir."*

For all my manipulation and pulling of strings on the
football front, my efforts to date to enhance my chances
of getting a licence for a pub back in Ventry had proved
fruitless. For nearly six years I had been waiting in vain,
all the time the tension simmered around the parish. You
see, local publican Páid Quinn had objected, I suppose

123

understandably, that the area couldn't sustain another pub. His own shop, situated down the road in the village would come under serious pressure if a well-known footballer was to open a premises in the vicinity. Strong case, no question. But as far as I was concerned, I was seeking to earn a living on the very turf where I grew up. I felt it was my right. The court hadn't seen it that way, at least not until now. A couple of weeks after the county final I faced into the Circuit Court in Tralee yet again. This time, however, I felt my case was strengthened considerably as I had purchased the licence from a pub three or four miles back the road in Baile Mór whose owners decided to sell it as a going concern. No dice. Judge didn't go for it and I was refused. This time I had to make a stand. I was fed up. Immediately after receiving the decision I consulted with my Junior Counsel, Paul Gallagher, who was operating under instruction from Paudie Lynch. We would appeal to the High Court. I wanted that licence.

Without the knowledge of my legal team, I decided to tap the Boss for some advice on the matter. I had been around the house too many times by this stage and if Haughey couldn't advise me then no one could. However, before I travelled to Kinsealy I had a chance encounter with Mick O'Connell in Tralee. Myself and Beatrice had travelled to the town for the afternoon and had just enjoyed a spot of lunch in the Imperial Hotel when Micko approached me on the street outside. O'Connell was an independent councillor with Kerry County Council at the time and had read of my recent refusal in the Circuit Court and impending appeal in the *Kerry's Eye* newspaper, "Páidí, I think you're being hard done by. Look, drop me a line, I'm very friendly with a Senior Counsel in Dublin named Hugh O'Flaherty. He could be your man for the appeal." I was gob-smacked. My hero-worship of O'Connell hadn't been diluted by our success. Now here he was offering me the hand of friendship, of encouragement. I think he felt strongly about my desire to live and work in my own parish.

Anyway, I was seriously buoyed by Connell's intervention. Didn't waste any time putting my request for advice in writing. The following week I travelled to Dublin to meet Fianna Fáil's leader of the opposition.

I explained my situation to Charlie, I was going to the High Court to appeal. "Do you think I'm right?" I ventured cautiously. "Well," he said thoughtfully, "let's look at the situation carefully. I'll have a word with my legal team and we'll meet after lunch. My gut feeling, Páidí, is that you are right to appeal it to the High Court, but let's examine all the possibilities." I was heartened by Charlie's response and felt secure in the knowledge that his advice would be sound. After lunch we met up again. My appeal was given the thumbs up. Now Charlie offered me a choice of two top-class barristers who could represent me in the High Court. The first was a man named John Cassidy, an expert on the liquor licensing laws. Sounded good. However, the second was, according to Haughey "a good Kerryman and a good GAA man". His name was Hugh O'Flaherty . . . the same man Mick O'Connell had mentioned to me. I made my decision on the spot. "This was my man." I needed no more convincing but, shortly afterwards, I was talking to the late Frank King who explained to me that O'Flaherty was indeed a good south Kerryman. And there was more. Flaherty's wife Kay was a Sligo woman whose father had umpired the 1947 All-Ireland final in the Polo Grounds. Staunch GAA folk. I was on solid ground here, I thought. Lynch, Gallagher and O'Flaherty. Optimistic.

Now there was one big drawback. In a small community like Ventry, people were forced to take sides. There was strain on all involved. I regret that. As the High Court case drew near after Christmas, tension mounted in the parish. In one camp: "Let Páidí build his pub"; in the other: "What about Páid Quinn's livelihood?" The choice was stark. In March 1985 I won my appeal in Tralee. Thankfully, the strain between myself and the Quinns evaporated quickly after the event. It was unfortunate that it had to come to that point, that a legal battle had to be fought. Yet it's a fact of life in rural Ireland. We're good friends now . . . an Irish conclusion to an Irish problem.

Shortly after my first wedding anniversary, work began in earnest on the pub at Ard an Bhóthair. In the past I'd baulked when I thought that responsibility might outweigh my commitment to football. Not now. Now, I was still training county champions West Kerry, about to assume the captaincy of the Kerry team for the first time and had just squeezed my head into the noose of a £150,000 mortgage. I coped. I had a lot of support around. Experience was also telling at last. The guards, Kruger's, six All-Irelands. I knew the pub was a winner. I mean, it had to work. GAA folk are proud, clannish. They'd flock to the place. Ideally situated on Bóthar an Rí, already a tourist Mecca and with the Kerry captain's name above the door . . . had to work. Did.

From Montrose to Baile na nGall

At this time, Diarmuidín Ó Súilleabháin adopted a supporting role. Big time. Aware that I was about to take the floor in the dressing room and control over my own destiny in Ard an Bhóthair, he dished out valuable advice with fraternal zeal. And, you know, a lot of the locals couldn't understand this. Diarmuid was considered contrary, cantankerous. "How can he tolerate Sé?" they'd ask. But the truth was that we never crossed swords. Ever. Never even argued about the taste of a pint. I learned so much about myself, my heritage, my sense of place from Diarmuid. He introduced me to some great people, great musicians like Joe Burke, who has remained a close friend since. More importantly, he put everything in context and coached me on how to carry it all. Language, traditional music, an Ghaeltacht . . . saol na Gaeltachta. "Páidí," he'd say, "you have to go deep to find the true man, you have to go to the middle of a fellow's belly for the best in him." Spiritual.

You see, Diarmuid had found his place, where he was

were he wanted to be, sa Ghaeltacht. He had turned his back on the bright lights, moved from the comfortable surroundings of RTÉ, where he operated as a newscaster, to work with Raidió na Gaeltachta in Baile na nGall. And he contributed in no small way to the rapid development of that station, a station that, I feel, has now surpassed all its lofty English-language rivals, especially in the field of sports broadcasting. Mícheál Ó Sé, Seán Bán Breathnach, Máirtín Ó Cíardha . . . they're the best in the business, great professionals, great characters.

There was a practical side to our friendship. Diarmuid coached me how to handle the public glare, the press. Taught me how to put the best foot forward at the time. Appreciate what I'd often taken for granted. With the pub due to open in July of 1985, he busily got to work organising media invites, musicians. Of course there was only one obvious candidate to do the official honours. CJ. By now my friendship with the Haughey family had blossomed, particularly so with Charlie and his daughter Eimear. It wasn't just expedience . . . good for Charlie to work the locality, good for Páidí to have such illustrious contacts. No. We were, and still are, genuinely good friends. I always enjoyed the Haugheys' company. They were remarkably easy-going. Despite their isolation on the Inis, they kind of had a handle on the locals. And vice versa. Local people had built the house on the island some years back and built a relationship in the process. Dan Bric had led the crew and regaled us all with tales of the Boss, choppers, fine wines. They'd spend weeks out there. "When would you realise it was time to come home, Dan?" we'd often ask. "When the sheep were winking at me," he'd reply. Charlie loved this. He returned the hospitality too. The doors of Kinsealy were always open to me. Times may have changed but our relationship hasn't. CJ opened the pub on a blustery July afternoon, shot down in the chopper. Some day. Couldn't go wrong. All-Ireland champions, Sam Maguire, Charlie Haughey. Stuffed. Diarmuid had all the angles covered too. Well received. *Tús maith . . .*

We played in the Ford Open Draw competition earlier that year. It had followed on from the Centenary Cup in 1984 and fizzled out soon afterwards. Carlow were our first opponents, in Tralee. My first match as captain of the Kerry team. Not for the first time, Micko thought he'd have a bit of craic with me. Handed me the ball. You see, he knew that this was one of the greatest honours I ever wanted. Thought I'd jump at it, shoot off . . . for an Open Draw game in spring, with Carlow! "Sssh, lads, hold on a minute," says Dwyer. "Our captain for 1985, P Sé's going to say a few words." I called his bluff. "No thanks, Micko, I have nothing to say now. When we play Cork in the championship . . . " Some of the players were surprised. I didn't want to let on, to Micko or any of 'em, that the captaincy meant as much as it really fucking did. I kept my powder dry. We ended up hammering Cork by thirteen points in the final of the competition in May on a rotten day in a near-empty Páirc Uí Chaoimh. Still, augured well. Our limbs may have been ageing but our brains were sharp. Well, sharp enough.

I was in reasonable shape going into the championship. Despite all the distractions the captaincy gave me the edge I needed. Put the effort in. Trained exclusively in Tralee that year for some reason. After skipping past Limerick we faced Cork in Páirc Uí Chaoimh again. They were still smarting from the humiliating hiding we dished out to them two months previously, so we needed to be on our guard. My first chance to take centre stage in the dressing room and ensure that we were on our guard. Well now I let fly. Fucking tore into the lot of 'em. There was no way I would lead Kerry to a Munster final defeat in Cork. In the midst of my fucking and blinding, I grabbed a ball, slammed it against the ground. Inadvertently, it bounced right up and smashed a light on the ceiling of the dressing room. By accident, my pre-match rant entered folklore. "Jeezuus Chruyssht, didn't Páidí smash up the fucking dressing room before they took to the field?" And, you know people believed that it had the lads wired

for the Cork game. Believed it myself. Subsequently I
learned the fuckers were laughing at my antics behind
my back! Sure hadn't they been around the block too
often? Goals from Bomber and Mikey, not the captain's
speech, proved the difference. I'd another piece of
silverware to plant behind the bar in Ard an Bhóthair.
Kept the bank manager happy.

A wet day in Croker for the semi-final against league
champions Monaghan. Nearly cost us. We didn't play
well. Eamon McEneaney bravely landed a famous 50 at
the close of the game to draw it. We were sloppy. I
insisted on kicking every ball, every free, every sideline.
Cranky. "Leave it off, I'll take it; throw it out to me."
Classic betrayal of a captain, you see it all the time;
overdoing it; demanding responsibility. I remember
Dwyer saying it to me afterwards and to this day it
makes sense to me, "If ever a ball goes dead, the player in
that constituency should kick it, there should be no
running out of position to kick sidelines or frees." Inter-
county players? Should be able to kick the fucking ball! I
get into the jigs now when I see the ball being tossed
back to one man every time, the fulcrum or the pivot as
he's sometimes referred to. It can kill the shape of a
team, diminish the responsibility of other players, slow
the play down. Doesn't make sense at all. I was full of it
in the drawn game against Monaghan. Bomber had been
in the States for a couple of weeks and returned home for
the semi. We didn't let him out of our sights after that.
And it was a different story when we squared up again.
Having been prodded the first day, we were much livelier
the second. Goals from Bomber and Powery in the first
half broke their challenge. Liston was sent off before
half-time but it mattered little. Later, Dermot Hanafin
switched to midfield while Jack O'Shea slipped in to
centre-back. Jacko had a massive second half. Monaghan
switched Eugene 'Noodie' Hughes to my corner but to
little effect. I'd tightened the screw. Picked up the man
of the match award afterwards. Near the end of that
game, Monaghan corner-back Fergus Caulfield scuffed a

free into Mikey Sheehy's grateful hands who proceeded to pop it over the bar. Fergus complained to Sheehy that he was standing too close to the kick. "You got away lightly," Mikey replied. Kind of summed up the day.

"Unaccustomed though I am . . ."

Dublin, All-Ireland final. Yet again. This time the old enemy stood between me and a lengthy spell for Sam Maguire in Ventry. I was trying not to let my role as captain burden me for the final. Tried to clear the head and concentrate on the one thing that really mattered. Performance. There was the temptation for a bit of cheap publicity for the pub. I opted for the cautious route. Still do. I'll always avoid the spotlight before the event and will continue to do so until such time as we're professional. I'll avoid it during the event as well. I cringe when I see the reporters shooting towards the dugout at half-time during the live games nowadays. If we were being thrown a thousand pounds then I'd have to learn how to talk to some young lad on the way into the dressing room, calm down and tell him what I think. But we're not. As amateurs, I feel players and managers are entitled to enjoy the freedom and security that anonymity provides in highly-charged situations. If someone wants to talk, that's their choice. If they don't, then that should be respected. It isn't.

Before the 1985 final, however, there were certain duties I couldn't avoid. A fortnight before the game, I was lying on the bed one evening having issued strict instructions to Máire that I wasn't to be disturbed when who shot up the stairs into the room only Diarmuid. "*Bhfuil óráid déanta amach 'gat*," he asked. "*N'fheadar cad 'tán tú chun a rá?*" The speech, had I prepared anything? "NO," I roared. He laid it on the line to me then, that it would have to be in Irish, "*as Gaolainn*". Well my first reaction was to tell Diarmuid to go and fuck off. "Will you leave me alone, haven't I enough on my plate?" He didn't let up. That was Diarmuid. He was so forceful and passionate that I reckoned that, had I refused, I'd have lost a friend. So he sat down with me and wrote a speech. Obviously the people of Kerry and Dwyer would need an early mention but the emphasis was on the west, the Gaeltacht, Corca Dhuibhne. He also knew that I was still training the West Kerry divisional side and pointed out that I should give the Private, Tommy Doyle, a leg up as he was likely to be nominated captain if we retained our county title. I gave the speech no more thought then. I came under fierce pressure before the game. Journalists besieged the place. I kept a lid on it. Safer.

Physically I felt good lining out in the All-Ireland final. I'd bulked up a bit, hadn't the stamina of old but I could sustain the short, sharp stuff no problem. Still, if pace and space are primary aspects of football, well, the latter was my forte. I drew on my experience to read situations, deliver the easy pass efficiently. Timed the hit. I didn't dive in blindly. If I made a break it was because I'd seen it a thousand times before, pictured it as I plodded through the sand on Ventry beach. I could also kick with both feet which helped. The game has been tweaked since. It's gone up a notch, no doubt. It would be difficult to rely on reading a situation alone nowadays . . . nowadays, the corner-back must be as fit and as agile as any man on the field. I managed. Keeping my man scoreless was always top of my agenda so, to that end, I was happy. Going into the Dublin game I was very conscious that the record of captains in finals was dreadful. Conscious of it now as a manager, I will always try to limit the responsibilities of the skipper, let him off. Dwyer's words after the drawn game against Monaghan were firmly imprinted in my head, the defender's code: *Mind your patch.*

I marked Kieran Duff. Started well, bottled him up, felt in control. We coasted through the first half, won every battle. Dublin's spiritual leader Brian Mullins was visibly, and understandably, weakened for allowing Jack O'Shea the latitude of the park. Jacko landed a penalty to give us a seemingly unassailable nine-point cushion at the break. We got the rub too as Jacko had picked the ball off the ground prior to that decision. As captain, the steps of the Hogan seemed tantalisingly close but I tried really hard to keep those thoughts out of my head. Gave my heated tuppenceworth at the break, which wasn't easy with our advantage. Started to go wrong after the interval. John Kearns turned the screw in midfield for Dublin, hauled them back into the game. Timmy Dowd then broke through for our second goal. Safe now? Jeezuus, no. Then it all went horribly wrong. A thicket of players rose to meet a high ball forward, broke to Joe McNally who crashed it to the net off the crossbar. Minutes later another high ball from Kearns arrived in my parish. I stepped out to shield my man from the breaking ball and Joe rose above Seán Walsh to punch his second goal. "I knew it, I fucking knew it. Speeches, captaincy . . . we're going to fucking blow it." With only a point between the sides I was sure Sam had slipped from my grasp. Then, we got another rub. A ball fell into midfield which broke from Tom Spillane's grasp. He punched the ball along the ground to his brother and, not for the first time – nor the last, Pat rescued us with a fucking unreal score. Had the ref blown it well . . . After Pat's score, we took control again. Bomber moved out around the middle; Jacko rallied. Survived, just about. Whistle went. Blur.

The first person I remember molesting me was Dwyer. He made the point, knew this was my moment. Then, as I was fighting my toughest battle of the day through a forest of well-wishers, who grabs me by the shoulder only Diarmuid. He'd left the press box early, where he'd been working for Raidió na Gaeltachta, and landed on the field. *"Bhuel, bhfuil tú ullamh?"* Ready for the speech? Grabbed a hold of me, shook me, gave me a quick summary, bang, bang, bang! Kerry . . . Dwyer . . . West Kerry . . . Corca Dhuibhne . . . the Private. Like Martin Luther King. *"A mhuintir Chiarraí agus a cháirde go léir . . ."*

There was no skipping the formalities this time

around. I kept a firm grip on the silverware as we headed south. It was a magical experience, arriving in Killarney at the head of the posse. After all the success this added a new dimension. On to Tralee, soaking it in. Captain of the Kerry team, All-Ireland champions. On Tuesday we pointed the bus west, it was time for me to take the cup home, Máire and Diarmuid by my side. Just outside Tralee the coach pulled in at Blennerville where Neidín Kelleher was waiting to take myself and Sam over the bridge on a pony and trap. We filled the cup in the Skelper Quane's. Inched our way towards the Blaskets. . . Annascaul, Lispole, into Dingle with fires burning. Regretfully, I didn't dwell in Dingle. In my haste to carry the cup home we snaked on through. Should have stopped, spent a few hours there. Hype, emotion, adulation, drink. Difficult to be rational. On through Milltown, veered left for Ventry. Through the village on to the crossroads. Ard an Bhóthair. Home. Boyhood dream comes true. All the hours in the *Duí*, in the churchyard, kicking balls with Batt Garvey, pretending to be Mick O'Connell, sneaking out of the Sem in 1970 to see Donie O'Sullivan take the cup home, listening to Mícheál O'Hehir's gripping commentaries on the wireless in the kitchen with Joe O'Shea, listening to Dr Jim talking about the Green and Gold . . . the Green and Gold. Doesn't get much better than that night. Unbelievable. The rumblings in the parish silenced in an instance. United in pride. Their man centre stage. And just in time, before our last curtain call.

The pub was hopping for weeks after. It was difficult to put a lid on it. When your name is above the pub door people expect you to be there. When you're the recent captain of the All-Ireland champions, people expect that bit more. I had to call a halt.

West Kerry had qualified for the county final again, having accounted for Shannon Rangers, Stacks and South Kerry along the way. Now, there was my promise to Tommy Doyle. Mercifully, there was a month's grace before we took on Feale Rangers in the decider. I could barely raise a gallop the day of the match. Played poorly.

It didn't really matter as we'd got the balance right. Fortunately the man in behind me, Bernard Dan Sullivan, was particularly solid, great west Kerryman, great Dingle man; unlucky not to win an All-Ireland with Kerry on the field of play; captained UCG. My real contribution was made off the field. I had won an amount of respect for imposing my simple philosohpy the previous year . . . players in their proper positions. Half-time, I buzzed around, made sure we knew our moves, raised the tempo with a few well-chosen words. All season I dangled the carrot that, if we won another championship, we'd travel to America. On 20 October, we won our second county championship on the trot defeating Feale Rangers 0–11 to 1–5. The wish I'd expressed from the Hogan stand four weeks before had been granted. The Private would captain the Kingdom in 1986.

I learned a lot from the West Kerry boys. There were some great characters . . . Connor, Sullivan, Maunsell, the Caseys. I picked their brains, shared their humour. Around this time, I started to define the idea of a smart man in my head. "A smart man," I thought, "is a man who's smart enough to realise that there's a man smarter than him." I hoovered up everything I could from players, often using their own wisdom against them. This would help in the future when the second leg of my journey commenced. So, too, would the respect I got back west for my exploits with the divisional side.

New togs please

We wintered well. Tigh Pháidí Uí Shé was the centre of the universe. Marvellous time. I picked up my fifth All Star in succession to cap it all off.

Facing into 1986, it wasn't football that occupied my mind. There were trips to the States with West Kerry and with the All Stars and another Kerry holiday to be organised. In fact holidays were occupying everyone's mind as there was an unmerciful row about Kerry's planned trip away. Rows seemed to be occurring with greater frequency . . . holidays, the cup. Anyway, some of my strokes were beginning to pay dividends. To add a bit of spice to West Kerry's celebration night after our first county success in 1984, I had invited New York chief John Kerry O'Donnell over to present the county medals. Thought 'twould be a good move. The West Kerry board went crazy. Couldn't afford it. I insisted. Anyway that Christmas, John Kerry flew into Shannon, spent a night in the Imperial in Tralee before heading to Dingle. He billed the west board for the lot, flights, expenses, everything. They went mad. "Jeezuus, Páidí, you're after stinging us badly here," was the consensus. I stuck to my guns. "Toughen, lads. Toughen." Then, in the spring of 1986, West Kerry travelled to New York to mark our second championship victory. While we were there, John Kerry invited us to play in an exhibition game against New York in Gaelic Park. A super crowd turned up for the match and afterwards the West Kerry board were gobsmacked when John Kerry turned and presented them with the entire gate. Had they quibbled with his expenses the previous year, he'd hardly have been so benevolent.

My dealings with John Kerry for that year weren't finished either. On the All Stars trip later in 1986, another unholy row broke out when O'Donnell opposed one of the appointed referees for the trip. Apparently, the New York hurlers had been 'blackguarded' by this referee and John Kerry refused to open Gaelic Park for the All Stars games. The sponsors, Bank of Ireland, were mortified. The embarrassment! Panic. Assuming the games were off, I'd already taken my cue and gone on the tear with my friend Toos Mac Gearailt's brother Peaitsín Toos. However, no sooner had I hit Manhattan than an SOS was issued for me. "Get Páidí, he'll sort it out with John Kerry." They eventually tracked me down and I was dispatched as a peace envoy to placate New York's GAA chief. I sat down with John Kerry, put the Bank's case forward . . . they were helping to honour the contribution of players. Anyway, after my opening shot he turned and asked me. "Páidí, with which bank have you your mortgage for the pub?" Jeezuus, I thought, where's he going here? I couldn't believe my ears. "Bank of Ireland," I replied. "Well then, if you're smart enough you can make this situation work to your advantage, get yourself a better deal. The bank are desperate to hold the games, you're in doing their dirty work. So . . ." He had me wired. I did as he said. Gaelic Park was opened.

Earlier that year, there had been a little tiff between the players and the board over a holiday but it had been quickly resolved. In truth, the board had always looked after us well, did their best with whatever resources they had. Harmony restored, the Canary Islands were next on the itinerary. While beached off the west coast of Africa, we spoke to Dwyer. Decided we'd go to the well one more time, see could we pull off another hat-trick. Jeezuus. Wouldn't be easy.

With so many distractions it was hardly any surprise our league campaign was pock-marked. When we finally got down to a proper grind, I was in some nick. For the first time in my career I needed bigger togs. Dwyer had always kept an eye on the lads who were fond of porter. Determined his attitude to pre-championship training. I had been part of the heavy-gang for a couple of years but, in 1986, it became the Dirty Half-Dozen. Aim of our mission? Weight loss. He drilled us hard but none was stupid enough to think we'd survive otherwise. I used every trick I knew to gain an advantage, to conceal my real state. We eventually snuck around the corner. Eased our way into the Munster championship.

Don't know how Dwyer did it. Year after year. Again he warned of the pitfalls that awaited us in Clonmel as we faced Tipp in our opener in June. Again we gave them a twelve-point hiding. I must admit that my heart wasn't really in it. I'd had my bellyful, was going through the motions. Fortunately, my instincts were good and steered my motions accordingly. Experience carried me. In Killarney the following month, when we played Cork, things fell nicely for the expanding Páidí. Just the match I was looking for. Didn't touch the fucking ball. Then again, neither did my man. I was marking Robert Swain and we fought an anonymous battle out in the corner. Kept him scoreless and myself happy. Overall, though, we were lucky enough to squeeze through by four points. The tide was beginning to turn in Munster.

In the meantime, Seán Boylan had engineered a Leinster breakthrough for Meath, so it was a novel semi-final pairing. A gift of a goal for Ger Power in the first half gave us a lucky platform, allowed us to loosen up. Meath were just the type of team to end our run; hungry, strong, with flair up front. Had they been slightly further down the road in their development, perhaps with an All-Ireland semi-final under their belts, they could well have closed the book on us. Their prominence over the next five years was proof of that. Still, one decent break was all we needed. Our dying kick was ruthless enough, especially up front where we were still better than any other county. Power looked like the youngest man on the field, Mikey showed all the class of old, Spillane . . . hungrier than ever. Bomber stroked over a beauty before half-time as if to remind everyone who they were dealing with. Ogie prospered as well while Willie Maher and Timmy Dowd added spice. Big Mike Galwey made an appearance too. All in stark contrast to Páidí Sé. I was fucking blessed to carry my legs out of that game. I was marking a very talented forward in Bernard Flynn and only a bit of cuteness on my part and a bit of inexperience on his, saved me from a right hiding. That was the pattern for 1986. Didn't change much in the final either.

The polish of the performance against Meath hid the rust beneath. We were there for the taking. It's kind of strange now that the Tyrone final doesn't register much emotion with me. Sure, the thought of a record eight All-Ireland medals for the gang of five was attractive, but records don't drive footballers. I was past it. I couldn't burn the candle at both ends like the old days. The enjoyment had been diluted. Smug? Disrespectful? "Jeezuus, Páidí, what about all the great players and teams who never tasted the ultimate success?" Ya, true.

But in context. I'd come to the end of my journey. This was our tenth All-Ireland final in twelve years and I was running on empty. Dwyer's special training hurt more than ever. My trips over the Clasach were token jogs half way up the hill. My head yearned for the days when I was the fittest man in the camp. Of course I didn't admit any of this. Even to myself. Few footballers face the end with their eyes open. I certainly didn't. My motivation was Tommy Doyle, our captain. West Kerry. I had a somewhat dubious club career with An Ghaeltacht but my commitment to the divisional outfit in the mid-1980s consumed me. It was just about enough to go on. *Just about.*

The final curtain

Final day. Blur. Red-and-white blur. From the moment Jack O'Shea cracked his penalty off the crossbar in the second minute of the game all I can remember is a red-and-white blur, a frenzied northern din echoing around Dublin 3. They swept forward relentlessly. I was on the back foot. Big time. The last thing I needed. We were behind 0–7 to 0–3 at the break, lucky to be only trailing by four. It was a bleak scene, the dressing room. End of the road? Well, some of us weren't quite sure. We raised the pitch in the room, but an air of uncertainty hung over most of us as we entered the red-and-white arena for the second thirty-five minutes. There was one exception. Just after the break disaster struck. I was hung out to dry when Tom Spillane got caught ball-watching and collided with Seán Walsh. Ended up on his arse as Damien O'Hagan broke away on his own with the ball. I was left two against one. As soon as I made the break to try and smother O'Hagan's pass, he slipped it to Paudge Quinn who fired it to the net. First goal I'd ever conceded in an All-Ireland final: 1–7 to 0–4.

After swapping points, Tyrone were handed their ticket home. Eugene McKenna was bundled to the ground in the square. *Penalty.* "If he puts this in the net we're gone." There wasn't a man in the Green and Gold that day that didn't tell himself that as Kevin McCabe stepped up with the ball. When he fired it over the bar the whole stadium seemed to exhale together. You sensed the fans' disappointment. The chink. "They've left the door open." Nine points down and we would have been looking into the abyss. Like a fucking tiger, Pat Spillane smelled the wound inflicted by the missed penalty. We'd barely got back into our positions when he delivered the mortal blow, a flicked goal. One split second of genius. Like a conductor rapping his stick off the platform, Spillane called us all to attention. Within minutes the Kerry orchestra was delivering its final, glorious performance. Harmony. Movement, finish. Sweet music. Sweet for me. Fuck it, now I'd could sit back and enjoy the concert. The torment of the first forty minutes was over. McKenna went off injured. Tyrone were gone. Hard to believe. Gone. Buckled. 2–15 to 1–10. A fifteen-point turnaround. Eight All-Ireland medals. Private read his script. Sam goes west again.

Where do I go from here? Of course, amidst the annual party and winter wind-down, there was all kinds of crazy talk about another four-in-a-row. And, you know, we marched on to the league final the following spring, were beaten in a cracker by Dublin. Looked like there was plenty of life in the old dog. Told ourselves that as we suffered a series of annihilations on our last trip to the States shortly afterwards. Looked like the Dubs might be around to slog it out with us too. Foolish hope. *Is mairg a dheineann deimhin dá dhóchas.*

Players are often most blind about their own weaknesses, especially veteran players. During the 1986 campaign, I had become extremely careless. I'd been indulged for long enough. Felt I'd have to retire my position myself, it'd never be taken from me. Under Billy Morgan's passionate command, Cork had closed right in on us. A strong spine had been boosted by the addition of Kildare duo Shea Fahy and Larry Tompkins. Significantly, young Niall Cahalane had proven himself to have the measure on Pat Spillane. When it came to the 1987 Munster final in Páirc Uí Chaoimh they were ready. Mightn't have wholly believed it themselves, but they were. A late Mikey Sheehy goal nearly cost them their breakthrough but a steady last-minute free from Tompkins tied it up. It was enough to give them the leg up. They knew now that they were, by far, the better team.

Billy tells a great yarn about the immediate aftermath of that drawn Munster final. We can vouch for it too, because you could hear him next door. Directly after the game, Morgan expelled all the officials out of the dressing room and huddled the players together. The only civilian allowed to remain in the room was the late Kid Cronin, the affable bag man with Cork. Lovely character. Kid was already well on in years, but he was included in the inner sanctum. Morgan grabbed a ball and started hand passing to each player in turn, questioning each in a high-pitched squeal. "Now, we're fucking going back to Killarney . . . and what are we going to fucking do there?" The replies varied little: "We're going to fucking finish 'em off." "We're going to fucking beat them." Every single one of them was well pumped now. Inadvertently, Morgan fired a hand pass to Kid Cronin who, startled, fumbled the ball. "Jesus Christ, Kid," Billy roared, "will you concentrate!"

On 2 August 1987 we surrendered our Munster crown to Cork for only the second time in thirteen years. What was more significant though, was the manner of our defeat in that replay. It was the first time since 1974 that we had been comprehensively outplayed by our neighbours. It was the end of the road. Not that any of us readily admitted it. I certainly didn't. After all I was playing as well, if not better, than I had the previous year. I would admit nothing.

"Who was going to take my place?" I thought. "There's no fucker going to move me out of the corner." Dwyer didn't seem to be in any great hurry to wield the axe either. Despite a lot of talk that it was time for him to step down, he decided to give it yet another shot. This suited me. "There's no way he'll drop me. Can't see beyond the old guard." I'd opted out for most of the league, but, as 1988 wore on, Dwyer upped the ante on the training field. Mikey and Seánie had already retired. I struggled on.

On 11 May that year, myself and Máire had our first child Neasa. There was great celebration around the Ó Sé household. Naturally, it was difficult to keep any perspective on the football front. At this stage of one's career it would have been easy enough to call a halt, leave it off. Training was becoming increasingly difficult, there were new responsibilities with a little girl at home, the pub . . . I stuck at it. Fortunately – and this is still the case – I had great support around the home from family and friends. This allowed me to keep at it.

Despite the struggle, I carelessly assumed that I'd carry my legs into the Munster final. I manned the usual berth against Waterford in the opening round. No change. Promising enough. Young Maurice Fitzgerald was ready to take charge of scoring. Ready for Cork. One more time. Then all hell broke loose. I was sitting in Bailey's Corner in Tralee with Diarmuid when news of the team for Sunday's Munster final in Páirc Uí Chaoimh came through to us. In goal, Charlie Nelligan; right corner-back, Mike Spillane; full-back, Tom Spillane; left corner-back, Morgan Nix . . . "What the . . . I'm on the bench? THE FUCKING BENCH. FOR CORK? JEEZUUS, WHAT THE FUCK'S MICKO AT?" I was boiling. Had I not seen it coming? No. Truthfully, no. Had I struggled in training? Yes. Had I lost form on the field? Yes. Was I past it? Yes. So had I not seen in coming? *No.* The end; don't see it coming. Blind. Blindly loyal to yourself, to your old standards, the old flame in your soul that made you better than every other fucker that ever chased twenty yards on your shoulder to win a ball.

There was no joking, no sniggering as I made my way to the bench in Cork on Munster final day in 1988. This time it was for real. Myself, Powery, Ogie and Bomber . . . enough gold on our sideboards to finance a small country . . . sitting in the dugout for a Munster final. Worse still, I got no run. Every Cork forward scored that day. I got

more sour with each kick. Despite a dazzling display
from Maurice, Cork bullied us, ended up beating us by a
point. A shemozzle erupted near the end of the game.
"Shcelping, against Cork, in Páirc Uí Chaoimh. Where
am I? On the fucking bench." Bad day. Things got heated
afterwards when our selector Liam Higgins stuck by me
and criticised Dwyer publicly for not throwing me on
against Cork. Must have hurt. Still Micko toughened it
out. So did I . . . for now.

Men are blind in their own cause.

10
Journey's End?

Ní thagann ciall roimh aois

I SAVED everything for the county. Always gave the best of the stuff to Kerry. My club, An Ghaeltacht, got short-changed. Like everyone else really. After Kerry football . . . everything suffered. Neglected. Even my club. I tried at times to conceal just how much the Green and Gold meant to me. I failed. Nothing came before the Green and Gold. The proof was there. My attitude to the Gaeltacht club was proof enough. Now, in my time of need, with my career petering out, who do I turn to? An Ghaeltacht. Oh I'd show the county management just how committed I was to getting back on the panel. It was working too. A few stirring displays for the club on the back of a lot of personal training and they took notice. The world had turned though. We played in a west Kerry league semi-final and Seán Walsh was dispatched to see how I was getting on. Walsh? Seánie Walsh, the youngster I minded when he came on to the Kerry panel first! I stood out at full-back, a bit of a problem area for the county at the time. Back on the Kerry panel I needed to impress them one more time, see could I get them to throw me a jersey for the Munster final. The Gaeltacht faced Lispole in the West Kerry league final in the Sportsfield in Dingle. I was well up for it. Warm day. The club hadn't won anything of note for fifteen years. Dominated in the late 1960s and early 1970s but, during

143

my best years, we hadn't figured. Chance to change that
now and follow my agenda to impress Dwyer. "Now," I
thought, "if I can't stand out here today . . ."

Despite the advantage of the wind, we're only hanging
on to Lispole. I'm happy enough though, marking my
pal, Kerry selector Liam Higgins. Let him spread the
word. Before half-time a gap opens up through the
middle. Think I'll go on an auld burst here, give 'em
something to talk about. Up the field, about thirty yards
from their goal. Nothing on so I plough into an opponent
as I'm about to kick the ball, claim the handy free.
Gabriel Casey, one of the three Casey brothers from
Lispole, first cousins of Brian Mullins, jogs past, remarks,
"Sign of an old man, Páidí, trying to win a handy free
like that."

After the break, things start to turn for us; creep ahead
of them, picking off a few scores. I'm taking the
kickouts, batin' the ball down the field. Now I'm taking
the piss. I fire a kickout into midfield towards John Long,
ref blows the whistle for a free. "Leave it, lads, leave it,"
I bellow jogging up to the halfway line. Take the free
myself and plant it over the fucking bar. Two kicks!
Then, Gabriel Casey comes soloing towards me. "Too
old, ey?" I'll show him. Meet him full on, floor him.
Picks himself up, takes the free himself. Wide. I jog up
alongside him, smiling. "Hey, I'm going to kick the next
ball out to you. You put up your hand, I'll kick it to you
and we'll see can you catch the fucking thing!" Five
minutes to go, we put over the insurance score. Two
points up. They need a goal. Doesn't look on, until we
lose possession in midfield. They break with a man free.
"Fuck it, they're going for the kill here. After all the
football I'm after playing!" Now, out of nothing, I'm
facing a two-on-one situation, with An Ghaeltacht's first
title in years at stake. I decide not to wait, not to be
drawn by the man in possession. I'll attack the source
early. Leave my man, tear out thirty yards at full pace.
Wallop! Lights out.

The late Denisín Higgins – a brother of my friend
Liam and socialist politician Joe, a tough,

uncompromising footballer – was the unfortunate at the other end of the worst collision of my career, and that includes the car crashes. Denis broke both his cheek bones, his nose and cracked his skull. I nearly severed my ear. Unconscious, I was stretchered off to the county hospital to have over thirty-five stitches inserted in my ear. Was sent off in the process by referee Tommy Sugrue. Some comeback.

Last stand

I had milked the controversy surrounding my omission from the Kerry team to the full. At a funeral in Cork not long after the Munster final in 1988, I did the rounds. "If they had only put me on Dinny Allen . . ." Nonsense; feel-good factor. I'd be embarrassed about it now if I hadn't learnt so much from the whole experience. Spending that Munster final afternoon with my arse on the bench was more valuable in the long run than another provincial medal. As a manager I often use it as a reference point. Dropping players or hauling them ashore during an important game is never easy. Established, talented players make it difficult for you. I think I'm better as a manager for having suffered that day.

Back in the spring of 1989 I wasn't as comfortable with the notion. Stung by Dwyer I decided to go at it. I trained as hard as I could. I talked as hard as I could. Having given the league a miss for the most part, I joined in at the latter stages. We flew to the North for a quarter-final against Antrim. I was given a run, left Dwyer pleasantly surprised. Shortly afterwards he put me through my paces in Tralee; width of the pitch; wire to wire. Surprised him again. I had found a new training ground, a sloped field down near the *Duí*. I erected five hurdles and shot down nearly every evening with five balls. Did the hurdles, picked up a ball, soloed back up the hill; jab-kicked the ball back down the hill to an imaginary wing-forward; four more kicks. I was nearly right, you know. Sure, I missed the competitive training, which is vital, but I was getting there. Was enjoying it too. Until, of course, I clattered into Denisín Higgins in the West Kerry league final. Realistically, could I now expect to make the starting line-up against Cork, only six weeks away? Still, the disappointment of my setback in 1989 should now be put into context. Poor Denisín died tragically some years later. I don't recall the whole period lightly.

Whatever chance I had now was surely gone. I lost valuable time convincing Micko that I could play a role against Cork. When I had the stitches and the collar brace removed, I rejoined the Kerry panel for training. It was the last kick. On my return I was put marking the Bomber in a game of backs and forwards. After five minutes I realised what was happening. Bomber was going easy on me. I imagined Dwyer having a word with him earlier, "Take it handy on P Sé for a while, he's been through the mill . . ." It was enough. I said nothing to anyone. Had a long, easy shower. I was finished with Kerry . . . finished with football. The following day I travelled to Kenmare to play in a county league game for the Gaeltacht. Stopped off in Tattler's in Killarney for tea and sandwiches. Máire travelled with me. I played for a half-an-hour below in Kenmare. When I joined Máire afterwards I turned to her and said, matter-of-factly, "I've played my last game of football. Let's go home."

It was the easiest decision I'd ever made. No fanfare, no glorious departure. Told no one. Just quit. I'd kicked my last ball in anger.

So, was this the end of the road for Páidí? No. From the moment I walked away from the playing field, a different fire was kindled in my belly. This was no journey's end, merely a stop-off.

On 23 July, Cork beat Kerry in the Munster final for the third year in a row. A week later Dwyer retired. It was over. Fifteen years steering the most successful course in the history of Gaelic football. Micko gone. Now, who was going to fill the void? This could be no ordinary appointment, I thought.

146

Retirement? No player likes it but some handle it a lot better than others. For some it's a release, a chance to take to the golf course, follow their commitments or other pastimes which had been neglected due to football. For me there was nothing to fill that particular gap. Sure there were family demands – our second girl Siún was born on 25 September. There were the demands of the pub, the shop, day-to-day stuff. But, for me, life without football was inconceivable. A gaping chasm. I needed to get back into the game as soon as possible. I would go for the manager's job straight away.

Now, Dwyer may have had a fair idea who was going to succeed him but I was fairly certain that, deep down, I would have been one of the men shortlisted by Micko. However, he was to have little impact on the outcome. There was a kind of acrimonious end to his reign as the county board, and not Dwyer, had announced his retirement. The executive would interview prospective candidates and appoint the new boss. I decided to throw my hand in. I would oppose Mickey Ned O'Sullivan for the Kerry job.

For all my experience as a player and as a coach with West Kerry, my pitch was a naive one. I was raw. I didn't realise the advantages Mickey Ned possessed; didn't realise just how far he was ahead of me. Sullivan had operated as a selector with Dwyer for a couple of years, had a degree in physical education. His CV was a masterpiece. With a yearning among the executive and the county as a whole for something new, Mickey Ned fitted the bill. TD Pat Rabbitte, a regular visitor to Ventry, helped me draft my own application and CV. My pitch came from the heart. I placed the emphasis on areas where I thought I could do a good job . . . football and pride. I met with a number of the board officers. I knew I had the backing of North Kerry chairman Bernie O'Callaghan. I informed them that I intended to bring John O'Keeffe into the management team, that I would pursue my simple football philosophy. It didn't wash. I didn't fit. They read me wrong, weren't sure I could handle the responsibility, too soon after my playing days, too close. Rejected. Mickey Ned was appointed manager of the Kerry team, comfortably.

Disappointed? Sure. No football. Well, fortunately, Derry Murphy stepped in again and invited me to take over as trainer of the West Kerry team for 1990. I snapped at the chance. It was a good move. After overcoming a number of tight games and a couple of replays with Feale Rangers and Austin Stacks, we ended up winning yet another county championship, hammering Mid Kerry in the final in September: 4–9 to 0–7. Although we had an experienced outfit, I ensured they were well drilled. I stuck to my philosophy too. We played simple football with a high level of technical skill, accuracy and pace. Still insist on the same principles with Kerry nowadays.

Cork annihilated Kerry in the Munster final of 1990. It was a bad day all round. They were on their way to a second All-Ireland on the trot, we were rebuilding. Regretfully, I went public with my criticism in the wake of that defeat. I was highly critical of Mickey Ned, even got personal. I regret that. I was sniping, following my own agenda. There was nothing honourable about what I did. My comments were born from frustration, even idleness. I admired Mickey Ned greatly as a captain, as a footballer. In hindsight I cringe when I think of my outburst. I'm a bit wiser now. It's not easy to walk the line.

Having led the divisional side to county success, there was a novel appointment awaiting me in the winter of 1990. Earlier in the year, young Kerry star Maurice Fitzgerald gave me a call, asked would I be interested in taking charge of the UCC football team. I took the job and spent two very enjoyable seasons with the students in Cork. Unfortunately it was probably the leanest period in my career as we won absolutely nothing. Personally, though, it was highly satisfying. It was new, gave me an opportunity to learn how to handle young lads, particularly lads out on their own in the world for the first time. These weren't minors. I learned that a manager needed to be careful, cute. Exams, finances, relationships, wildness . . . had to chart a course through the lot. The experience would soon stand to me. Big time.

As Dublin and Meath were holding the nation spellbound, Mickey Ned and Kerry earned a reprieve in 1991 when they defeated Cork in the Munster semi-final. After taking the provincial title against Limerick, they fell to a two-goal burst from Peter Withnell in the All-Ireland semi-final. It was enough to keep the knives covered. Meanwhile, my minor football commitments had kept me content enough for the time being. However, I was beginning to lurch a little. Without any involvement with Kerry, I felt neither here nor there. I didn't apply myself properly to family life. Without football everything seemed out of sync. Sounds utterly selfish. I suppose it is. But I cannot deny my nature.

Despite my crabby attitude towards football at the time, life wasn't that bad. Business was good, our two young daughters were thriving, everyone was healthy . . . until tragedy struck.

On Sunday, 1 December 1991, Gaeltacht won the west Kerry championship when they defeated Annascaul. Historic victory but not one I remember fondly. Late that night Diarmuid Ó Súilleabháin's car spun off the road while travelling over the Clasach on his way home from my place. I was about to leave for Raidió na Gaeltachta early on Monday morning to do an interview when word came through. Diarmuid was dead. The most shocking moment of my life. Like most men, I can count your true friends on one hand. My tally was significantly reduced that winter's night. I told things to Diarmuidín that I wouldn't say to anyone else. He was extremely kind to me. I will never forget his belief or his support. This man opened my eyes to more things about myself than anyone had ever done. Huge loss. Immeasurable. At his funeral in Cúil Aodha I was asked to deliver one of the *Guí an Phobail.* For the first time in my life, my legs started to go from under me. Typical of the locality,

Diarmuidín's funeral was deeply passionate. Spiritual. Devastating. *"Seán Ó Duibhir an Ghleanna . . ."*

The outsider

I could feel myself drifting from the source. I was trying to keep the hand in but I needed more. In the summer of 1992 Kerry seemed, once again, to have kept the snipers at bay when they turned Cork over for the second year on the trot. That was, until the Munster final disaster. I was up north at the Ulster final the day Clare scored their historic victory over Mickey Ned's side. I couldn't believe it. I knew we were drifting, that the team was lacking. But I couldn't see that coming. There would be some serious fallout. The flak started to fly. I didn't have to snipe this time around, people were tripping over one another to have a go. Now, I'd take a step back. Get myself ready. Throw myself into the shake-up once more. After the battering the county board had taken, the executive decided that, rather than leave themselves open again, the clubs would elect the manager.

Now, I thought, I must be in with a chance. I had a share of managerial experience – three county titles and a stint with the students in Cork. Should be enough for a decent hearing, at least. The opposition was formidable but not unbeatable. I was still naive. The opposition: Séamus Mac Gearailt, my former clubmate from the Gaeltacht had a lot of experience with the successful county minor teams; Con Riordan from north Kerry, who'd also won a county championship; and Ogie Moran, eight All-Ireland medals, a degree in physical education but limited experience as a manager. Once again Bernie O'Callaghan was in my corner but I'd underestimated the support for Ogie. He was a popular figure and had a strong base. I put my case forward to the delegates. The night of the count, I was advised by a political friend to have someone present to tally my votes, to ensure I knew exactly where I stood regardless of the overall outcome. Afterwards I knew exactly. At

the bottom of the fucking pile. I came last. Ogie Moran
was the new Kerry boss. I was now the outsider.

There's merit in knowing your place. I couldn't walk
away, the demons were sitting stoutly on my shoulder. I
had to get back some time. No way I could forget the
whole idea, as much as those around me may have hoped
I would. Then I got a break. At a Gaeltacht match back
in the pitch at Gallarus one night, I met Séamus Mac
Gearailt who suggested that I put my name forward for
the job of managing the Kerry Under-21s. I thought about
it. "After so many kicks in the bollox there's no way one
more kick's going to make any difference," I said. Seán
Walsh challenged me for the job. I genuinely didn't think
I'd a hope, was sure another cartel would scupper my
chances. I was mistaken. Before Christmas in 1992, I was
elected Under-21 manager by a single vote.

As manager I was now permitted to choose my own
selectors. I set about the job, making sure all areas were
properly covered. Number one on the list was the late
Bernie O'Callaghan, my old selector, ally and friend. He
was also a great friend to Kerry football as he shared my
passion for the Green and Gold. Fierce Kerryman, great
football man. He would cover the north of the county.
The next man up was Séamus Mac Gearailt who'd
encouraged me to apply for the job. Mac Gearailt's
experience with the minor team would be a huge
advantage, he was also with Na Gael club in Tralee. I
was a bit lost in south Kerry so I contacted an old
political friend of mine, Paddy Gallagher. I told him I
was looking for a good southern representative. He
recommended Jack O'Connor, who'd achieved success
with the Kerry vocational schools. I'd played minors
with Jack's brother Paddy. Jack had returned from the
States and built a pub in Dromod; worked hard, a grafter.
I met him in Killorglin and he agreed to join the team.
The last selector, Johnny Culloty, would cover the east
Kerry beat for me. Johnny was an easy choice for me. I
always felt the better for an hour of his company. When I
submitted my selection to county chairman, Seán Kelly,
he was pleasantly surprised. Any talent that was out

there, these boys would get it in. He knew it.

We met early in the New Year of 1993. Johnny Culloty brought a list of the minors from the previous two or three years and we set about putting a panel together. Everything went well. In fact so well that we reached the All-Ireland final in our very first year and were unlucky to be beaten by Meath by a point. It augured well. Things weren't as good on the senior front for Ogie, though. Cork won back their Munster title, only to fall to Derry in the All-Ireland.

Before the National League final of that year, the *Irish Independent* asked me if I would be interested in a stint as a Gaelic football analyst with the newspaper. I thought about it a while and decided to give it a shot. Long term it would do no harm. A chance to keep an eye on the bigger picture. In fact, it worked out better than I'd hoped. I got to meet a lot of people around the country, kept the profile up, saw a lot of football. The experience would help my canvas next time around.

A pretty good year, all considered. Finished on a high too, as Máire gave birth to our son Pádraig, our third child, on 16 December. Pretty hectic Christmas.

The new year promised much but deceived us. Our Under-21 squad wasn't as tight as the year before, didn't have as much work done. We lost a few key men through injury, particularly Séamus Moynihan, which didn't help. Moynihan was as good as I'd seen. Didn't need any second opinion. Crashed out to Cork in the first round of the Munster Under-21 championship. Back to the newspaper for the rest of the summer. Wasn't a bad thing really. I got to tag most of the big teams of the day: Down, Dublin, Cork, Derry. Unfortunately Kerry didn't rank among them. Their shortcomings were becoming alarmingly obvious to me. The style was wrong. I yearned for a crack at the whip, to strip the side bare and start again. Get the basics right. The ambition was growing. So was the frustration. Sitting in the press box at one particularly poor Leinster championship clash on a wet day in Croker, I turned to my journalist colleague, gave him a little reminder on the shoulder before declaring, "If they'll only give me the fucking job, I promise you, as sure as I'm sitting here I'll bring the Sam back to Kerry." Wishful thinking, many thought, fuelled by a couple of brown pints in Mulligan's. I'd made my promise. It was recorded too.

We'd turned the corner in 1995. We'd a fierce panel, loads of talent . . . Ó Cinnéide, Ferriter, Hassett, Ó Sé. Great spirit too. Oh we'd every chance this year, I thought. We even beat the seniors in a challenge game. Great chance. Worked out well. We turned the tables on Cork and booked an All-Ireland semi-final date with Donegal. In the meantime, Kerry seniors had been beaten yet again by Cork in the Munster final. Unfortunately, Ogie Moran's spell in charge, for me, was marked by the ill-fated comeback of Bomber Liston – against my advice. Beaten for the third year in a row, the knives were now out for Ogie. Suddenly the spotlight turned to Páidí Ó Sé and his Under-21s. Everyone knew I wanted the job, now the Under-21 championship had become my test. Pass it and they'd consider my candidacy. Became a public spectacle. "He'll get the senior job if he leads the Under-21s home." We beat Donegal comfortably on a scorcher of a day in Tuam to book an All-Ireland place against a talented Mayo side. As it turned out my agony was prolonged. We drew with Mayo in the All-Ireland final in Tullamore. Blew it really, had plenty of opportunities to win the game. I didn't quibble. In the end, Mayo could have won the game. Had they done so . . . who knows? Journey's end? We got a second crack, in Thurles. This time we made no mistake. All-Ireland Under-21 champions 1995.

Next step? The journey would continue.

11
Walking The Line

Bíonn gach tosnú lag

THEY THOUGHT they had me figured out. I know it.
Plenty of people scattered throughout the county
squirmed at the thought of me walking the line with the
Kerry senior team. "That west Kerry lunatic!" Now, we
had won an Under-21 All-Ireland playing an exciting
brand of football. Traditions were adhered to while
modern trends were followed. This confused my
opponents. "It can't be Páidí, can it? He could never
produce a team like that?" Never being too far from the
edge it took that Under-21 success in 1995 to convince
the officials and the public. I was now the front runner
for the Kerry job. Had we lost the replay against Mayo . . .
well who knows?

Public opinion had swung behind me. Having helped
land three county championships, support from west
Kerry was never in doubt. The experience had to stand to
me some time. I mean, to manage a divisional side you
have to bring several clubs together, get them pulling in
the one direction. Now, however, the support from the
west was much more vocal. Working as an analyst with
the *Irish Independent* kept my profile constant as well as
keeping me abreast of developments in the game, players
and tactics. The national media now conceded I was the
man for the job. This, in turn, put more pressure on
people in Kerry to throw their weight behind me. Having

154

been burned twice I ensured that, this time round, I would play a politically correct game. I got a lot of sound advice at the time from TD Pat Rabbitte. His fierce passion for football gave him an interest in my candidature for the Kerry job. He preached caution. I listened.

After our Under-21 victory, myself and the selectors met for a meal in Tralee and decided we would apply *en bloc* to take over the senior outfit. I would go forward as trainer (manager in Kerry) and they would come in as my selectors. However, it wasn't that straightforward. Séamus Mac Gearailt had also applied for the senior job on the two previous occasions, just as I had myself. He now felt he was due a crack at the whip. The two of us met with the county chairman Seán Kelly who proposed that I go forward as trainer while Séamus be appointed coach. This package was then presented to the county board delegates for ratification. You know, I believe there was way too much made about this codology afterwards. As far as I was concerned, we were all in it together – myself, Jack, Bernie, Tom and my old clubmate Séamus. My job was to pick their brains and ensure that everything we did benefited Kerry football. Sometimes that took some picking, but it worked.

I don't think my appointment was ever really in doubt, certainly not with the chairman. I mean the county was desperate. We were facing a decade without an All-Ireland and we'd won one Munster title in that period. There was panic among football folk in the Kingdom. My much-publicised passion for the Green and Gold was now seen as vital if we were to rehabilitate the fortunes of the county. The pressure was also mounting on Seán Kelly. He'd have to deliver to survive. It would have to be Páidí. After Dublin's All-Ireland victory in 1995, I was appointed 'trainer' of the Kerry team. Séamus Mac Gearailt was named as 'coach' while selectors Bernie O'Callaghan and Jack O'Connor also came on board. Johnny Culloty declined to let his name go before the delegates and stepped down. He was replaced in time by Tom O'Connor from Kenmare. Our task now was to secure a place for Kerry back at football's top table.

My first outing as senior boss was against Kildare in a National League match in Tralee. We lost. Fortunately Dermot Earley was steering the ship at the time and it wasn't Dwyer who handed me my first defeat. In our next game we beat Brian Mullins' Derry up north. Took the initial heat off anyway. The league followed this pattern until immediately after Christmas when we got down to some serious training. I took charge of the sessions myself. Along the way I got as much advice from many different quarters to help me prepare the team. Limerick rugby, international athletics . . . anything to give us an edge. As the game was becoming physically more demanding, there was no doubt that international practices were becoming more relevant. A crowded midfield was increasingly resembling situations in rugby. How do rugby players move the ball out of such situations? Maybe a short back pass would actually move the ball more quickly into the forwards, as it would give the player behind time to direct a long kick into the corner. Worth looking at, I thought. Athletics? Well, how do you improve a fellow's pace? I mean, you can get them super-fit, get them to run all day, work the weights over the winter. Will they be faster? A lot of people gave their advice and help willingly, people like former Irish coach Mick Doyle, former international runners like Tom O'Riordan and Eamonn Coghlan. Great help. Encouragement.

We qualified for the knockout stages of the League, which suggested some progress, and, although we fell to Cork after extra time in Páirc Uí Chaoimh, I was reasonably happy.

We opened our Munster championship campaign against Tipp who gave us a torrid enough afternoon. After a sticky forty minutes, things eventually came right for us and we pulled away. The Tipp experience was a blessing really. No more than it had done twenty-one years previously, it helped our focus for the Munster final against Cork. Our preparation for that game went

well. I really hadn't thought of what lay beyond Cork,
everything was geared for that July date. It had to be.
Rehabilitation had to start with Cork. Unfortunately, in
1996, it ended there as well. There was a lot of pressure
going into the Munster final. My first big test. I had
applied the same principles to managing the senior team
as I had with West Kerry a decade previously: best
players in their best positions; constant honing and
practising of basic skills; conservative defenders; use of
two feet; pride in the jersey. Kept the 1970s and 1980s
out of it as much as I could. I got my first payback. We
edged past Cork in Páirc Uí Chaoimh by 0–14 to 0–11
thanks to Maurice Fitz and a couple of lucky breaks from
Clare ref Kevin Walsh. Great feeling. Really enjoyed it.
This was a very proud moment in my life. I would take a
Kerry team to Croke Park.

It's only a step from the sublime to the ridiculous

One Munster final does not a Kerry manager make,
however. What transpired over the next few weeks,
culminating with our disastrous All-Ireland semi-final
experience against Mayo, would teach me more about
management and preparation than any victory could
have done. I learned enough to do me a fucking lifetime.
When I think of it now it makes me shudder. Raw.
Unprofessional! Losing to Mayo in Croke Park changed
the way I approached the job completely. You see a
number of mistakes were made and I take full
responsibility for them. Full responsibility. I couldn't get
Cork out of my mind, my focus was way too narrow.
When we beat them I let rip. Celebrated with gusto.
Even worse, I celebrated with the players. We only had
three weeks to prepare and I didn't keep a tight rein on
discipline, especially my own discipline. Huge mistake. I
didn't keep a tight rein on the media. Huge mistake. We
billeted the team in the Burlington Hotel the night
before the Mayo game, which backfired completely. The
Burlo had become the prime location on the eve of big

games in Dublin. I was a regular there on such occasions, don't know how I didn't cop it. The place was black with Kerrymen, Mayomen, footballers . . . and our panel trying to relax before an All-Ireland semi-final. Huge mistake. Worst of all, we played Mayo in a challenge game early in the summer, I took little notice. Should have. Should have avoided a challenge with a team from the province due to meet the Munster champions in August. Big mistake. Never take your eye off the ball. Mayo manager John Maughan was that bit more experienced and had his homework done. I analysed nothing from that game, took no notice of their personnel. I paid the price, Mayo 2–13, Kerry 1–10.

Jeezuus. Never again. When the dust settled and I'd shouldered the first batch of criticism . . . "Oh, I told you so . . . weren't the team on the piss out west for a week after the Munster final?"

"Páidí, ah he can only bang tables, only preaches pride in the jersey, how could he prepare 'em right?"

I'd turn this around. Fuck it, would I turn this around. From now on it would be an iron fist. I thought of Dwyer and the advantage he had of being a non-drinker. How he could keep people guessing, keep 'em on their toes. I may be a bit of a rake, but from the winter of 1996 I vowed that there wouldn't be a more disciplined panel in the country. And I'd start with myself.

You know, everything fell into place after that. By keeping a handle on my own behaviour, I learned to keep a distance from the players while ensuring they were looked after in a thoroughly professional manner. That distance is vital. I actually got to know the lads better that way, as I was viewing them from a step back. I ensured the opposition in future would be scrutinised and analysed. To this end the selectors, Tom, Jack, Séamus and Bernie worked tirelessly. We also threw the spotlight on ourselves, dissected our own performances. I embraced all the modern approaches to the game – training techniques, dietary advice, video analysis, statistics – while always trying to simplify matters, cut out the bullshit that tended to accompany these new methods. All venues, both playing and accommodation, would be checked out. Our attention to detail would be absolute. Our liberal attitude to the media was tightened. Caution would apply to all dealings with the press. This instilled a great sense of discipline in the camp. From now on, any interviews would be conducted in a professional manner. If this pissed off the media, denied them their fodder, well so be it. If they think we're a boring shower of unconfident, reticent fuckers, well so be it. We'd do our fucking talking on the field from now on. End of story.

The differences between the top teams in Gaelic football was narrowing by the year. Any advantage which could be squeezed out of a situation needed to be grabbed. Equally we could provide the opposition with no edge, no ammunition. Discipline in all areas of our preparation would ensure this. I led by example. With a new focus, I drilled the team hard in the spring of 1997. I had a good feel for it, could condition players differently, took account of individual physical requirements. We reaped the rewards instantly. After squeezing through a tight National League clash with Cavan, we qualified for the knockout stages of the league. I think this was probably the turning point for the team. The damage I had inflicted in 1996 had been repaired.

My philosophy hadn't changed. I insisted on a high level of skill from *all* my footballers – backs and forwards. Kick with both feet, punch with both fists, good in the air, strike a ball cleanly, intelligently. With such a young squad the advantage of having Maurice Fitzgerald in our ranks could not be underestimated. His influence was extraordinary – strike of a ball; elegance of fielding; clinical distribution. We had huge potential. I knew it. Moynihan, Crowley, the Hassetts, Darragh Sé ... Now, I had to ensure that it was harnessed, realised. To this end, our new, regimental approach to preparation worked a treat. But we never stopped practising our skills. Johnny Crowley, now one of the most lethal forwards in the game, constantly practised catching the ball over his head. Saw it as a weakness early in his career. Never stopped working on it.

We took the closing stages of the league by storm. Down and Laois both fell to us in Croker. We travelled to Páirc Uí Chaoimh and defeated Cork in the final on their home turf. Secured our first national title. Great boost, especially for the younger players on the panel. Kept one up on Cork as well. But the most significant aspect of our National League success over Cork was that we were back training two days later. New regime.

All the while I was getting to know the players, communicating much better with them, listening to their needs, deflecting pressures. Anything I could do behind the scenes to make their lives easier, I did. Opened up the channels with their families too, especially their mothers.

After the league success, we plotted our approach to the championship. Collectively, we were very committed. Serious. I left them in no doubt just how serious. "Lads, I want this team to be training in the dark by the end of the summer. When I was younger I was told that there were two marks a Kerryman puts in his diary, Munster final day and All-Ireland final day. That's what we're faced with in this county. That's the measure. Let's stay tuned in. Don't drop the guard."

Once again we began our campaign in 1997 with a right tough joust with Tipp. We only really carried our legs out with a late burst. No harm though. I was a lot more clued in, got great capital out of our difficulties with Tipp. A week later, I travelled to Cusack Park in Ennis and saw a well-drilled Clare side, managed by John O'Keeffe at the time, shock Cork with a late Martin Daly goal. Couldn't believe my eyes. Mick Curley reffed the game, played a heap of added time. So I had to change tack. In truth it was a lot easier. Having witnessed Clare's dramatic victory, we were well guarded against any complacency. Our preparation for the Munster final was meticulous. We had an easy, comfortable morning in Limerick, a light stretch and warm-up at the back of our hotel. Everything going smoothly. Until someone complained of an upset stomach, then another . . . and another. Fuck it. Food poisoning. Fortunately, we pulled through but it was another sobering experience. After all our preparation, discipline, fine-tuning . . . that it could be jeopardised so easily.

Fifty years later

The same day we retained our Munster title at the Gaelic Grounds, Cavan defeated Derry in Clones. There was great excitement about this novel semi-final pairing, falling, as it did, exactly fifty years after Kerry and Cavan played the All-Ireland final in the Polo Grounds in New York. Personally I steered clear of the hype surrounding the game. I had more pressing matters. After the Munster final, defender Stephen Stack, one of the veteran players on the panel, arrived back to my house in Ventry to say he was packing it in. He hadn't been handed a starting role for some time and hadn't been one of the players asked to warm up on Munster final day. Decided he'd had enough. Wished Kerry luck. I counselled against it. "Don't do it, you never know what'll happen, Stephen," I warned, "it's only July now, toughen it out for another four or five weeks. See what happens. You might get in yet. You just might get in, you never know in this game. Don't be up in the Hogan Stand in September cursing yourself for opting out." Stephen missed a night's training but after a couple of days mulling over it, arrived at the next session. He started to improve immediately, was mentioned in dispatches by Bernie O'Callaghan. Just as well. The week of the Cavan game we lost both our corner-backs – our captain Mike Hassett through injury and Killian Burns with a wasp sting. Three weeks after his aborted retirement, Stephen Stack was named in the starting line-up for the All-Ireland semi-final. Played well.

Our preparation for the Cavan game was solid. To a man we were clued in. We had the advantage of having played a couple of games at headquarters earlier in the season. We studied them closely. Decided that the game would be won off the ball, by tackling, harrying, giving nothing away cheaply. This applied particularly to our half-forward line of Denis Dwyer, Liam Hassett and Pa Laide. And, you know, it's a great crux for the modern manager. Getting your half-forwards to work tirelessly off the ball while not neglecting their primary duty of taking or making a score. They must be very athletic, very fit, but they must also be highly skilled. Hard line to get right, ask any manager. Fortunately, we had the right personnel.

In light of our experiences in the Burlo in 1996, and after discussions with John Glynn, MD of the Doyle Hotel group at the time and a good friend, we decided to switch to the Tara Towers Hotel in Booterstown on Dublin's south-side. It was an ideal choice. Quiet, out of the way, beside Blackrock College, the beach and still only fifteen minutes from Croker with a garda escort. Ideal.

Maurice again did the business for us against Cavan. Made a huge impact when he moved out around the middle in the second half. His fitness levels were excellent that season, having played through most of the league campaign. They had put it up to us before the break, put our other deputy at corner-back, Seán Burke, under fierce pressure. However, another big difference between our situation at half-time and the same situation a year previously is that we didn't panic. I didn't panic. Denis Dwyer was concussed, we had an ambulance pulling up to the dressing room door, we'd just conceded a goal. But there was no panic. We stuck to our plan. Remained focused. We would work even harder when we didn't have the ball. Maurice stemmed the flow. Moved out around the middle and the '40'. His delivery for Michael Frank Russell's goal will live long in the memory, as it was one of the most perfectly flighted balls I think I've ever seen kicked. Myself and the selectors were conscious of not pressurising Mike Frank too early in his career. His huge potential was obvious. We gambled. And won. Kerry were back in an All-Ireland final for the first time in eleven years. Now our new discipline would kick in, big time. We shot straight back to Kerry. We were back together the following night for a team meeting. Trained on Tuesday.

The atmosphere in the camp was excellent in advance of the final. Everything was tight. A couple of good challenge games got the players going. The selectors never stopped working, brought fire to our meetings, particularly Bernie O'Callaghan who was of the old school, always had his arguments well worked out in advance. He'd fight his corner too, always, I might add, with a view to putting the best fifteen on the field. I was conscious that I wanted no player put out by the suffocating attention of the media, so we arranged a press morning on the Saturday, a week before the game.

From our point of view, the press morning was a great success. It was criticised in certain quarters, but I asked players to make themselves available, be sensible. The older members could mosey around, give the younger boys a dig-out. The media presence doesn't consist of seven or eight scribes anymore. Everyone wants a piece of the action. There could be a hundred people swarming around looking for a quotation, all conscious that pages and pages needed to be filled for a week, that slots on radio stations needed to be padded out. I agree that some formal control needs to be placed on media/player contacts. A few years ago it was open season. I changed that. I will not allow, or certainly won't encourage, a player to do anything that might blur his focus in advance of a game. The stakes are higher now than ever before. I didn't raise them, the media did. Back in 1996, I never refused an interview. I wasn't going to revisit that disaster zone.

We decided to make a full weekend of it at the Gleneagle Hotel. I've changed my mind about the value of weekends away together since, probably too tiring for a player. Anyway we felt we needed them at the time. Bonding a young squad tightly is important. Served us well in 1997. We trained on the Friday night, met the journalists on Saturday morning, watched videos in the afternoon then went back to Fitzgerald Stadium for a full-scale trial game. No one held back. High intensity. Stephen Stack ended up with a half-a-dozen stitches over his eye after colliding with Rory O'Rahilly. After the game, we returned to the hotel where we met up with our sponsors, Kerry Group, got kitted out with our clothes for All-Ireland weekend. It brought back memories for me, got very excited. Kind of childish, I suppose. I always felt very professional as a young fellow when we got our suits for All-Ireland day. Got the same feeling that evening in the Gleneagle. We were then informed that we would be flying home after the final. That news lifted everyone. Magic. I could see them, smiling, giggling about taking Sam down by plane. Then, they went to bed.

With the informal, light-hearted stuff out of the way and the players in the sack, it was time to get down to business. Myself and the management team finished the night with our final selection meeting. It was time to pick the starting fifteen for the All-Ireland final.

I'd love to divulge in detail what was thrashed out at these meetings but it would be a betrayal of confidentiality. Sparks flew. I can assure you. Our captain Mike Hassett had recovered from injury but had lost his place. He had been commuting from his new job in Wicklow for training sessions. Massive commitment. It was the hardest thing I've ever had to do, inform Mike that he wouldn't be starting. The chances of captaining a team in an All-Ireland final is something that rarely presents itself to a footballer. When, in Mike's case, you have it snatched from your grasp . . . cruel. But football's a harsh master. He'd lost form, we had to act. Mike's talent was never in doubt. He's one of the best I've ever trained. Has the lot. Can kick well with both feet, good hands, good tackler. The fucking stark reality of being a manager is that none of that matters if you think something isn't right. If you don't act, you're betraying yourself. I've been accused at times of lacking courage as a manager. I won't breach the confidentiality of any selection meeting just to prove a point. We made our decisions. Stephen Stack was in, Killian Burns was in the other corner and Billy O'Shea was included up front.

With the difficult task dealt with, we had an easy final run-in. Our physical preparation was practically perfect. Best I'd ever been involved with. We wound down during the week, talked about the task ahead. Since taking charge of the Kerry team, I've always tried to avoid reference to my own playing days. Never wanted to piss players off with tales of success from the past. Yet, every so often, I need to share some of the nuggets I picked up along the way. One area I referred to was winning a game. Sounds ridiculously obvious. But it eludes a lot of great players and teams. I admitted that the game was now faster, that players were fitter, more dedicated, more professional. However, if a team was found wanting, it was quite often because they didn't have the knack of winning a game, didn't know how to do it. I suppose it is avoiding panic when things turn against you, surviving the spell when your opponents are on top, to keep doing the simple things well, don't be throwing caution to the wind. Take Spillane. How often – when things looked bleak for Kerry, when we'd conceded a succession of scores without reply – would he pop up and squeeze an angled shot over the bar? Sometimes, it was only a catch or a good clearance. Point was, it was a signal to the rest of the players. Calm down, win the game.

Another area I referred back to was the old mind game; visualising difficult situations for yourself. It worked really well for me so I was prepared to try it out with the lads, especially coming up to an All-Ireland final. "Go for a walk," I told 'em, "and imagine yourself in Croke Park. Think of a hard situation. Say, you're a wing-back. Your man makes a burst to the far side of the field into space. The ball is kicked into that space. Your man is running on to it. Lads, you're fucked if you have to react to that situation coldly. If you've thought about it you just might catch him, cut out the threat early. Edge. Give yourself an edge."

24 September 1997 – a promise kept

We travelled by train to Dublin. Everything nice and
easy. Our hotel proved the perfect location once again.
Quiet, not too many supporters around. Easy meal, walk
down by the beach. We could even sit in the foyer, read,
chat. Easy. We had a team meeting late on Saturday
night. Afterwards, I lay on the bed for a few hours.
Couldn't sleep, couldn't stop thinking about the game.
Fuck it, I was confident but I couldn't stop thinking . . .
about Maughan, thinking about his speech in our
dressing room in 1996. Struck a few delicate chords.
Mentioned 1992, mentioned Clare . . . seemed to hint he
had something over Kerry. Couldn't get it out of my
mind. I'd save it for my last spiel. Before they hit the
turf.

Just as with Dwyer, I had a *piseoga* about mass on the
Sunday morning. Nothing special. Go to the local
church. Nothing special. No balls and jerseys. No! Quiet
prayer for those that wanted it.

I've always gone with my instinct. I can feel it. I felt
we would win as our bus sped towards Croker. Felt it.
We were so tuned in. So right, physically, mentally.
Maurice was buzzing. Of course a game can turn in the
most peculiar way. The final was barely a few minutes
old when Mayo drastically changed their starting line-up
following a hamstring injury to Dermot Flanagan. Then
Billy Shea broke his leg. *Maurice*. Bizarre sequence of
events. Then there was Maurice. And Maurice again. He
was absolutely magnificent. This was his stage. It had
been a long time coming. Magnificent. Now, he had a
solid platform. Solid. Breen, Flaherty, Hassett, Darragh,
Moynihan, Stack, Dwyer . . . solid. We had our anxious
moments in the second half after conceding a penalty.
They came at us. That's when our preparation came into
its own. No panic. Then there was Maurice. Wonderful
moments. Kerry 0–13, Mayo 1–7. Wonderful occasion.

I savoured it. Didn't break out immediately. Held
back. Sat at the banquet with Máire and the kids in
Jury's Hotel, with the players, friends calling in.

Especially nice to see those who believed, those who kept faith. Many had doubted. Many still did, buying into fact that my public role with the team was still somewhat blurred. Fuck them. I'd proved to myself that if I kept my guard up and trusted my instincts I could chart a course for a team to reach the ultimate prize. Proud night. Personal.

After hitting the sack that night, I lay staring at the ceiling, utterly content but restless. It was about 3 am. I couldn't stop thinking about Dwyer. "He's over now in the Burlington, I wonder if there's any chance he'd still be awake . . ." Up I hop. Tog out again in the post-match blazer, hop in a hack and over to the Burlo. Unfortunately the Mayo camp are stationed there. Get a fair bollocking from a couple of well-cut supporters. Understandable really. "What are ye doin' here, Ó Sé, trying to rub salt into the fucking wounds? We're depressed enough without having to see you." Unfortunate. Didn't mean that at all, just wanted to see Dwyer. Needless to say it led to accusations of stirring it. Receptionist contacts Micko and I shoot up to his room. We adjourn downstairs to a corner of the empty restaurant. I swap pints for pots of tea. Spent the next two hours 'til dawn talking about the match; football; Kerry; All-Irelands. Deep down . . . I felt Dwyer knew I was the man to turn Kerry around. "Discipline, P Sé," he said. "If you're tuned in . . . always go with your gut feeling, trust your instinct. Don't mind what any of 'em are saying. Go for it." I didn't lick it off the road. As enjoyable a couple of hours as I've ever spent in my life.

Better than being a player? No. Next best thing.

1997. All-Ireland champions. League champions. "Ah, 'twasn't Páidí that won it for 'em. Couldn't have been. How could he be the brains behind the operation? Only for Maurice . . ."

Still learning.

12
Evolution

Seachain na húdaráis gan eolas

WHY DIDN'T I just go playing golf? Why bother inhabiting the edge with all these fuckers sneering at me? Well, because it's the only place to be. Golf? Far more complicated. You know I tried it. All the lads were talking about the 'small ball', how it filled in after they finished playing football. So out to the local course with me, to Ceann Sibéal with the stunning backdrop of the Three Sisters. Found out I was actually a *ciotóg*. Now, the only other *ciotóg* who was a member, as far as I could work out, was the late Paddy Bán Brosnan. So Paddy introduced me to the game, gave me a few tips, reckoned it was handier for a *ciotóg* to show another *ciotóg*. For some reason, well probably for several, I could make no fist of it at all. Bán couldn't figure this out. Lost cause, he thought. Then, about six months later Christy O'Connor Junior was back in the pub at Ard an Bhóthair; invited me out to Ceann Sibéal for a round that evening. We played nine holes and afterwards, Christy adjourned to Paddy Bán's in Dingle for a pint. So, he was chatting to Bán, telling him he'd been back west playing golf with a friend of his.

"Would it have been the fella behind in Ventry you were out with?" Bán enquired.

"God, you know it was Paddy," replied Christy. "And, you know, he wouldn't be bad at the golf if he'd only keep his head down," he explained.

Bán continued, "Christy, I gave him a remedy for that problem ages ago, trouble is, he didn't listen to me."

"What was that, Paddy?" asked Christy.

"I told him his head should be tied on to his balls!" Golf!

You have to keep evolving. The game has gone so technical now, you can't afford to stand still. Curtains if you do. After 1997 this became increasingly obvious. All the top teams were striving for the edge. Everything was scrutinised. Everything. If a team was working a ball one way, then the other would match it, outdo it, do it faster. Faster. The pace of the game has changed even since 1997. As champions I could demand little more, at least not in the short term. One of the reasons many of the top sides – sides with loads of talent, courage, organisation – fail to retain the Sam Maguire is that they lose this vital edge. When I studied a video in 1997, I would pick out the man who missed a ball, missed a tackle, misdirected a kick, hit a chance wide. Three years later I would source the original pass, trace the difficulty back, query why another option wasn't chosen, why the ball wasn't worked a different way. It's like fucking snooker . . . you have to think five or six shots ahead. Crazy. Of course if you ignore the basics for one second, you're goosed. No point in ripping a sequence of moves apart if all you discover at the end is a fella who can't catch the ball over his head, who can't kick with his weak leg, can't direct a 30-yard pass, can't direct a 30-yard shot over the bar. No point.

Shortly after our All-Ireland victory over Mayo we shot out to New York for a week to play Cavan in a National League game, a commemoration of the 1947 clash in the Polo Grounds. Several plane-loads of Kerrymen made the journey. Some craic. Didn't hold back. Got the blessing of John B Keane in Listowel on our way to Shannon. There were many hilarious moments during an epic week, none better than mine and Pat Bán Brosnan's escape from the Bronx. Having steered a dodgy late-night taxi in the wrong direction, we hopped out at the first sign of civilisation. Wrong move.

There was Páidí Sé, in a suit and tie, Pat Bán, son of Kerry legend Paddy Bán and a former county minor, sporting a badge – PAT BÁN BROSNAN, KERRY – standing on a Bronx sidewalk in the middle of a couple of hundred gangster rappers! Jeezuus Chruysht! Not that it bothered either of us. If I'd carried my legs past Hickey & Co. in the 1970s, I could out of this, I thought. Pat Bán agreed. "Jeezuus, P Ó. I go fishing for a living. Far more dangerous than the streets of the Bronx. They'll have to shoot me." I wonder what the locals made of the pair of us, walking in the middle of the road, trying to flag down a stray taxi. Eventually, a police car appeared. On seeing us, they slowed down, lowered the window, looked at us quarely. "We're a bit losht, officer," I ventured. "You certainly are, sir," the bemused cop replied. Went down well when we eventually got back to Rosie O'Grady's.

Maurice gave another exhibition to take the first brace of league points out in the States, kicked a point from the corner flag, unreal. We won our next outing after arriving back too. However, the wheels came off then. Nothing I could do. I had to take the foot off the pedal, had to cut the lads some slack. The preparation is so intense. Our league form plummeted. So much so that we actually ended up being relegated to Division 2 for the first time in our history.

There were other problems. In the space of a few months I lost my entire management team. Firstly tragedy struck on our arrival home from the States when Tom O'Connor's wife died suddenly. Then Séamus Mac Gearailt and Jack O'Connor both resigned citing personal reasons. My main ally, Bernie O'Callaghan, was the only one remaining. I invited Frank O'Leary from south Kerry, and Seán Counihan from east Kerry to come on board. No sooner had we got together than another tragedy struck immediately after Christmas when Bernie O'Callaghan suffered a stroke. Bernie had always batted on my account. More importantly, he was a friend. Despite several fallouts – over players, approaches, techniques – we always made up. He understood. His health deteriorated after that and he died a week before the Munster final. Terrible tragedy. Huge blow to Kerry football as well.

Around this time, word was out that I was a most difficult individual to get on with, that I dictated at all selection meetings, that I always wanted my own way. Sure, there was some truth in it. But wasn't I the fucking manager? Of course I delegated, listened, threw things around, took the stick. But the buck has to stop with someone? As far as I was concerned, I was leading from the front. The 1995–1997 selection team was diligent, hard-working. Most of us had been together from the outset with the Under-21s. As I learned, they learned with me. We travelled together. When I changed tack after 1996, they responded. It was a good team. No doubts. But I regret, big time, that I allowed the definition of my position to be blurred from the outset. Should have toughened that night in Larkin's restaurant in Tralee back in October 1995. Would have saved a lot of hassle. We never broke ranks, the selectors. So I had to grin and bear the public speculation as to my exact role.

When a manager has a 'bad' reputation for being . . . well, a manager, you know something's not right. I must admit, though, the county board officers never lost faith. As the team's performances deteriorated and Division 2 stared us in the face, the board stuck with me. In hindsight I can understand why. As far as I'm concerned, the 1997 All-Ireland success had more to do with Páidí Ó Sé than 2000. I've never put as much work into anything in my life. The Kerry executive understood this.

New county chairman Seán Walsh stood in for Bernie O'Callaghan as we tackled the championship in 1998. We had drifted badly over the winter but things started to turn as the evenings lengthened. Understandably, we were a little behind the rest but our panel was still a match for any. As the players' fitness levels rose, so did their spirits. Unfortunately we had to plan our campaign without the two Hassett brothers. Both withdrew from the panel when Mike was denied a medal in the wake of his demotion for the 1997 final. It was a huge blow, on two fronts. I reiterate that, after Moynihan, Mike was

the best I ever trained under age. Liam had matured
nicely on the '40' and his ability to forage and distribute
was lost to us that summer. Big time. Still, we had to
persevere. If someone needed to be dropped, I wouldn't
shirk responsibility. I'd have to live with the
consequences. We defeated Cork for the second time in
three years in the Munster semi-final in Killarney. A real
cliffhanger. Everything seemed to be falling into place
again. Had three points to spare on them, 1–14 to 1–11,
after great displays by Liam Flaherty, Johnny Crowley,
Mike Frank and Darragh. Beat Tipp to take our third
Munster title on the trot. Maybe now, I thought, I can
buck this trend of champions being unable to retain their
title. And with a whole new team of selectors as well.
Having overcome quite a bit of adversity to secure a date
in Croke Park in August, who stood in our way but
Dwyer. Fucking Dwyer. Why did I deserve this? Kildare
shocked Meath in the Leinster final. Dwyer had a crack
at the big time with his rehabilitated Lilywhites.
Jeezuus.

The haunting of Páidí Ó Sé

You know, I maintain that, had anyone else been
managing that Kildare team in 1998, we'd have beaten
them by seven or eight points. The longer I was in the
job, the better I felt I was becoming. More confident. But
if anything was going to put me in the jigs it was the
sight of Dwyer on the line. I couldn't believe this was
unfolding. No point denying it. Dwyer looms large in my
life. He's been a constant for nearly thirty years. Less
than twelve months earlier I'd shared a couple of my
happiest hours with him when he told me how well I'd
done, leading Kerry back to glory. Told me to trust my
instincts. Now he stood in my way. I would have to try
every trick in the book to stop this man. Turn the tables
on him. Step back into the past, see what I could find. I
knew Dwyer well, really well. Knew if he pissed
crooked. But I feared him. When it came to match day,

high on my priority was securing the dugout closest to the Canal End for the Kerry team. Why? *Piseoga*. I knew Dwyer wanted it. Even if his team was dispatched to the Hill Sixteen end of Croker for the pre-match warm up he'd insist on the Canal End. He achieved far too much success at that end for him to overlook it. I moved in advance with a phone call. Then, on the day, I had ear-marked a few officials to start dumping our gear into the dugout over an hour before the game. There was a bemused look on the crew already planted there for the curtain-raiser.

Still, one-upmanship wasn't enough. Kildare played a high-intensity, short-passing game. Very high fitness levels and mobility compensated for whatever shortcomings they had. To counter them we needed our half-forwards working harder than ever, cutting off their moves at source. I perhaps underestimated this need. Always conscious of not detracting a half-forward from his primary duty, I didn't pay enough heed to matching Kildare's constant movement. In trying to avoid being too negative, I conceded ground. You see last year's plan is this year's video. What we'd done to overcome Cavan and Mayo was now old school, especially to Dwyer. Preparation . . . no matter what stroke of genius you think you can apply in the heat of battle there's no substitute for it. Our forwards didn't squeeze Kildare tightly enough. To this end, Liam Hassett's loss proved costly.

Fucking dreadful start. Dreadful. We could have killed that game in the first quarter, missed several good scoring chances, a couple of gaping goals in particular. I had Darragh Sé primed for Niall Buckley who ended up not playing. They moved Dermot Earley to the middle, which upset us. Shouldn't have but did. Maurice was still our prime mover. Having scuffed a few early frees, Tipp-convert Brian Lacey suffocated Maurice for the remainder. Whether we were over-reliant on Fitzy at the time is a moot point. Had we taken the early chances it would have become irrelevant. We also had a goal disallowed in somewhat dubious circumstances by

referee Mick Curley. As the game got tighter, I struggled
on the line. Hesitant, with switches, with changes.
Dwyer had me.

My heart sunk with the final whistle. I'm not a bad
loser but the circumstances of this defeat . . . knew what
lay ahead. Anyway, I toughened, shot into the Kildare
dressing room after the game. Wasn't that bad an
experience actually. I knew Dwyer wanted to beat Kerry,
big time. Sure, he was dishing out loads of "Oh, I'm sorry
that it had to be Kerry" afterwards. Truth is, Dwyer
didn't give a fiddler's fuck that it was Kerry. This was
one of the best days in his life. Make no mistake about
that. I know Dwyer, he was only too happy that it was
Kerry. Still, I had to take it on the chin, so in I marched.
Dwyer called the jubilant throng to attention. "Lads,
everything I know about football," I said, "I learnt it
from this man here, Mick Dwyer. And lads, I was a good
pupil. But when I retired from the game I thought, 'that's
the end of Mick O'Dwyer now.' Little did I think that
ten years down the road that he'd come back to fucking
haunt me." They got a good kickout of that.

This was hard. You can ignore critics, knockers,
begrudgers and gobshites, but when your old master
teaches you a lesson, you can't hide. Dwyer trumped me.
They squeezed a victory out of us. You know what was
worse? There was an element of support in south Kerry
for Dwyer and his son Karl since their move to Kildare.
Understandable. Karl had prospered, despite being
overlooked in his native county. He'd overcome
adversity and pressure, proved a lot of people wrong. I
admire Karl for that. What I couldn't understand was
how these elements in south Kerry supported Kildare
against Kerry despite the fact that Maurice Fitzgerald,
from Caherciveen and Denis Dwyer, from Waterville,
lined out with the Kingdom. This bothered me.

I had to face some flak in the wake of the Kildare
defeat. Said I was bad on the line. However, when the
dust settled the fact was we'd lost a tight game by a point
having played badly. Had we converted a fraction of our
chances early in the game, I'd have been a hero. I know

that only too well. As Babs Keating once told me, "The difference between a pat on the back and a kick up the arse is very, very small."

Approaching the Galway–Kildare final, my gut feeling was that Galway would win. Unlike Dwyer, I reserved my counsel. I didn't give my opinion to anyone until a couple of minutes before the ball was thrown in when I predicted a Galway victory on Raidió na Gaeltachta to Seán Bán Breathnach who had me in as an analyst. This is where I differ from Micko. If the roles were reversed Dwyer would turn up the pressure on me by predicting a comfortable Kerry victory! Deep down, Dwyer is very conscious of his record with Kerry. Doesn't want the gap to close too much. I know that and all those close to him know it.

Poor Dwyer though. After all the shennanigans surrounding the dugouts for the semi-final, he decided to stay with the Hill Sixteen end for the All-Ireland final after the success it had brought him against Kerry. Backfired. He still hasn't won an All-Ireland from the Hill dugout. *Piseoga!*

On my way home from that final, I was about to step on the Tralee train in Heuston when I chanced upon a gang of about six forlorn Kerrymen sporting the Kildare colours on the platform. "You're laughing this evening," one of them said to me in passing. "Things worked out well for you." Penny didn't drop for a while. Later, as we passed through Portlaoise I met one of the six. Tackled him. "What did you mean by your comments?" I asked.

"Obviously you were delighted to see Kildare beaten," he said.

I was furious. "It shows you how much you know about football," I replied, "how much you know about Páidí Sé. Fuck all. Because if you think that I was up for Galway, that I was delighted to see the man who was partly responsible for putting eight All-Ireland medals in my arse pocket beaten . . . go and take a fucking jump on the tracks because you're out of order." Some of these guys will always be in the winners' enclosure.

Wasn't a great deal to look forward to that winter.

Division 2 football. Antrim, London, Limerick, Kilkenny. Jeezuus, when I think of it, we played Kilkenny in a competitive fixture in Ballyraggert. Wouldn't be the greatest environment for preparing for the road ahead. We actually lost our first Division 2 game of the season away to Roscommon just to add to the whining chorus. We won the next seven on the trot to ensure an end to our spell in the basement. Actually qualified for the quarter-finals before bowing out to Meath in a lively fixture in Limerick. Once again, Meath. Early yardstick.

In the wake of our setbacks in 1998, I invited John O'Keeffe into our backroom team to coach and supervise the winter training. He wasn't, at this stage, one of the appointed selectors but I felt that he had a huge amount to offer Kerry football. He'd finished his stint with the Banner so I moved to get him involved. Johnno's a super character. Full-back of his generation, he brought great experience and a vast knowledge about modern training methods. Unwittingly, Johnno's arrival may have put a bit of strain on the selectors *in situ*, after all I had shunted him in, he hadn't been elected. I regret that I may have caused some friction, but I certainly make no apologies for reintroducing this man to Kerry football. We're very different in character and temperament but Johnno's as good as I've ever worked with.

Time out

What he couldn't bring – perhaps none of us could – to the championship of 1999 was hunger. Plain and simple. Raw hunger, passion. We were going for our fourth Munster title on the trot. Didn't want it enough. Cork had done their homework, identified our strengths and weaknesses. You have to keep evolving, changing tack, looking for different players to raise the tempo, catch the opposition off guard, produce something they've never seen before. And it's not always glamorous stuff.

Sometimes you're looking for one of your so-called ordinary players to do something unexpected. It might only be cutting across his own square and catching a ball cleanly over his head. This is where you cut an edge.

After a lame National League campaign we hadn't sharpened enough. I could feel it. But it was very difficult to halt the slide. After squeezing past Tipp in May, we then gave a weakened Clare side an awful reddening, beat them by fourteen points in the semi-final. That didn't help. We were overwhelming favourites to retain our Munster crown. On a soaking July day in Páirc Uí Chaoimh, we surrendered it to Cork after a fair bit of scelping. You know, the morning of that game, down at the Blarney Park, my gut told me we weren't right. Hunch. "This ain't going to go right for me," I thought. Little things. We'd prepared as well as we could, the selectors had done their stuff, but, with home advantage, the hungrier team won. Cork were league champions, had achieved high fitness levels, very motivated. Sometimes there's nothing you can do. Aodhán Mac Gearailt scored two fine goals in the first half, but we flattered ourselves at the break. I got a fierce hammering for taking him off in the second half. Trusted my instincts. Have to. Switched things around. Didn't work. We conceded two soft goals after the break, Maurice had an off-day from placed kicks, physically we were second best. We were, consistently, badly positioned to win breaking ball, to win the knock downs. That's hunger, focus. Weren't tuned in, went nearly a half-an-hour without scoring. No shortage of scelping. Beaten 2–10 to 2–4.

Shortly after our Munster final defeat, we suffered another major blow. Maurice broke a bone in his ankle playing for South Kerry in a county championship game against the Gaeltacht. It was a big setback for him personally and the county's morale collectively. Yet, he was determined that he wouldn't close the chapter on football, not after losing to Cork. Mentally, there are few footballers as strong as Maurice Fitz. He applied himself diligently to his recovery. However, the injury would have serious ramifications for myself and Maurice down the line. It set in place a train of events that would test me as a manager.

In the meantime, I had to contend with the fallout after the summer of 1999. The gloss of our All-Ireland success had flaked away by this stage and questions were being asked at home. Very difficult to turn to your critics and say "by the law of averages we were going to lose that game against Cork". Ya, that'd go down well all right. I certainly didn't lose faith. We needed a rest, players and management. Knew it. Whet our appetites for the long road. More importantly I, once again, got great support from the county executive. That support made life a lot easier, took the pressure off.

There was a change of personnel on the line that winter. The delegates were anxious to ratify John O'Keeffe's role with the management team. I had brought him on board as a technical advisor in 1999 but the attitude of the delegates was: "If Páidí Sé thinks so much of John O'Keeffe and we are reappointing Páidí, then why not throw O'Keeffe in as part of the package, as coach, in charge of physical fitness?" This, in turn, had a knock-on effect as one of the selectors, Paul Lucy, was from the same club as Johnno, Austin Stacks in Tralee. It was felt that it would be wrong to have two men from the same club on the management team. This was unfortunate for Paul who hailed from a great dynasty of footballers, many of whom, like Vincent and Jimmy Lucy, were tragically plucked away from life in their prime. Anyway, I didn't get involved. Appointing the selectors wasn't my responsibility anymore. That was the job of the county board delegates. Frank O'Leary opted out of another stint while Seán Counihan and Eamon Walsh put their names forward again. However, there was some stiff competition. Jack O'Connor, who resigned after 1997, threw his name back into the hat. Jack, a faithful, hard-working selector in the past had spent a few years with the Under-21s. I sensed that Jack was being kept in reserve, in case I lost the plot completely with the senior team. Kept tabs on me. Now, with my future secure, he wanted a piece of the action again. Won his place. Welcome addition. Another candidate was Eddie 'Tattler' O'Sullivan from the Dr Crokes club in Killarney. Eddie had been involved with Kerry on a couple of occasions, with Dwyer and Mickey Ned. Eamon Walsh was returned and the Tattler defeated Seán Counihan for the final slot. So the new team consisted of myself, Johnno, Eamon Walsh, Jack O'Connor and Eddie O'Sullivan. Allied to this team was the strong support of county chairman Seán Walsh and secretary Tony O'Keefe.

Sadly in the wake of his defeat, Seán Counihan broke ranks and had a go at me publicly, said I refused to act on suggestions from the selection team during the Kildare defeat and the 1999 Munster final setback. The management team had got a lot of stick after both of those defeats. Took it collectively. However, Seán felt compelled to separate himself, give his side of the story, extricate himself from the criticism. Personally, this was disappointing. I've no problem taking the blame when things go wrong but I steadfastly refuse to get drawn on the matter. I just wonder did Seán think I had coaxed Tattler to put his name forward? I hadn't. I mean if I was so keen on Eddie, I'd have appointed him myself a couple of years previously. Still, I don't think a manager or a selector should break ranks. It's like cabinet confidentiality – vital for the success of any government. Same with a management team. Tight. Don't break the code. In Kerry we don't do that. I thought it was an error of judgement on Seán's part. I don't harbour any resentment about the incident, mind you, I still meet Seán socially. Very nice guy. Don't harbour anything. That's Seán's business.

The new blood added impetus. No doubt. Shook things up. I was delighted to have Johnno on board. His calibre gave our management a very polished, professional edge. Training would be unrivalled. I faced the new millennium with great hope. I knew it wouldn't be difficult to add the edge this time around. The hunger would return. Players needed a break, from the drill, from each other. Now we were fresh. Our opening National League game at the end of October was against Cork, still smarting after their All-Ireland defeat by Meath. After the final, I had upped the ante a little bit, criticising a lot of the Cork forwards. Knew this would add a bit of spice to the league game. We hammered them 0–19 to 0–7. Oh, we were back in business all right. It may have been early days, but the gut feeling was already good. One more time, as belief in my tenure was beginning to wane, I would prove 'em wrong again. One more time.

13
Yours Is Success

Éist le fuaim na habhann is gheobhair breac

POLITICIANS? NEVER hid my fondness for politicians. We've always been a Fianna Fáil house but my interest stretches across party boundaries. At fourteen I was out canvassing with Timothy Chub O'Connor in Dingle. Elections held me spellbound. Getting to know Charlie Haughey at such a young age opened a window for me, a window revealing a fascinating world of power, counts, canvasses; a world lived out on the edge, sharp-witted, ruthless. Watching them operate, charm, move . . . always working, always connecting, feeding off people, gathering information. Taoisigh . . . I've known several. Charlie, Albert, Bertie. Different characters but all equally intriguing in their own right. Charlie the intelligent, Albert the selector, Bertie the streetwise. The feel they have for people, feel for situations. Fascinating. Power; very seductive.

Then there's the wit, the yarns. Besides a long friendship with the Haugheys, I have shared many happy times with countless politicians, most of whom express a deep interest and passion for football. Sort of a social *quid pro quo.* I suppose, the GAA and Irish politics have never been too far apart. Feed off one another, in every way. Even Charlie himself knows the score, won a Dublin senior football championship medal with Parnells. Knows about taking on officials too, had a famous set-to with a linesman at one game, got a twelve-month ban for his trouble. Bertie; never far from Dublin football; huge fan. I mean, in what other country can you rub shoulders with a prime minister at a local club match? Brian Cowen's another. One of the most capable ministers of his generation. Knows his football, no mistake. I've been close to Cowen for years and can testify to that. Early in 2000 when our full-back Barry O'Shea suffered a serious knee injury we were toying with different ideas about what to do. I met Cowen socially one evening and was talking about our dilemma. He was asking me about our prospects, said he fancied us big time. "Páidí, I can see nothing stopping Kerry this year, if . . . if ye can sort out your full-back difficulties. Who do ye have in line for the full-back slot?" he asked.

"Séamus Moynihan," I replied.

"Problem solved," said Cowen.

Hard man to catch out. Tried it before the All-Ireland final a few months later. I was in a roguish mood one afternoon, decided to ring Brian for a chat. We got talking about the forthcoming clash with Galway and I asked, "Jeezuus, Brian, what'll we do if Pádraig Joyce goes out the field, will I get Séamus to follow him?" He didn't fall for it. Great stories. Cowen tells a great yarn about his party colleague, the colourful Killarney TD John O'Leary. After a Fianna Fáil Christmas party in Jury's Hotel in Dublin years back, Cowen and O'Leary, intent on stretching the evening a little further, hit a local nightclub on the old strip. After entering the premises, Cowen beckoned to O'Leary. "What'll ye have, John?"

O'Leary replied forthrightly, "Brian, I'll have a creamy pint of stout, from the middle of the barrel."

After a brief flurry of activity at the bar Cowen turns and says, "They've no beer here at all, John, only wine."

"Oh," says O'Leary, "I'll have a pint of wine, so."

Sure, I've been touted as a potential candidate on several occasions. But there's no room really, not with football. Like the idea. Well, like the idea of parts of the job. The canvas, working on people, working for a community. I'd love to do something for the parish, for

Ventry. Turn my attentions back towards home. Maybe in time. Maybe in time I'll get a chance to turn my energies back to my business as well. Managing Kerry doesn't allow much room for business. Professional really, in an amateur world. Same for players. Politics? Well . . . I don't know. Football I know. While bidding for the Kerry position and since becoming a manager though, I've taken a good shot of advice from various politicians about running the show. Fortunately many of the country's top people gravitate towards Kerry. Have the advice on tap. Doesn't appeal to young people that much though. Pity really. I suppose I ignore a lot of the things that turn the younger generations off. I immerse myself in the social side of politics. Make no secret of that. I love nothing better than the company of politicians and football folk, sharing stories over pints. Wasn't too long ago that I ran into Fine Gael TD Paddy Sheehan. Lovely character, from Goleen, southwest Cork. Great wit. Told me a great yarn about an encounter across the floor of Leinster House the day Charlie resigned as Taoiseach on the 11 February 1992. Given the profound impact Charlie has made on the political landscape of the country, this final joust is a triumph for the unimportant. Sheehan, recounted the story with delight, scribbled it down for me . . .

> "A Cheann Comhairle. Seeing that the Taoiseach is departing his high office within the next few hours, before he goes I want to put the records of this house straight. When is the Taoiseach going to extend the powers of the Castletownbear Harbour Master over the waters of the Bearhaven Sound?"
>
> The Ceann Comhairle, Paddy Sheehan said, hit the bell a scelp you'd hear it in Ventry. "Deputy Sheehan, you're out of order, resume your seat or leave the house." Deputy Sheehan replied to the Ceann Comhairle, "Can't you see that the Taoiseach is on his feet and he's ready to answer." So the Ceann Comhairle beckoned to

Taoiseach and Charlie's reply was, "Deputy
ˎeehan, the battle between us is now over, we
ll return our swords to the scabbards."

ıl. Irrelevant.

ᴏᴋᴀy, I'm not blind. I see politics is a big turn-off for a
lot of folk. In recent times the climate has changed, but I
won't turn my back on old friends. Never. The busy,
local activist is now the man. Still, I'm not for turning. I
admire those who choose to live out there on the edge.
No pipe and slippers for them. Live on their wits, on
guard.

Early warning

I'd always know when I was working well, when I was
clued in. Máire would tell me. If I was any way off the
mark, if I was letting something slip, Máire would tell
me. Lay it on the line. There could be no half-measures,
nothing disjointed. It was like an early-warning system
at home. If I wasn't clued in for a game, for an incident,
for a problem, Máire would spot it, put me in my place
fairly quickly. "If you're going at this job, do it right. If
you're going to manage this team, do it to the best of
your ability." Likewise, across the road. My mother
might be in her mid-eighties now, but she'd also know.
Always spend a half hour before a big game chatting to
Beatrice, listening. Great for the head. If I was going off
the rails, had a quare idea about something . . . wouldn't
go any further than Ard an Bhóthair. No let-up. Kept me
tuned in.

After our lively opening to the National League in
1999 I felt good. Mood was right back in Ventry, sort of
an early buzz of expectation. Before the Christmas break,
we played a cracking game with Dublin in Parnell Park.
We lost by a couple of points after missing two penalties,
but it was heartening stuff nonetheless. From that
evening many sensed we'd be the team to reckon with
for 2000.

However, after hammering an Armagh side just back from their holidays, we suffered a setback in our second outing of the New Year against Roscommon, when full-back Barry O'Shea did his knee. We had been trying different players like Tom O'Sullivan in that role before Christmas but this would now force our hand. We topped our group in the league and qualified for a semi-final meeting with Meath in Thurles. This will test us, I thought. I watched from behind the wire, part of my punishment for pitch incursions in the championship the previous summer. We played Mike McCarthy on the edge of the square against Meath. Mike had been a very successful full-back under age, but had subsequently developed as a corner man. This became very obvious that day when we leaked four goals in a roller-coaster of a game. Played some super football that left me satisfied enough. All-Ireland champions Meath went on to burn themselves out over a two-game final against Derry. I was glad to be out of it. Winning league titles is fine for a developing squad. It's really a hindrance to championship preparation after that. Better to do the fine-tuning with a couple of low-key, but sprightly, challenge games. National League? It's like preparing a greyhound for a race. Give it a few good kills early in the season. You don't lose sleep over losing league games, especially away from home. Playing badly in a challenge game in June? Then you worry. What was striking about our league semi-final defeat that April afternoon in Thurles was that Kerry supporters actually came away from the game reasonably happy. Must have been doing something right.

Anyway, the fine-tuning we required at No. 3 was pretty obvious. I thought about this for a while. Our captain, Séamus Moynihan, was carrying a knock and only appeared as a late substitute against Meath. Moynihan is as complete and versatile a footballer as I've ever encountered. Never a man to feel I was wasting talent by playing a good ball-player in defence, I decided to sound this one out. Moynihan at full-back. After discussing it with the selectors, I asked the Tattler, Eddie

O'Sullivan, to hop the idea off Séamus quietly, see would he slip into the full-back line temporarily. After losing to the Royals, we played Kildare in a challenge game a fortnight later. Séamus started in the corner but after a while, we moved him to full-back. We lost by a point but, as the Minister for Foreign Affairs stated shortly afterwards, "Problem solved."

The Tattler proved a great father figure on the management team around this time. He could dip into a deep well of experience having worked on several Kerry teams. Very astute. I think Tattler, no more than Johnno, came on board with this idea that I was a difficult guy to work for. That myth persisted. After a couple of months I think he understood otherwise. In fact, at the All Stars function in Dublin before Christmas, I got chatting with former GAA president Joe McDonagh, a good friend of Eddie's, who confirmed just how differently he now felt about me.

With Tattler's subtle prompting, the problem of the vacant full-back position was accounted for. Other problems, however, persisted. Maurice Fitzgerald made his comeback to the panel after Christmas following his ankle break in August. Unfortunately, he suffered a huge setback almost immediately. And, you know, we made a big mistake with Maurice. Having survived a savage session on Banna Strand with Johnno one Saturday, Maurice lined out in a full-scale game against Tralee RTC in Killarney the next day. Shouldn't have let him. He was sore going into the game. What happened? Broke his ankle again – in the exact same place. This rocked Maurice, big time. Rocked us all. I mean, I wasn't hopeful for him at this stage. There was a lot of mileage on the clock. Maurice, after all, had made his championship debut back in 1988. He had been to the fore in his club for years before that. And, as you can imagine, every fucker in the county trying to take the head off him for over a decade. Had to take its toll.

To me the situation was clear-cut. I knew Maurice was, once again, determined to persevere, to overcome the injury and work his way back. Football meant far too much to him to let something force him out of the game on anything but his own terms. No broken ankle was going to finish him. Yet, we had to plan without him. Supremely talented as Maurice is, he couldn't take a full, active part in much of our pre-championship training.

By the time our first game arrived, on the 18 June, Maurice had only done bits and pieces with us at the latter stages of our programme. We had to hit the ground running, we faced Cork in the Munster semi-final. Now Maurice, like any good footballer, wasn't going to approach the championship saying, "I'm only good for twenty minutes or so." He wants to play for Kerry, from the start, wants to be there in the second half, in extra time if needs be. I can't overstate how important football is to him and his family. But I had to call it as I saw it. Maurice wasn't physically ready for the rigours of seventy minutes of championship action as far as we were concerned. If this caused great resentment, well, then I'd grin and bear it. I don't harbour any bad feelings for Maurice. I believe you should always make it difficult for a manager to drop you. Never make it easy. I have also the highest respect for his football. I don't think there has *ever* been a footballer with his skill. For mental strength he is also peerless. Watch him with a pressurised kick. You'll often notice him changing ball. Won't use a county ball, insists on a new, official Croke Park ball, with the requisite 13oz of air inside. Unreal. Knows the flight of a ball better than any man alive. But this situation, in the summer of 2000, was so clear to me it wasn't even funny. My job as Kerry manager concerns our team performing collectively to our maximum potential. Yes, of course, Maurice's unrivalled skill was part of that collective effort. But to harness it, we had to make sure Maurice was physically capable of delivering. It was clear to me. Start him and we couldn't be certain. Bring him on when the game has opened up? Definitely. Regretfully, the idea of a rift grew in momentum publicly almost from the Cork match. Given how successful our tight controls on the publicity surrounding the team had worked, there was no way I was going to start explaining at length my decision. I'd stand or fall by what happened on the pitch. If I called it wrong, so be it. I added no fuel to the rift theory.

Last man back

Going into the Cork game, much of the focus centred on Moynihan's new role as full-back as well as Maurice's exclusion from the starting line-up. I was very confident nonetheless. Our run-in had been excellent. Despite Moynihan's new detail, we had a very settled look to the team: Mike Frank top of the right; Dara Ó Cinnéide full-forward and consistent free taker; Johnny Crowley left corner; Liam Hassett on the '40' with a view to coming deep around the middle, even behind midfield. Aodhán and Noel would do the running on the wings. And, you know, one of the big factors in 2000 was the development of Darragh Sé. More than ever he was becoming a leader on the field. His improvement was constant . . . fielding, distribution, running, taking a score. Starting to dominate games. Off the field too, at team meetings, he was becoming very influential. At the back we were now closing in on a very tight unit. With Séamus shoring up the middle, Mike Hassett was returning to his best form, putting huge pressure on Killian Burns at right corner-back. The way you want it. On the far side, Mike McCarthy was developing a reputation as one of the game's top defenders. Solid half-back line. No going forward at every opportunity, no fucking around up front on the opponents' 14-yard line. Tom O'Sullivan on the right, Eamon Fitzmaurice in the middle and Tomás Sé on the left. My kind of players.

I've always been a big advocate of conservative defending. I believe that a half-back who constantly goes forward is merely covering up some weakness, usually that he can't defend. Mind your fucking patch. End of story. Now, that doesn't mean that your quality of football can be compromised, far from it. Just because I don't want a defender kicking points doesn't mean I will tolerate bad distribution, headless stuff. No. The opposite. Good distribution from this sector will win you games.

It was an attractive mix. Obviously, we had great strength on the line, too. Now, I wanted us to do everything at pace. Everything. We had to give ourselves an edge. Accurate football, attractive football. Natural. No contrived tactical manoeuvres. Yes, we would pull our centre-forward a little bit deeper, allow Dara to come out, give Russell and Crowley room. Room for the diagonal ball, arguably the most effective pass in Gaelic football. Doesn't have to be goal-side. A diagonal ball from a wing-back, midfielder or a half-forward played over the shoulder of the opposing defender, out in front of the corner-forward. Out towards the sideline, no problem. Then it's one on one. This is when it comes down to skill, basics . . . football. Now, you're playing. Now, you're putting the opposition under pressure. Now the corner-forward can take on his man, throw it out to an in-rushing half-forward, knock it across field to the far corner or just lamp it over the bar.

We have the best handlers of the ball in Kerry. Always had. Sounds a little snobbish but it's true and, regardless of recent setbacks, I still believe it. I suppose it's tradition. Football in Kerry is like hurling in Kilkenny. Kids carry a ball around with them, never stop kicking, catching, off walls, out in fields. The same philosophy is applied to the inter-county set up. There's a common belief that football, unlike hurling, doesn't require a high level of skill and artistry. Don't subscribe to that in Kerry. It gives us a great advantage. Great versatility. Allows us to move players around. I always tell the lads: "Whatever position a Kerry footballer is dragged into, a corner-back might be dragged out to midfield, to the far side of the pitch . . . he should feel comfortable." Allows us to play the game at a very high tempo, a good catch can save a lot of work. Of course you still need a platform. Fitness; courage; strength, physical and mental.

Goes without question. But when victory comes down to the tiniest detail, that marginal edge, I put my trust in instinct. Do the basic things well. Positive. Contest it bravely, catch it cleanly, look up, kick it accurately. If you can't catch it cleanly, ensure that your man doesn't. On your toes for the breaks. Hit hard, fair, no quare carry-on, no mouthing. All sounds so fucking simple. Well it isn't. With so little separating the top teams in the game nowadays, with so much work to do to ensure that everything is covered, to vary the recipe, it's very easy to lose sight of the simple things. Now for 2000 everything at pace. *Everything.*

Eighteenth of June. Hottest day ever in Killarney. Jeezuus. Couldn't even warm up on the Crokes pitch, had to keep the lads in the shade, conserve energy, fluid. "Keep the boots off." Hot day like that, better to prepare without the boots. I think your ankles swell in the heat. I remember Mick O'Connell twenty-six years previously, in the days when we didn't know anything. On a hot day, he'd do his first couple of laps, his warm-up, in an old pair of wellies, cut to the ankle. Then, he'd lace up the boots. Gave the ankles a chance. Felt very confident facing Cork. The talk the week before had been magic. Despite all his setbacks, Maurice's influence in the dressing room was unbelievable. You know, he matches his incredible skill on the field with his talking off it. And I don't mean stirring it for me! He was absolutely brilliant at team meetings, brilliant feel for the game. Helped coax an awful lot out of players. I felt very confident. More than ever, we had a lot of very strong personalities in that dressing room: Séamus, Darragh, Maurice.

Amazing first half that day. Incredible displays from Darragh Sé, Liam Hassett, Dara Ó Cinnéide. Incredible. Two penalties. Two great kicks from Ó Cinnéide. Wasn't all one-way. Colin Corkery always saves the best for Kerry. Gave Killian a tough half hour, brought Mike Hassett in before half-time. We went to sleep after the break, hard to avoid it when you're ten points up. Cork started chipping away, early goal, Corkery again. Bit like Kerry and Dublin in 1985. After tormenting them for so long . . . all of a sudden there were only a few points between the teams entering the closing stages. Maurice came in for the last quarter, caught some good ball around the middle. Fortunately we capitalised on a stray pass from Steven O'Brien, won a free, settled. It's what I'd been talking about, the knack of winning games. We were good at it in the 1970s and 1980s. Oh, you'll hear the pundits nowadays talking about a team's inability to 'kill off' the opposition. It doesn't generally work like that. I mean, if a team like Cork are ten points down, what do you think they're going to do? Fucking go for it, that's what. Any of the top sides in the country will react that way. You weather the storm, ensure that, at some stage, your good habits will yield the important score. Finish strongly. We did against Cork, had five points to spare: 2–15 to 1–13. Happy out.

Afterwards there was a lot of flak about Moynihan. "Wasted in at full-back, influence missed around the middle," was the consensus. As far as we were concerned, he'd kept his man scoreless. We toughened. He was staying put.

We'd no real trouble with Clare in the Munster final in Limerick a month later. They'd gone back a bit and could only live with us for a while. Without ever really getting out of the traps, we cruised to a 3–15 to 0–8 win. Crowley and Mac Gearailt tormented them. We whipped off Moynihan early in the second half after he'd picked up a knock. Again, he'd looked most comfortable at No. 3. Hardly surprising for a man of his ability. You know, I began to realise at this stage just how much this meant to Moynihan, or the 'Pony' as he is affectionately known. After he'd lifted the Munster cup that afternoon in the Gaelic Grounds, he became incredibly focused on going the distance. Fucking unreal. Absolutely obsessed with going the distance. Stepping off that plane in Farranfore with the Sam in his hand. True captain.

Armagh v. Kerry – Part 1

Now the stakes were raised considerably. On 20 August 2000, we faced an Armagh team down for their second semi-final in a row. Powerful side. Had folded to Meath a year previously after missing a rake of chances. Knew this would be tough. I left nothing to chance. Compiled the most detailed video ever in preparation. Their strengths, weaknesses, our form, where we could improve. Most thorough ever. Selectors worked overtime. We had a fair idea how it might go, how they played . . . three midfielders, Tony McEntee's roving role, Barry O'Hagan pushing up. We detailed Tom Sullivan to man-mark Tony McEntee, didn't want the Armagh man going deep, winning easy possession in his own defence. Equally, when he ventured forward, Tom was to stick to him. As it transpired, Tom took the instruction to the letter of the law, so much so that he probably sacrificed too much of his own game.

Before we played Armagh, I took the Kerry team to Dublin for a walk out on the pitch in Croker, get used to the absence of the Hogan Stand. After travelling to watch the drawn Dublin–Kildare game, one thing struck me about the play – the majority of the action seemed to be drawn towards the New Stand side of the field, probably because of the absence, at that time, of a defined barrier on the far side. Made sure that our boys would consciously avoid this happening. Also noticed that the pitch seemed to have been made slightly bigger. Anyway, I was concerned that the players had a feel for the surroundings.

The Armagh game was a blistering clash. Unbelievable. And, you know, not too far off what both sides had in mind. A typical, crisp opening yielded 1–3 for us without reply but I knew it was only a matter of time. They packed the middle, put a powerful squeeze on us, clawed us back, turned the tables. A few harsh calls by referee John Bannon seemed to keep us on the back foot. But it would be hard to blame the ref. What goes around comes around, and Bannon played enough time for us to rescue the day. We brought Maurice on early in the second half and he turned the game for us, before it turned back again. One of those days. His goal in the final quarter was extraordinary. Genius. Only matched by his courage to go and kick a highly pressurised equaliser in injury time. This is his stage. Regardless of what way our relationship is perceived . . . we would not have survived that day without his stunning contribution. Nor would we have lived to fight again were it not for Moynihan. His performance was incredible. Driven like no man I've ever come across, his determination to succeed singled him out that day. Sure, he tried to do too much. Never shirked responsibility to attack a ball, instinct of a half-back. But I've never seen a player so utterly committed for the entire seventy minutes.

Personally, I found the going tough on the line, felt like I was being marked at times. Tense afternoon. Reflecting what was happening on the pitch, I suppose. The game turned so many times. Bizarre. In truth, I thought we were gone when Kieran McGeeney kicked them into the lead following their late goal. Thought that was it. But sure enough, my theory about the far touchline, the size of the pitch, may not have been too far off the mark. We survived that day because Barry O'Hagan dropped their final shot short, didn't club right, allowing Declan O'Keeffe to fire it out to Denis Dwyer who won the free for Fitzy. Bizarre. 2–11 each.

Armagh v. Kerry – Part 2

We hadn't left Croke Park when the calls for Maurice to start in the replay began. Few noticed that he limped from the ground courtesy of a toe injury he received during the game. Couldn't train between the drawn game and the replay. Naturally, that was ignored. Once again, we had to go on what we saw behind the scenes. Toughened it out once more.

Again, little separated the sides in the replay a
fortnight later, but I had a much better afternoon. Mike
Hassett came in this time and did the marking job on
Tony McEntee, leaving Tom Sullivan to play his own
game. We switched Ó Cinnéide out to the '40', see would
his style counter the effect of McGeeney. Tomás added a
bit of steel to our defence. Again the game see-sawed,
went to the wire. Yet I felt more composed. Didn't feel as
suffocated on the line. The selectors were excellent; cool
and calculated. Everything worked out. I stayed more
composed. Never more so than when the game was
forced into extra time. Probably my best moment of the
championship. I dug into my own past, to the Munster
final of 1976. *An rud 's annamh is iontach,* what's
seldom . . . Extra time. Warned against fatigue, warned
against the tired mind. Talked it out. "Don't foul, don't
grab a jersey, don't take anything for granted, don't take a
shortcut just because your fucked. If we keep mentally
alert, we'll win." Reiterated the advice at the break in
extra time, primarily because Séamus had just handled a
ball on the ground, giving away a free moments earlier.
Talked it out. Relaxed. Much better day. Aodhán Mac
Gearailt had struggled earlier in the game. Came back on
in extra time. Rarely will you get a second chance in an
All-Ireland semi-final. He did. Was a different man when
he came back in. Stage belonged to Mike Frank Russell.
Every time the Ulstermen threatened, Russell upped the
bar. Steered us to the All-Ireland final. Kerry 2–15,
Armagh 1–15.

Kerry v. Galway – Part 1

The pattern of speculation didn't alter after we'd secured
our place against Galway for the 24 September
showdown. Would Maurice start and would Séamus
Moynihan remain on Pádraig Joyce? We didn't budge.
Same plan, same response. Preparations went well
initially but a couple of things threw us off kilter as we
approached the final. Eddie O'Sullivan's brother died

suddenly. That was tough on the Tattler. Then, I think the strain of the Maurice debate started to seep through the squad a little. Had to. The lads looked up to Maurice and he wasn't happy. It was hard to blame him. Any man that has put so much into football, has lived football from the O'Connell heartland of Caherciveen, developed his game to such a high standard; I mean, he was hardly going to be happy with his place on the bench. I could sense the tension on the train to Dublin. I toughened. I was steeled not to let his disappointment in any way affect our focus. But he confounded me later on in the hotel by making the most telling contribution to the team meeting. Wonderful speech. Coaxed the players, great encouragement. Great passion.

The drawn final wasn't anywhere near as intense as the clashes with Armagh, yet it followed a remarkably similar pattern. We stuck to our plan, everything seemed to be going right, and the wheels came off. Lucky to carry our legs out in the end. Had Derek Savage thrown that last ball out . . . who knows. It's important you don't get carried away with victory or defeat. Jeezuus, I could crow about vindication, but "the difference between a pat on the back . . ." It is so fucking tight at the top level. Potential, form, class, injuries . . . you call it as you see it. But when a game explodes you have to ride it out. You can switch a man who isn't playing well, then take him off, bring on a great player, he may or may not do the business, cajole, encourage. But, at times, you're helpless. Very strange feeling. Sure, the line is important but maybe not as important as the philosophy, the belief in how you play. Thankfully, the support from Johnno, Jack, Eddie the Tattler and Eamon was immense.

Survived. Fourteen points apiece.

Kerry v. Galway – Part 2

Go at it again. I was confident we could up our performance to the necessary pitch to take Galway at the second asking. Made sense to me. Mike Hassett was

195

improving with every game. He was a very big asset to us. His residence in Wicklow where he worked as a teacher was obviously a hindrance, but, after a summer's training with Johnno, he was beginning to make a telling impact. Knew his graph would continue to rise. Analysed the drawn game, took into account the criticism that we couldn't deal with a team running at us, that we fouled too much, gave away handy frees. Decided to improve our tackling. Went back to the well again. "The closer you are to the big prize, the closer you are to your man." They took it on board. We spoke to Séamus as well. Had to change his game a little. Against Armagh he was covering everything – his man, the square, everything. Galway were a slicker team, they'd draw the tackle, slip the pass off at the last second. I wanted Séamus to back off a little, be cautious. Séamus pleaded that he wanted to contribute more out the field. Begged. He was so hungry. Wanted that prize so much. I had to match his passion. Took him back to 1982, where I'd made my greatest contribution out the field, and we'd lost the game. Knew he'd respond. Through all the intensity of the semi-finals and finals, Moynihan was a rock. A constant. A leader. By example . . . brave, intelligent, passionate. Inspirational.

Found myself increasingly dipping into my past. I suppose this is where the experience comes into its own. Having gone through the mill so many times, I went with my gut feelings. Things that fucking annoyed me when I was a player, when I was anxious . . . fans hanging around, saying stupid things at the wrong time, stupid jokes. Ensured this wouldn't happen now. Wanted the players to be as relaxed as possible. No mobiles going off during meetings. Small things. Keep everyone comfortable. Wasn't happy with the journey on the train to Dublin the first day. Decided to change tack. The first day we'd shared two carriages, the players, management, county board officials, wives. Wasn't happy. This time we got one carriage, for players only. Everyone else travelled on a different train. Tight.

The night before the game we decided to switch Tom Sullivan onto Michael Donnellan. Tomás Sé had followed him the first day but we felt O'Sullivan's pace would be better suited to Donnellan's running, would yield less frees. Was probably a little late to break it to the lads, but we trusted their maturity. Worked out as well.

With our homework done the replay went like a dream. A most enjoyable afternoon on the line. Players responded to everything we mentioned. Shrugged aside the setback of the early goal. Brilliant. Noel Kennelly's confidence took a bit of a dent following Declan Meehan's goal so we decided this time that we'd move Maurice in before the break. This wasn't, as was suggested, because I feared the consequences. It was a calculated response by the management team to what was happening on the field. And it worked. Gave Maurice a chance to come into the dressing room at half-time already in the game, warmed up. He was outstanding in the second half, particularly his fielding and distribution. Full-forward line was lethal. Further out Liam Hassett . . . unreal. Everyone contributed. The way I like it; all tuned in to their jobs – focused, alive to everything. Delighted for all of 'em . . . Mike Hassett, Maurice, in particular. And, of course, the Pony. More than any of us, the All-Ireland success of 2000 belonged to Moynihan. Hunger. Put himself on the line, for his team, for the selectors, for me . . . for Kerry. 0–17 to 1–10.

Didn't crow about it. Quiet satisfaction. Wasn't concerned about vindication. Those who understand, who know . . . they're respectful. Those who don't, well, they don't matter. Respect. Respect for what John O'Keeffe, Eddie O'Sullivan, Jack O'Connor and Eamon Walsh had given for twelve months. The sacrifice, the workload, copying videos, watching players, trusting their judgement, driving thousands of miles.

The players? Total commitment. Total. I don't think enough people see it from the players' perspective. They give everything. Give up so much for the collective good.

Have to get more than just a holiday. Have to. Training, travel, injury, mental preparation, stress. I mean, you bare your soul on a football field. In front of 65,000 people. Just because they love the game shouldn't mean they're taken for granted. Families. Huge burden on life at home. Without support in that sector it's impossible to deliver. Can't insulate your family from all the hassle, from the non-stop telephone calls, from the demands, the abuse.

Takes its toll. Every year you have to evolve, stay one step ahead. That means more energy, a greater battle of wits. But when you believe, when you've good people around you, sharing the burden . . . it's not so bad. Surprising what the winter does to the appetite.

Go at it again. See what the 'back door' will throw up. Go at it again.

14
Eastern Promise

Gach aoinne ag cur a bhó féin thar abhainn

Winter 2000–2001

THE WHITE heat of Croke Park has started to cool in the memory along with the evenings. Time to take stock, recharge. Ask the annual question: is it worth it? The journey? I've never known life without football. From childhood, the *Duí*, the Sem, minors, Under-21s, 1975, four-in-a-row, captaincy, West Kerry, newspaper, sniping, bidding for the manger's job, getting the manager's job, Under-21s, training, meetings, interviews, seniors, selections, rows, All-Irelands, celebrations. No stops. Endless grief.

Well maybe not endless. There's always winter. They can't see you in the dark, gives you a chance to become human again. I'm starting to appreciate it more by the year. Quiet winter nights, at the counter in the pub discussing situations with Sally Long, Tony Sé, Michael Andrew. Every so often the conversation will pause, we'll hear the rain lepping off the windows, wind howling in from the bay, crackle of a roaring fire. Then we'll laugh . . . someone will hop the ball. "*An cuimhin leat an cluiche san . . .*" Remember the game. Happy out.

Tough? Yerrah, it's tougher on the family really. I'm driven by the demons on my shoulder but it's tougher for them. There's a lot of work, a lot of family stuff at Ard an Bhóthair bypasses me. When I get stick they take it badly. Máire has deputised for the Kerry manager for years and, before my wife, it was my mother Beatrice. They've all stuck by me. Máire, Neasa, Siún, Pádraig. They're passengers too. And, you know, it's not just the nephews who've taken to football, my own crew are all involved. Neasa and Siún are both playing with the local ladies football team while Pádraig Óg's mad for it. He never leaves a ball out of his hand. Máire, of course, is always on hand to ferry them to games. *Dúchas.*

Now, the end of another championship gives us a chance to reacquaint ourselves as the evenings lengthen. Even thinking of our children rekindles football tales for me. Can't escape it. Our three children were all born in the Bons' in Cork and we were always looked after by our good friend Dr Con Murphy, a fierce Cork GAA man. Football shadowed me everywhere, even to the maternity hospital. The poor kids, wrapped up in football tales from the time they were in the cradle. Can't resist the yarns. When our eldest, Neasa, was due, I remember driving to the hospital in Cork with Máire. After she had settled in the ward, I headed down town – I wouldn't be one to witness the delivery. Old-fashioned. Anyway, as I was making my way down the corridor, past the labour suite, I met this forlorn figure outside, togged out in the cape and mask. He gazed at me and the penny dropped. "Are you Páidí Ó Sé?" he asked.

"I am."

"Páidí, I'm a Corkman, a football man, from Declan Barron country. But after seeing what I did back inside there, it wouldn't cost me a thought to stand on the corner of the square against Humphrey Kelleher." The Humper, Cork full-back in 1973, tough man, never far from the blood and guts of battle! I wasn't finished with football talk yet. I left the hospital and headed for the Western Star pub to wait for word. In the meantime, Dr Con had let a shower of the Cork lads know exactly when the baby was due. When I arrived at the pub, Con, Jimmy Barry Murphy and the boys were there. Needless to say, the discussion wasn't long drifting from the imminent arrival of our first child. Soon, the chat

centred on an alleged mangling Jimmy Deenihan gave
Jimmy Barry one afternoon. Pulling and dragging. Oh
JBM was giving out stick. I was having none of it,
defending Deenihan big time. "God, lads, Deenihan was
a great all-rounder," I ventured. "He was very good at
rugby, very good at soccer, a very skilful player. We'd see
it, whenever we'd be having a five-a-side, warming down
at training. Never saw that side of him now, Jimmy
Barry." I wouldn't back down. Anyway, the phone rang.
Wasn't it the Bons. I shot off for the hospital leaving the
lads roaring behind me. "You better hope 'tis a footballer,
Sé."

She's a footballer all right, lads, Neasa.

Football. My wife Máire has never been far from it.
Shortly after landing back from our honeymoon at the
end of March in 1984 I joined up with the Kerry panel for
my first outing in ages. I think we travelled to Beaufort
for a game. I went on an awful tear with Lynch
afterwards, arrived back in Ventry at an unearthly hour.
Máire had a good look at me walking in. "Jesus, is this
what I'm after marrying?" I was telling Lynch about it
the next morning. "You know, Paudie, there was a lot to
be said for all the years with Beatrice . . . she'd arrive out
to the car, no matter what hour, take my gear in for me
and give Mick Dwyer a right good scolding; 'God, Páidí,
he's working ye way too hard at the training.'"

Some day I'll step off, end the journey. Don't really
know when. Then I'll turn the demons' attention to
Ventry, to the pub, the family, my business. I'll see if I
can land a few prizes for the team at home, see if can I
make life that bit easier at Ard an Bhóthair. I suppose
some day managers, maybe even players, won't have that
nagging feeling of leaving something undone at home, in
their work. Something will give somewhere down the
line. I'm a traditionalist, like most GAA folk of my
generation, but I'm also a realist. If I approached the
Kerry job with anything less than total professionalism,
I'd be hung. If a player is sloppy and unprofessional about
his approach, he won't last long either. The game won't
go professional, in a financial sense, not yet. But you can

only have professionals dressed as amateurs for so long. It'll probably happen some day. In the meantime, my wish is that players get looked after, by their sponsors, by their employers. I think the GAA needs to rethink how it promotes the game. It's supposed to be a countrywide effort. In some parts, however, it's only token stuff. Needs to be more than just coaching or a couple of summer camps. Senior colleges are still the prime areas to develop good footballers.

Why have some areas deteriorated so much over the years? Because teachers don't pick up the slack? Because lifestyles have changed so much? The GAA needs to move into places like the senior colleges and secondary schools and ensure that the right individuals are in place to develop the game properly. You know, like them or loathe them, good county board officials are vital for success, on and off the field. I think we've been very lucky with our executive in Kerry over the last few years. I'd hate to have to work with the resources some managers are expected to work with. They don't stand a chance. Maybe I'm biased, but I don't see a better way of promoting the game in a county than through a successful, well-resourced senior team. Especially with a revamped format . . . more games, more television, more coverage, more sponsorship. Nowadays, you need huge resources. Travel, injury-care, equipment, accommodation . . . these are basic requirements, not luxuries. We now play our games in a stadium to rival the greatest in the world. We can't quibble about travel expenses. Must do more, more for players.

Winter means peace for Páidí Sé, a time to unwind, to travel to Dublin for a few blow-outs, attend functions, like the All Stars. I love that craic, telling yarns to a huddle in Morrissey's in Leeson Street, dressed in monkey suits, recalling a story about a medal ceremony in Aherlow. This is the easy stuff. Of course it's easier when you've won something, as it keeps the begrudgers and experts off your back for a while. Unfortunately that's only a temporary situation. As soon as you slip up, may be only a late point or a dodgy decision, you'll get it in the neck. "Told you so, brutal on the line, Páidí."

Sun never sets

By Christmas, I had enough of the monkey suits and ceremonies. Listened to enough wisdom to do me for a lifetime. Early in the New Year we shot off to Thailand for a good stint in the sun with the family and the panel. Enjoyed a bit of black magic winding each other up, a bit of craic with the lads. The team holiday is payback time. 'Tisn't a huge payback but it is enjoyable nonetheless and it breaks the back of January. Better to be sunning myself on a beach in Thailand than getting the bollox blown off me in Ventry. The All Stars trip is another small reward for players and, sometimes, managers as well. After steering Kerry to an All-Ireland last year, I was invited out to Dubai for the All Stars trip which meant that, shortly after landing back from Thailand, I was off out to the sun again. I was baked brown by this stage, beached by the pool like a fucking otter. One of the nice things about collective GAA trips is meeting other players and managers in less pressing circumstances. Enjoying a bit of craic together. I enjoyed chatting with Galway manager John O'Mahony. Good guy.

Wintered well.

Not that bad really is it? The journey? You see, after wintering for a few months, after getting the sun on the back, you're ready to go at it again. You want the buzz, you want to see, one more time, can you raise the pitch and land that fucking canister again. And if you're going at it again, you have to do it right. All-Ireland champions 2000. Counts for fuck-all if Cork bate us in Páirc Uí Chaoimh this year. Oh, I'm going at it again all right. Out of hibernation. Tanned, fat . . . but hungry. Have to change something this time round, change tack, look for some player to give me something different. I have to up

it, have to be more fucking tuned in than last year. At it
again. If we can get these boys anyway right, we'll be in
the shake up . . . we'll carry our legs against Cork.
Fellows are fighting for places, pressing for positions.
Never made the big passion play in the dressing room
despite what they all say about me. Now I'm thinking . .
. this year. Maybe this year, maybe this time, it'll shake
them up after winning an All-Ireland.

March 2001: back to back

If it wasn't for this fucking foot and mouth, I could have
a good look, see have they got the winter out of their
systems. Need matches, got to get myself and Maurice
out of the papers.

Can they put All-Irelands back to back? We'll see.
Matches . . .

Rain is hopping off the windscreen as I wind my way
from training. It's late; had a chat with the management
afterwards, sorted out a few things with county secretary
Tony O'Keeffe. Off into the stormy night. West. I'm
almost in Lispole before I stop dreaming. Auto-pilot.
What can I do to get this crowd right? Back-to-back
titles. If they want it. What'll this bloody back door
throw up? What's Maurice going to do? Ah! Turn up the
CD of Dessie O'Halloran for company – "*I'm waiting for
you, say you love me, say you love me.*" Wind my way
back through Dingle, around the back of Garveys, masts
are dancing in the gale, making that eerie clinking sound
around the marina. Sheets of fucking rain batin' in off
the bay. Wouldn't like to think any of the boys are out in
that. The Dingle fishermen. Great folk. Jeezuus, when I
think of it. Those boys looked after me something fierce
when I was up in Dublin in 1975. In the old Daly's Bar
on the Quays. Dingle fishermen, walking over O'Connell
Bridge. Proud. Bán and the boys, looking out for young
Páidí. Throws me back in time again. The Dubs . . . love
the Dubs. Hickey, Mullins, Hanahoe, Cullen, McCarthy,

O'Driscoll. Love their fans, "Howaye, Pawdee, ya bollix. I suppose yiz'll bate us ou' the ga'e again dis year." Don't know what it is, exactly, that relationship between Dublin and Kerry. Unlike any other. Maybe we'll meet this summer. Has to happen some time. Like the old days. Stop reminiscing. Joe Burke's accordion accompanies me out to Milltown, over the bridge, up the hill. Left for Ventry; deserted; past the caravan park, past the towering reeds, the *giolcach*, through the river now careering down the road. Need a fucking keel on this car. Boys are clearing up behind in the bar as I pull up to the pub. Mooch on in, help for a couple of minutes, turn off the jukebox. The way it is. Throw on a pot of tea, quick chat about the evening's custom. Token business. "Good luck, lads."

It's 2 am. Walk across to the house. Rain blinding me. Head won't rest. Back to back . . .

Journey continues.

Epilogue

Toughen

3 September 2001

THE EVENING sunshine above the clouds isn't long
disappearing as we descend into the gloom over the bogs
outside Castleisland. Touchdown. Kerry International
Airport, drenched in September mist. No fanfare, no
canister, no adoring hoardes bedecked in the Green and
Gold. Just as well. Don't fucking want to see anyone.
Jeezuus, how the tide can turn. Darkness falling on the
Kingdom. Fitting really. Just received the hardest kick in
the bollox of my career. Hop into the cart at the airport,
receiving a couple of consoling glances en route. Raise a
smile, "Ah sure, these things happen." Feel strange.
Shook. Know there's a fire raging somewhere inside.
Take its toll yet. Feel tired, put the head back in the car.
Can't think, can't analyse. Don't need to. Knew it at a
quarter to four that afternoon.

I've devoted my life to Kerry football, had a hand in 14
All-Ireland victories between playing, Under-21, senior,
management. I feel I know the game. Now, I've just
spent a year talking about changing tack in Kerry, about
raising the tempo to keep the opposition guessing, about

trying to move on from last year's victory. Last year isn't worth a fuck to a team. Last year's performances are video fodder for our opponents. We never stopped preaching this message and emphasising the importance of finding a new edge. I thought we could pull it off, back-to-back All-Irelands. Sure, we suffered a couple of blows along the way, like losing our centre-forward Liam Hassett. But you shoulder that stuff and get on with it. There were no early wobbles in the Munster championship and we took Cork again after a dodgy start to land our fifth Munster title in six years. Happy enough. Knew we still needed to up the bar. Had to keep raising it. Had to.

Fond memories

Being drawn against Dublin got me going again, just like old times. Oh they told me it wasn't the same, that Dublin versus Kerry wouldn't match the intensity of the past. "Won't be like the old days," they said, "there are no characters now." Sure, it was a different context, a novel venue. The Dubs . . . in Thurles, cars backed up to Kildare an hour before the game. Then, after all the rubbish about not looking to the past, what happens? It's Dublin versus Kerry of old. Serious drama. Great stuff.

The Dubs were always in your face and it was no different this time, sixteen years on since I captained Kerry in our last championship meeting. Really brought back fond memories for me, though I wasn't reminiscing when they landed their second goal. I really thought we were gone that first day in Thurles. Gone . . . until Maurice stepped up and caressed that sideline kick over the bar. No man in Ireland could have matched that. Didn't quite need any such magic in the replay. We were much better second time around. I was very happy with our performance until Tomás Sé got sent off early in the second half. That hurt me, big time. I felt strongly for Tomás, knew it would cost him dearly down the line. I suppose most players would have been sent off for what

Tomás did but I still felt he was a marked man. That's why I made my pitch to the referee afterwards. Now he'd miss an All-Ireland semi-final against Meath. Tomás is just the type of player you need against Meath. Really annoyed me losing him. I get hammered from time to time about my allegiances to family, to my nephews, to west Kerry, to the Gaeltacht club. I don't hide my fondness for the nephews but they play for Kerry on merit. I helped coach the boys from the cradle, made sure they never left a ball out of their hands. Proud? Of course I'm fucking proud. They're great footballers. But when things go wrong, or if one of them has an off day, then the critics say, "Páidí is blinded by family, can't see beyond the nephews or past west Kerry". I'm not the most die-hard Gaeltacht clubman that ever was but I'm happy enough to have influenced those around me.

Harsh realities

I felt comfortable against Dublin in the end. It mightn't have looked that way but I always felt we'd carry our legs out the second day. We shot off immediately after the Thurles replay to watch Meath squeeze the life out of Westmeath, the gallant newcomers to the 2001 championship. Meath? Know what you get – every time. Never play to the watch, never play to the scoreboard. They just play, always concentrating on their performance whether in front or behind. Meath? Squeeze you at the back, tear you apart in open space up front. Knew exactly how Meath would play. Crowd midfield, break as much ball as possible, hunt you all over the pitch, cross-field ball to Murphy or Geraghty, others buzzing around, harrying defenders. That's Meath. Knew it. Kerry? All-Ireland champions, rich tradition, high skill levels, good organisation. Favourites to buck the trend and land the elusive back-to-back title. I was confident that we had our homework done. No one in our dressing room was under any illusions as to what Meath were about.

So was I surprised with the reddening we got? Well, I wasn't in the least bit surprised with Meath, it was our own boys that left me bewildered. Didn't see us collapsing like that. Couldn't envisage an early surrender. My first reaction was one of immense disappointment for the players and management. I mean, we're in one another's pockets for six months so, directly after the game, I felt for those around me sitting with their heads bent. It was a seriously crushing blow. However, as the evening passed my emotion changed from disappointment to hurt. I felt let down. We'd dropped our heads early in the game, we didn't win the *carpet* ball, the difficult stuff on the deck, the breaks. Not Páidí Sé. That upset me. I mean, Meath were exceptional but our performance really defies analysis. I was hurt.

Maybe I'm too conservative, as a manager, as a tactician. Maybe I should have unleashed the beast, as they say. Maybe my emphasis was wrong. Meath are the modern yardstick. When they're on their game they play intense football, hard and true. I remember Dwyer at half-time in the 1986 All-Ireland when we were being given the run around by Tyrone. Really upped the ante, threatened to walk out on us. Got us going. Rallied the troops.

So we've feet of clay in Kerry. No back-to-back titles.

Defeat? You've got to toughen, specially when it's a bad one. All you can do is let go for a while, unwind. Bit like victory really. I mean, it's the same as it ever was. Treat the two impostors the same. Plough on, take the hit, stand over everything. Now's not the time for bloodletting. Take the breather. After a while we'll look at this situation one more time, see can we turn it around. Oh we'll see what comes out of all this. One more time.

You know it's funny . . . victory or defeat, it leads you back to the same place. Home. Once you step out of Croke Park, away from the panel, you're back with your own. Start to see things their way again. I live the life of a professional football manager. Máire and Beatrice provide that luxury for me. The pub, the shop, the kids. I spent seventeen years in the Kerry jersey and I've spent the last six ranting and raving about Kerry football. Just like Micko. But you can't serve two masters. Máire has always picked up the slack, put up with my humours, good days, bad days. Lucky man.

Defeat sharpens the senses. At least until you dull them again. We'll do that for a while. Back home, with the lads. Surrounded by my own. Ventry.

Practically on two wheels as we pull out of Farranfore. Shoot down through Firies, on for Castlemaine, turn right, then a sharp left. Few of the old haunts won't get a visit this time. County is fucking traumatised. Press on for Inch, Lispole . . . west. No stops. Less than five hours after being torn asunder by Meath in the All-Ireland semi-final we land back at Ard an Bhóthair. Friendly faces. *"Ná bí buartha fén situation san, a Phí Ó. Beimid thar n-ais arís an bhliain seo chugainn."* Support.

Journey over.

For now.

Páidí Ó Sé
Record Card

Páidí Ó Sé
Record Card

Underage Titles
4 x Kerry Colleges (O'Sullivan Cup) – 1971, 1972, 1973, 1974
2 x Munster Colleges A – 1972, 1973
1 x Munster Colleges B – 1974
3 x Munster U-21 Championship – 1993, 1995
3 x All-Ireland U-21 Championship – 1973, 1975, 1976

Senior Titles
8 x All-Ireland Championship titles – 1975, 1978, 1979, 1980, 1981, 1984, 1985, 1986
11 x Munster Championship titles – 1975, 1976, 1977, 1978, 1979, 1980, 1981, 1982, 1984, 1985, 1986
4 x National Football League titles – 1974, 1977, 1982, 1984
4 x Railway Cups – 1976, 1978, 1981, 1982
5 x All Stars Awards – 1981, 1982, 1983, 1984, 1985
2 x Kerry County Championship titles (with West Kerry) – 1984, 1985

Managerial Record
2 x All-Ireland Senior titles – 1997, 2000
5 x Munster Championship titles – 1996, 1997, 1998, 2000, 2001
1 x National Football League title – 1997
1 x All-Ireland U-21 title – 1995
2 x Munster U-21 titles – 1993, 1995
3 x Kerry County Championship titles with West Kerry – 1984, 1985 (player-manager), 1990

All-Ireland Final Teams 1975–1986

1975   Kerry 2–12; Dublin 0–11
Kerry: P O'Mahony, G O'Keeffe, J O'Keeffe, J Deenihan, **P Ó Sé**, T Kennelly,
G Power, P Lynch, P McCarthy, B Lynch (0–3), D Moran (0–2), M O'Sullivan
(capt), J Egan (1–0), M Sheehy (0–4), P Spillane (0–3) *Subs*: G O'Driscoll (1–0) for
O'Sullivan

Dublin: P Cullen, G O'Driscoll, S Doherty (capt), R Kelleher, P Reilly, A Larkin,
G Wilson, B Mullins (0–1), B Brogan, A O'Toole, T Hanahoe, D Hickey,
J McCarthy, J Keaveney (0–6), P Gogarty (0–2) *Subs*: B Doyle (0–1) for Brogan,
P O'Neill for McCarthy, B Pocock (0–1) for Reilly

1976   Dublin 3–8; Kerry 0–10
Dublin: P Cullen, G O'Driscoll, S Doherty, R Kelleher, T Drumm, K Moran,
P O'Neill, B Mullins (1–1), B Brogan (0–1), A O'Toole (0–1), T Hanahoe (capt) (0–1),
D Hickey (0–1), B Doyle, J Keaveney (1–2), J McCarthy (1–1) *Subs*: F Ryder for
Hanahoe, P Gogarty for Doyle

Kerry: P O'Mahony, G O'Keeffe, J O'Keeffe (capt), J Deenihan, **P Ó Sé**, T Kennelly,
G Power, P Lynch, P McCarthy, D Moran (0–2), M Sheehy (0–3), M O'Sullivan
(0–1), B Lynch (0–1), J Egan (0–1), P Spillane (0–2) *Subs*: C Nelligan for O'Mahony,
S Walsh for McCarthy, G O'Driscoll for O'Sullivan

1978   Kerry 5–11; Dublin 0–9
Kerry: C Nelligan, J Deenihan, J O'Keeffe, M Spillane, **P Ó Sé**, T Kennelly,
P Lynch, J O'Shea (0–1), S Walsh, G Power (0–1), D Moran (capt), P Spillane (0–1),
M Sheehy (1–4), E Liston (3–2), J Egan (1–2) *Subs*: P O'Mahony for Deenihan
Dublin: P Cullen, G O'Driscoll, S Doherty, R Kelleher, T Drumm, K Moran,
P O'Neill, B Mullins, B Brogan (0–1), A O'Toole, T Hanahoe (capt), D Hickey,
B Doyle, J Keaveney (0–8), J McCarthy

1979   Kerry 3–13; Dublin 1–8
Kerry: C Nelligan, J Deenihan, J O'Keeffe, M Spillane, **P Ó Sé**, T Kennelly (capt),
P Lynch, J O'Shea (0–1), S Walsh, T Doyle, D Moran, P Spillane (0–4), M Sheehy
(2–6), E Liston (0–1), J Egan (1–1) *Subs*: V O'Connor for O'Keeffe
Dublin: P Cullen, M Kennedy, M Holden, D Foran, T Drumm, F Ryder, P O'Neill,
B Mullins, B Brogan, A O'Toole (0–1), T Hanahoe (capt) (0–2), D Hickey (0–2),
M Hickey, B Doyle (0–3), J McCarthy *Subs*: J Ronayne (1–0) for M Hickey,
G O'Driscoll for McCarthy, B Pocock for O'Toole

1980   Kerry 1–9; Roscommon 1–6
Kerry: C Nelligan, J Deenihan, J O'Keeffe, P Lynch, **P Ó Sé**, T Kennelly,
G O'Keeffe, J O'Shea, S Walsh, J O'Shea (0–1), S Walsh, G Power (capt) (0–1),
D Moran, P Spillane (0–1), M Sheehy (1–6), T Doyle, J Egan *Sub*: G O'Driscoll for
Power

Roscommon: G Sheerin, H Keegan, P Lindsay, G Connellan, G Fitzmaurice,
T Donnellan, D Murray (capt), D Earley (0–1), S Hayden (0–1), J O'Connor (1–2),
J O'Gara (0–1), A Dooley, M Finneran (0–1), T McManus, E McManus *Subs*: M
Dolphin for Dooley, M McDermott for Hayden

1981   Kerry 1–12; Offaly 0–8
Kerry: C Nelligan, J Deenihan (capt), J O'Keeffe, P Lynch, **P Ó Sé (0–1)**,
T Kennelly, M Spillane, J O'Shea (1–0), S Walsh (0–1), G Power (0–1), D Moran
(0–2), T Doyle (0–1), M Sheehy (0–5), E Liston, J Egan (0–1) *Subs:* P Spillane for
Egan, G O'Keeffe for M Spillane

Offaly: M Furlong, M Fitzgerald, L Connor, C Conroy, P Fitzgerald, R Connor
(capt), L Currams, T Connor (0–1), P Dunne, V Henry, G Carroll, A O'Halloran,
M Connor (0–4), S Lowry (0–2), B Lowry (0–1) *Subs:* J Mooney for T Connor,
J Moran for Henry

1982   Offaly 1–15; Kerry 0–17
Offaly: M Furlong, M Lowry, L Connor, M Fitzgerald, P Fitzgerald (0–1), S Lowry
(0–1), L Currams (0–1), T Connor, P Dunne, J Guinan, R Connor (capt), G Carroll,
J Mooney (0–2), M Connor (0–7), B Lowry (0–3) *Subs:* Stephen Darby for M Lowry,
Seamus Darby (1–0) for Guinan

Kerry: C Nelligan, G O'Keeffe, J O'Keeffe, P Lynch, **P Ó Sé (0–2)**, T Kennelly,
T Doyle, J O'Shea (0–1), S Walsh (0–2), G Power, T Spillane (0–3), D Moran,
M Sheehy (0–3), E Liston (0–2), J Egan (capt) (0–3) *Sub:* P Spillane (0–1) for Moran

1984   Kerry 0–14; Dublin 1–6
Kerry: C Nelligan, **P Ó Sé**, S Walsh, M Spillane, T Doyle, T Spillane, G Lynch,
J O'Shea (0–1), A O'Donovan (capt), J Kennedy (0–5), D Moran (0–1), P Spillane
(0–4), G Power, E Liston (0–3), J Egan *Sub:* T O'Dowd for Egan

Dublin: J O'Leary, M Holden, G Hargan, M Kennedy, P Canavan, T Drumm (capt),
P J Buckley, J Ronayne, B Mullins, B Rock (1–5), T Conroy (0–1), K Duff, J Kearns,
A O'Toole, J McNally *Subs:* M O'Callaghan for McNally, K Sutton for Ronayne

1985   Kerry 2–12; Dublin 2–8
Kerry: C Nelligan, **P Ó Sé (capt)**, S Walsh, M Spillane, T Doyle (0–1), T Spillane,
G Lynch (0–1), J O'Shea (1–3), A O'Donovan, T O'Dowd (1–1), D Moran (0–1),
P Spillane (0–2), M Sheehy (0–3), E Liston, G Power *Subs:* J Kennedy (0–1) for
Power

Dublin: J O'Leary, M Kennedy, G Hargan, R Hazley, P Canavan, N McCaffrey,
D Synott, J Ronayne (0–2), B Mullins (capt), B Rock (0–3), T Conroy, C Redmond,
J Kearns (0–2), J McNally (2–0), K Duff *Subs:* T Carr (0–1) for Redmond,
PJ Buckley for Mullins

1986   Kerry 2–15; Tyrone 1–10
Kerry: C Nelligan, **P Ó Sé**, S Walsh, M Spillane, T Doyle (capt), T Spillane,
G Lynch, J O'Shea, A O'Donovan, W Maher, D Moran (0–2), P Spillane (1–4),
M Sheehy (1–4), E Liston (0–2), G Power (0–1) *Subs:* T O'Dowd (0–2) for
O'Donovan

Tyrone: A Skelton, J Mallon, C McGarvey, J Lynch, K McCabe (0–1), N McGinn,
P Ball, P Donaghy, H McClure, M McClure (0–1), E McKenna (capt), S McNally
(0–2), M Mallon (0–4), D O'Hagan (0–1), P Quinn (1–1) *Subs:* S Conway for Lynch,
S Rice for McKenna, A O'Hagan for M Mallon

1977 All-Ireland Semi-Final

Dublin 3–12; Kerry 1–13
Dublin: P Cullen, G O'Driscoll, S Doherty, R Kelleher, T Drumm, K Moran,
P O'Neill, B Mullins, F Ryder, A O'Toole (0–4), T Hanahoe (0–3), D Hickey (1–1),
B Doyle (0–1), J Keaveney (0–3), J McCarthy (1–0) *Subs*: B Brogan (1–0) for Ryder,
P Gogarty for McCarthy

Kerry: P O'Mahony, J Deenihan, J O'Keeffe, G O'Keeffe, D Moran, T Kennelly,
G Power, **P Ó Sé**, J O'Shea, J Egan (0–2), P Lynch (0–1), P Spillane, B Walsh,
S Walsh (1–2), M Sheehy (0–7) *Subs*: T Doyle for B Walsh, P McCarthy for J O'Shea

Munster Final Teams 1974–1988

1974   Cork 1–11; Kerry 0–7
Cork: B Morgan, B Murphy, H Kelleher, D Hunt, KJ O'Sullivan, J Coleman,
C Hartnett, D Long, D Coughlan, N Kirby (0–1), D Barron (0–1), D McCarthy
(1–0), J Barry-Murphy (0–3), R Cummins (0–4), J Barrett (0–2) *Subs*: K Kehilly for
Coleman

Kerry: P O'Mahony, D O'Sullivan, P O'Donoghue, D Crowley, **P Ó Sé**, J O'Keeffe,
G O'Keeffe, P Lynch, (0–1), J Long, E O'Donoghue (0–1), M O'Sullivan (0–4),
G Power, J Egan, S Fitzgerald, M Sheehy (0–1) *Subs*: J Walsh for Fitzgerald, B Lynch
for E O'Donoghue, M O'Connell for Walsh

1975   Kerry 1–14; Cork 0–7
Kerry: P O'Mahony, G O'Keeffe, J O'Keeffe, J Deenihan, **P Ó Sé**, T Kennelly,
G Power, P Lynch, P McCarthy (0–1), B Lynch (0–4), M Sheehy (0–4), M O'Sullivan
(0–1), J Egan (0–2), J Bunyan, P Spillane (1–1) *Subs*: D Moran (0–1) for P Lynch,
G O'Driscoll for B Lynch

Cork: B Morgan, B Murphy, H Kelleher, M O'Doherty, KJ O'Sullivan, K Kehilly,
C Hartnett, D Long, D McCarthy, D Allen (0–3), S Coughlan, A Murphy (0–1),
J Barry-Murphy, D Barron (0–1), R Cummins (0–2) *Subs*: D Hunt for O'Doherty,
JColeman for O'Sullivan, J Barrett for A Murphy

1976   Kerry 0–10; Cork 0–10
Kerry: P O'Mahony, G O'Keeffe, J O'Keeffe, J Deenihan, **P Ó Sé**, T Kenelly,
G Power, P Lynch, P McCarthy (0–2), B Lynch, D Moran, M O'Sullivan, J Egan,
M Sheehy (0–5), P Spillane (0–2) *Subs*: S Walsh (0–1) for B Lynch, J Walsh for
O'Sullivan

Cork: B Morgan, S O'Sullivan, B Murphy, D O'Driscoll, J Coleman, T Creedon,
K Kehilly, D Long (0–2), D McCarthy, C O'Rourke, S Coughlan 90–1), B Fields
(0–2), J Barry-Murphy (0–1), D Barron (0–1), D Allen (0–2) *Subs*: S Murphy for
Fields, K Collins for McCarthy

Replay Kerry 3–20; Cork 2–19 (aet)
Kerry: P O'Mahony, G O'Keeffe, J O'Keeffe, J Deenihan, **P Ó Sé**, T Kennelly,
G Power, P Lynch, P McCarthy, D Moran, M O'Sullivan (1–2), P Spillane (1–3),
B Lynch, M Sheehy (0–11), J Egan (0–1) *Subs*: S Walsh (1–3) for O'Sullivan

Cork: B Morgan, S O'Sullivan, B Murphy, D O'Driscoll, J Coleman, T Creedon, K Kehilly, D Long (0–1), D McCarthy (0–1), C O'Rourke (0–4), D Allen (0–1), S Murphy (0–5), J Barry-Murphy (1–3), D Barron (0–3), S Coughlan (1–0) *Subs*: K Collins for O'Sullivan, B Fields (0–1) for O'Rourke, O'Rourke for Coughlan, C Murphy for Fields, K Murphy for Creedon

1977 Kerry 3–15; Cork 0–9

Kerry: P O'Mahony, J Deenihan, J O'Keeffe, G O'Keeffe, D Moran, T Kennelly, G Power, **P Ó Sé**, J O'Shea (0–2), J Egan (1–0), P Lynch (0–1), P Spillane (1–3), B Walsh (0–5), S Wlash (1–1), M Sheehy (0–3)

Cork: B Morgan, S Looney, T Creedon, B Murphy, D O'Grady, J Coleman, K Kehilly, D Long (0–2), S Coughlan (0–3), M Mullins, D McCarthy, S Murphy, D Allen (0–1), J Barry-Murphy (0–1), S O'Shea (0–2) *Sub*: S O'Sullivan for Looney

1978 Kerry 3–14; Cork 3–7

Kerry: C Nelligan, P Lynch, J O'Keeffe, J Deenihan, **P Ó Sé (0–1)**, T Kennelly, D Moran, J O'Shea, S Walsh, G Power (1–0), T Doyle (0–2), P Spillane (0–4), J Egan (0–2), E Liston, M Sheehy (2–5) *Sub*: P McCarthy for J O'Shea

Cork: B Morgan, B Murphy, G Desmond, K Murphy, J Coleman, T Creedon (0–1), B McSweeney, D McCarthy, C Ryan, D Allen (2–2), D Barron, S Murphy, J Barry-Murphy (1–0), R Cummins (0–3), J Barrett *Subs*: J Kerrigan for K Murphy, D Linehan (0–1) for S Murphy, V Coakley for Coleman

1979 Kerry 2–14; Cork 2–4

Kerry: C Nelligan, J Deenihan, J O'Keeffe, M Spillane, **P Ó Sé**, T Kennelly, P Lynch, J O'Shea, V O'Connor, G Power (2–4), T Doyle (0–1), P Spillane (0–5), M Sheehy (0–3), E Liston, J Egan *Subs*: D Moran for Doyle, S Walsh (0–1) for Moran

Cork: B Morgan, T Creedon, K Kehilly, B Murphy, J Crowley, C Ryan, J Coleman, V Coakley, J Courtney (0–1), P Kavanagh, D Barron, D McCarthy, J Barry-Murphy (1–0), D Allen (1–2), C Kearney (0–1) *Subs*: S Murphy for Coakley, S O'Sullivan for Coleman, T O'Reilly for Kavanagh

1980 Kerry 3–13; Cork 0–12

Kerry: C Nelligan, T Kennelly (0–1, own point), J O'Keeffe, M Spillane, **P Ó Sé**, G O'Keeffe, D Moran, J O'Shea, S Walsh, G Power (1–2), T Doyle (0–1), P Spillane (0–5), M Sheehy (0–3), E Liston (2–1), J Egan (0–1) *Sub*: V O'Connor for J O'Shea

Cork: B Morgan: S O'Sullivan, K Kehilly, J Evans, J O'Sullivan, T Creedon (0–2), J Kerrigan, C Ryan (0–1), C Collins, S Murphy, D Allen (0–5), T Dalton (0–1), J Barry-Murphy, J Allen, D Barry *Subs*: T O'Reilly (0–2) for S Murphy, M Healy for S O'Sullivan, V Coakley for J O'Sullivan

1981 Kerry 1–11; Cork 0–3

Kerry: C Nelligan, J Deenihan, J O'Keeffe, P Lynch, **P Ó Sé**, T Doyle, M Spillane, J O'Shea (0–1), T Spillane, G Power, D Moran, P Spillane (0–3), M Sheehy (1–5), E Liston (0–1), J Egan (0–1)

Cork: B Morgan, M Healy, K Kehilly, J Evans, M Moloney, C Ryan, J Kerrigan, T Creedon (0–1), C Collins, D Barry (0–1), S Hayes, T Dalton, F O'Mahony, D Allen (0–1), D Barron *Subs*: M Creedon for Morgan, J Lynch for Hayes

1982   Kerry 0–9; Cork 0–9
Kerry: C Nelligan, T Kennelly, J O'Keeffe, P Lynch, **P Ó Sé**, G O'Keeffe, G Lynch, J O'Shea, S Walsh (0–3), G Power, D Moran, T Doyle, M Sheehy (0–5), E Liston (0–1), J Egan *Subs*: J L McElligott for Moran, M Spillane for Kennelly, V O'Connor for J O'Shea

Cork: M Creedon, T Creedon, K Kehilly, J Evans, M Monloney, C Ryan, J Kerrigan, M Burns (0–2), D Creedon, D Barry, D Allen (0–2), T Murphy, T O'Reilly (0–1), D Barron (0–2), D McCarthy (0–2) *Subs*: E O'Mahony for O'Reilly, M Connolly for Murphy

Replay   Kerry 2–18; Cork 0–12
Kerry: C Nelligan, G O'Keeffe, J O'Keeffe, P Lynch, **P Ó Sé**, T Kennelly, T Doyle, J O'Shea (0–1), S Walsh, G Power, T Spillane (0–4), D Moran (0–4), M Sheehy (2–4), E Liston (0–4), J Egan (0–1) *Subs*: V O'Connor for J O'Keeffe, JL McElligott for Power

Cork: M Creedon, T Creedon, K Kehilly, J Evans, M Moloney, C Ryan, J Kerrigan, M Burns (0–1), D Creedon, D Barry, D Allen (0–4), T Murphy (0–1), E Fitzgerald (0–3), D Barron, D McCarthy (0–2) *Subs*: T O'Reilly (0–1) for Ryan, C Corrigan for Moloney

1983   Cork 3–10; Kerry 3–9
Cork: M Creedon, M Healy, K Kehilly, J Evans, M Hannon, C Ryan, J Kerrigan, D Creedon, C Corrigan, T Murphy (2–2), E O'Mahony, D Barry, D Allen (0–2), J Allen, J Cleary (1–6) *Subs*: T O'Reilly for Barry, E Fitzgerald for O'Mahony

Kerry: C Nelligan, G O'Keeffe, J O'Keeffe, P Lynch, **P Ó Sé**, T Kennelly, M Spillane, J O'Shea (2–0), V O'Connor, G Power (0–1), D Moran, T Doyle, M Sheehy (0–7), E Liston, J Egan (0–1) *Subs*: JL McElligott for J O'Keeffe, S Walsh (1–0) for Power

1984   Kerry 3–14; Cork 2–10
Kerry: C Nelligan, **P Ó Sé**, S Walsh, M Spillane, T Doyle, T Spillane (0–1), G Lynch, J O'Shea (0–1), A O'Donovan, J Kennedy (0–4), G Power (0–2), P Spillane (2–0), M Sheehy (0–3), E Liston (0–1), W Maher (1–0) *Subs*: D Moran (0–2) for Power, J Egan for Maher

Cork: J Kerins, M Lynch, M Healy, J Evans, N Cahalane, C Ryan, J Kerrigan (0–1), D Creedon, C Corrigan (0–1), T Nation, M Burns (0–2), D Barry (1–4), D Allen (0–1), J Allen (0–1), T Murphy *Subs*: K Kehilly for Healy, B Coffey (1–0) for Corrigan, C O'Neill for Burns

1985   Kerry 2–11; Cork 0–11
Kerry: C Nelligan, **P Ó Sé**, T Spillane, M Spillane, J Higgins, T Doyle, G Lynch, J O'Shea (0–1), A O'Donovan, J Kennedy (0–1), D Moran (0–1), P Spillane (0–2), M Sheehy (1–3), E Liston (1–2), G Power *Subs*: T O'Dowd (0–1) for O'Donovan

Cork: J Kerins, N Cahalane, C Corrigan, J Evans, T Mannix, C Counihan, J Kerrigan (0–2), B Coffey (0–2), M McCarthy (0–1), P Harrington, T McCarthy (0–1), T Nation (0–1), T O'Sullivan, C O'Neill (0–1), D Barry (0–2) *Subs*: M Beston (0–1) for Harrington, J Boylan for Coffey, C Ryan for Nation

1986   Kerry 0–12; Cork 0–8
Kerry: C Nelligan, **P Ó Sé**, S Walsh, M Spillane, T Doyle (0–1), T Spillane,
G Lynch, J O'Shea (0–2), A O'Donovan, J Kennedy (0–4), T Dowd (0–1), P Spillane,
M Sheehy (0–4), E Liston, G Power *Subs*: W Maher for P Spillane

Cork: J Kerins, T Nation, C Corrigan, J Evans, N Cahalane, C Counihan, D Walsh,
J Kerrigan, M McCarthy, T McCarthy, B Coffey, D Barry (0–4), J O'Driscoll (0–1),
C O'Neill (0–3), R Swain *Subs*: P Hayes for Corrigan, T O'Sullivan for
M McCarthy, T Mulcahy for Coffey

1987   Cork 1–10; Kerry 2–7
Cork: J Kerins, A Davis, C Corrigan, D Walsh, N Cahalane, C Counihan,
T Nation, S Fahy, T McCarthy, P Hayes, L Tompkins (0–8), J Kerrigan, J O'Driscoll
(1–1), C Ryan (0–1), J Cleary *Subs*: B Coffey for Hayes

Kerry: C Nelligan, **P Ó Sé**, S Walsh, M Spillane, T Doyle, T Spillane, G Lynch,
J O'Shea (0–2), A O'Donovan, T O'Dowd, D Moran (0–1), P Spillane, M Sheehy
(1–4), E Liston (1–0), G Power *Subs*: D Hanafin for Moran, M McAuliffe for
O'Dowd

Replay Cork 13; Kerry 1–5
Cork: J Kerins, A Davis (0–2), C Corrigan, D Walsh, N Cahalane, C Counihan,
T Nation (0–1), S Fahy (0–2), T McCarthy (0–1), P Hayes, L Tompkins (0–3),
J Kerrigan, J O'Driscoll (0–1), C Ryan, J Cleary (0–2) *Subs*: T Leahy (0–1) for Hayes,
D Culloty for Kerrigan

Kerry: C Nelligan, **P Ó Sé**, S Walsh, M Spillane, T Doyle (0–1), T Spillane,
G Lynch, D Hannifin (1–0), A O'Donovan, J Kennedy, J O'Shea (0–2), P Spillane,
M Sheehy (0–1), E Liston, G Power *Subs*: T O'Dowd for Kennedy, M McAuliffe for
O'Dowd, V O'Connor (0–1) for O'Donovan